AF552675

THE COAST & THE SEA

Marine and Maritime Art in America

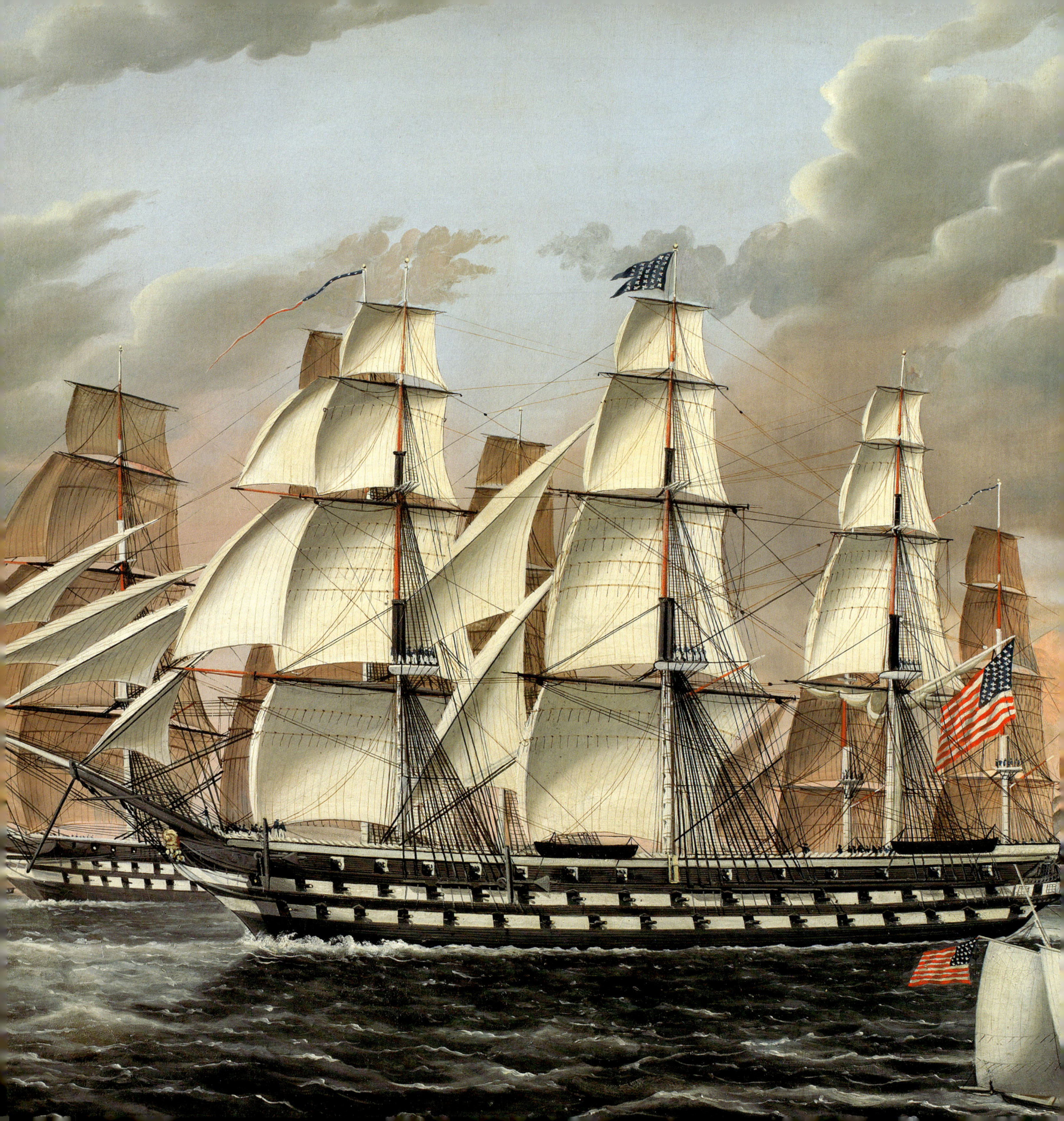

THE COAST & THE SEA

Marine and Maritime Art in America

at the New-York Historical Society

Linda S. Ferber

New-York Historical Society
in association with
D Giles Limited, London

Published on the occasion of the traveling exhibition *The Coast & the Sea: Marine and Maritime Art in America* at the Society of the Four Arts, Palm Beach, Florida (January 24–March 9, 2014), The Baker Museum (April 19–July 6, 2014), and the New York State Museum (October 24, 2015–February 22, 2016).

First published in 2014 by GILES
An imprint of D Giles Limited
4 Crescent Stables, 139 Upper Richmond Road
London, SW15 2TN, UK
www.gilesltd.com

Cataloging-in-Publication Data is available from the Library of Congress.

ISBN: 978-1-907804-31-1

For the New-York Historical Society:
Project Curator: Linda S. Ferber, Vice President and Senior Art Historian
Project Editor: Fronia W. Simpson
Photographs are by Glenn Castellano

For D Giles Limited:
Copyedited and proofread by Sarah Kane
Designed by Caroline and Roger Hillier, The Old Chapel Graphic Design

Produced by GILES, an imprint of D Giles Limited, London
Printed and bound in China

All measurements are in inches and centimeters; height precedes width.

Front cover Francis Augustus Silva, *New York Harbor*, 1880 (fig. 50, detail)
Back cover Thomas Buttersworth, *Escape of HMS "Belvidera" from the U.S. Frigate "President,"* ca. 1815 (fig. 16, detail)
Frontispiece James Guy Evans, *U.S. Ships of the Line "Delaware" and "North Carolina" and Frigates "Brandywine" and "Constellation,"* ca. 1835–60 (fig. 14, detail)
Copyright and Contents pages Thomas Birch, *Escape of the U.S. Frigate "Constitution,"* 1838 (fig. 18, detail)

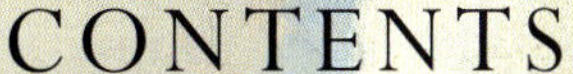

CONTENTS

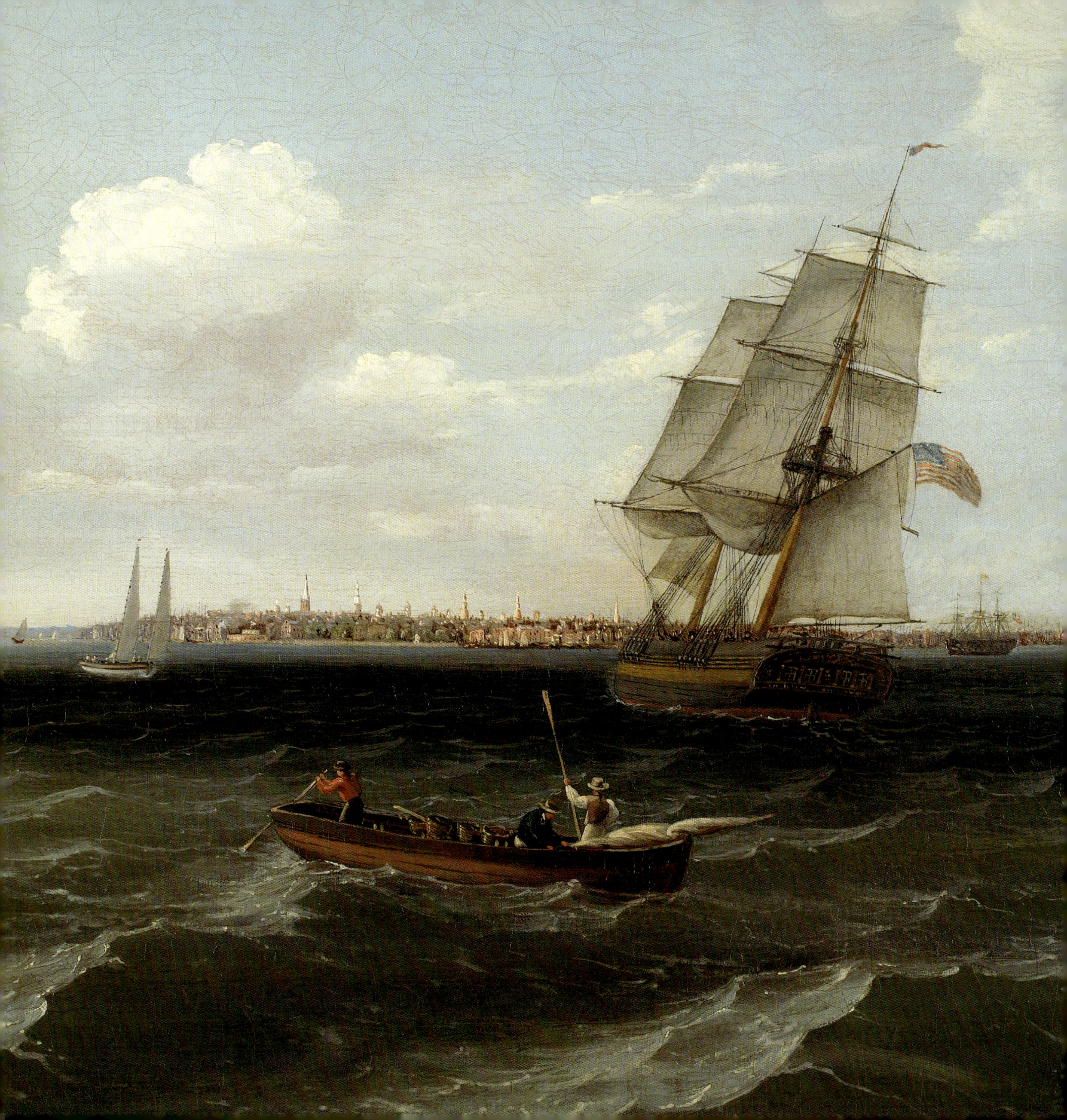

FOREWORD

It seems entirely appropriate to celebrate a renovated and reinvigorated New-York Historical Society with *The Coast & the Sea: Marine and Maritime Painting in America*. New York City's destiny has always been linked to the Atlantic. Her great harbor has been the source of commercial wealth and cosmopolitan ideas since the founding of New Amsterdam in 1626. This landmark exhibition drawn from the Society's own deep collections of maritime art, artifacts, and documents introduces us to a marvelous corpus of paintings and objects that will be new to many viewers. The volume also expands our understanding of the culture of those who built these collections (and New York City) as well as their aspirations and agendas.

The exhibition is part of "Sharing a National Treasure: The Traveling Exhibition Program of the New-York Historical Society," our ongoing campaign to bring our remarkable collections to the attention of national and international audiences. We are delighted that our first partners on what will be a national itinerary are appropriately located in Florida, a state with some 1,260 miles of tidal shoreline. They are the Society of the Four Arts in Palm Beach and The Baker Museum in Naples. The exhibition will also travel up the great estuary of the Hudson River to be shown at the New York State Museum in Albany.

Thanks are due to a stellar New-York Historical Society team. My spectacular colleague, Dr. Linda S. Ferber, Vice President and Senior Art Historian, selected the works and developed the ideas and themes that drive the exhibition. Dr. Ferber worked in close concert with colleagues in the Museum and Library, whose individual roles and contributions she acknowledges in her preface.

We extend our special thanks to the board of trustees for the generous support that made this publication possible. Roger Hertog presided as Chair when the project was initiated, and our succeeding Chair, Pam Schafler, will open the exhibition. The New York Community Trust Joanne Witty and Eugene Keilin Fund generously supported the publication. We are also grateful to Irma R. Rappaport and the Thomas and Diane Jacobsen Foundation.

Louise Mirrer
President and C.E.O.

Thomas Birch
New York Harbor, 1831
(fig. 13, detail)

PREFACE & ACKNOWLEDGMENTS

The New-York Historical Society holds a large and important collection of marine paintings and maritime artifacts, a reflection of the fact that the early history and culture of the United States are closely bound to the Atlantic and the eastern seaboard of North America. Wealth generated by maritime enterprises supported New York City's cultural development, prompting the rise of schools of marine and landscape painting as well as portraiture and a booming print industry. It is interesting to note that a number of the artists represented in *The Coast & the Sea* were themselves mariners at one time. Thomas Buttersworth served in the British navy, James Guy Evans may have served in the American, while Mauritz Frederick Hendrick De Haas held an artist's commission in the Dutch navy. De Haas's pupil, Julian Oliver Davidson, followed his mentor's example by sailing around the world to prepare for his career. Carlton Theodore Chapman had run away to sea as a youth. Their paintings and many others ranging in date from 1728 to 1904 will be surveyed in this volume, which explores the rich visual traditions of both marine and maritime painting and, in the process, demonstrates the often permeable boundaries that marry them. Both traditions have inspired stirring works by academically trained artists as well as those working in vernacular traditions, be they sea painters, ship painters, or portrait painters. While this survey includes a number of icons, many lesser-known works are also brought to light. Most works are American, some are European, and many of them were collected by New Yorkers.

Numerous colleagues have contributed to the investigations culminating in this publication. First among them is Sophie Lynford, who has played a critical role in conducting the research that provides the foundation for much of this text in addition to undertaking the myriad tasks critical to producing both this volume and the exhibition. Not only has her work been invaluable, but her enthusiasm and efficiency have greatly facilitated the many challenges of assembling all of the elements required to produce this catalogue in remarkably short order. Sarah B. Snook's research skills have been enlisted on behalf of this project and, as always, are deeply appreciated. Natalie Fleming's exhaustive survey of our marine and maritime collections during her 2011 museum internship has provided a rich resource. Margaret Hofer, Debra Schmidt Bach, and Mike Thornton have offered welcome guidance in the selection of maritime objects and instruments. Marilyn Kushner, Mary Beth Kavanagh, and Joe Festa have done the same in the selection of prints. Working in concert with Stephen Kornhauser, Chief Museum Conservator, to resurrect both paintings and frames were conservators Kenneth M.

Moser, Lenora Paglia, and Patricia S. Garland, interns Margarita Sergeyevna Berg and Caitlin Breare, and Julius Lowy, Inc., and Eduardo Larrea.

Colleagues who have generously provided information include Patrick M. Conner, Marybeth De Filippis, Stephen Edidin, Stuart P. Feld, Kevin Fewster, Dan Finamore (who deserves my deepest gratitude for reviewing the manuscript), Barbara Dayer Gallati, Thomas Gochberg, Harold Holzer, Richard Johns, Thomas P. Kugelman, Deirdre Lawrence, Benedict Leca, Ray Lent, Kenneth Maddox, Janet Maddox, Mark Mitchell, Harry Newman, the Old Print Shop, Roberta J. M. Olson, Bryan Oliphant (who deserves special thanks for so enthusiastically sharing his expertise on all things maritime), Kimberly Orcutt, Bonnie Ayers D'Orlando, Valerie Paley, Thomas B. Parker, Franklin Riehlman, Nigel Rigby, Zachary Ross, Ralph Sessions, Pieter van der Merwe, Bruce Weber, Heidi Wirth, and Paul Worman.

N-YHS staff in both the Museum and Library supported every aspect of bringing this project to completion. Special thanks go to Chris Catanese, Director for Museum Administration, who fielded a host of museum issues while I worked on this book. I am also very grateful to Maurita Baldock, Alan Balicki, Dayna Bealy, Kate Burch, Glenn Castellano (for his splendid photography), Joseph Ditta, Roy R. Eddey, Eleanor Gillers, Tammy Kiter, Susan Kriete, Sean Lally, Maureen Maryanski, Alexandra Mazzitelli, Brenna McCormick-Thompson, Cheryl Morgan, Edward O'Reilly, Jillian Pazereckas, Ione Saroyan, Elizabeth Shulman, Mariam Touba, Laura Washington, and Timothy Wroten. The design team included Marcela Gonzalez, Kira Hwang, Brianne Muscente, and Gerhard Schlanzky. The exhibition and registrarial team included Miguel Colon, Victoria Manning, Heidi Nakashima, Jeffrey Porterfield, Daniel Santiago, and Scott Wixon. We are grateful to Dan Giles and his wonderful team as a great publishing partner, and to The Old Chapel Graphic Design for the handsome book design. Fronia W. Simpson's editorial skills and insights, as well as her diplomacy, are deeply appreciated.

Linda S. Ferber
Vice President and Senior Art Historian

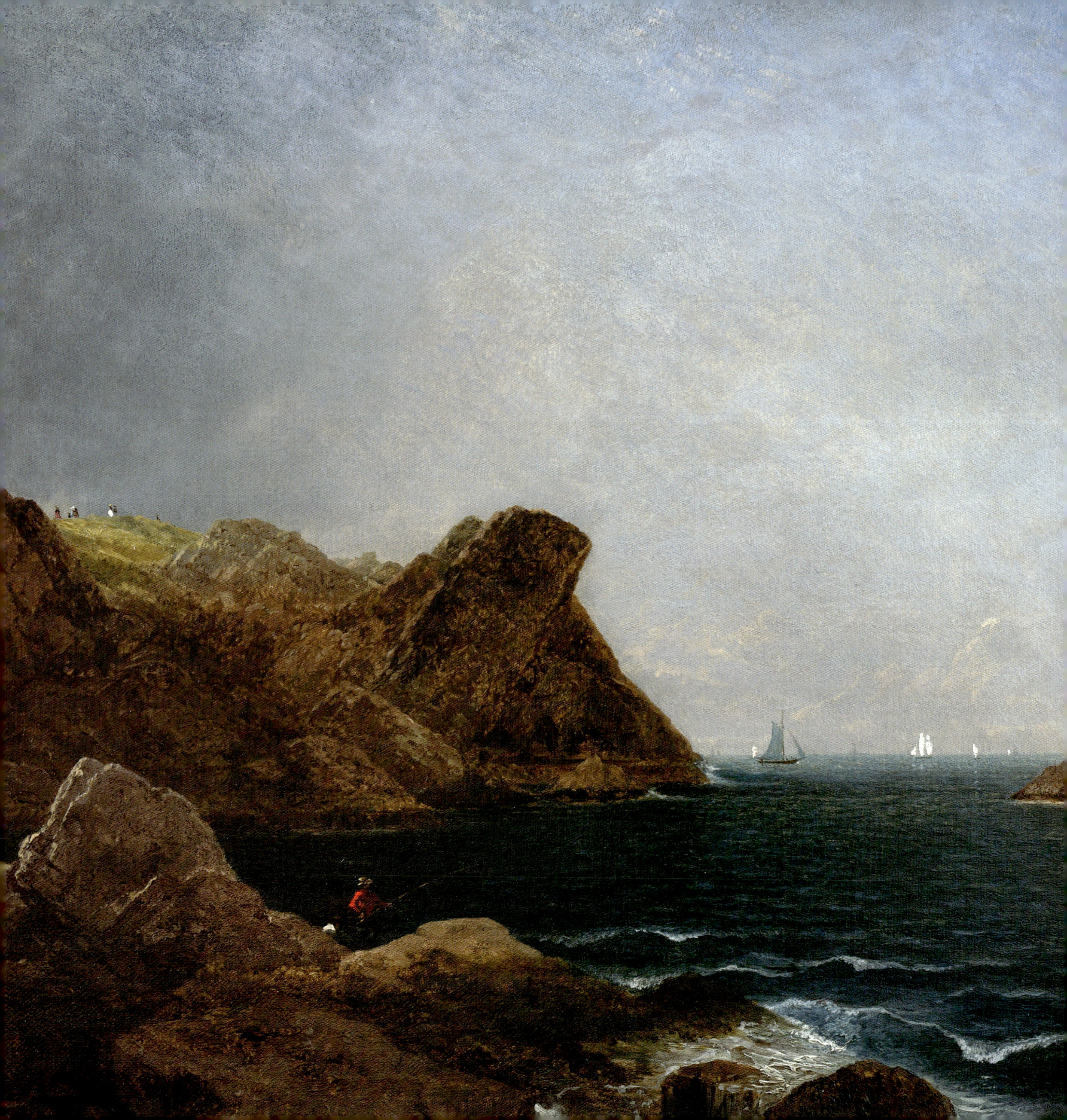

ON THE EDGE

Marine and Maritime Art in America, 1728–1904

Linda S. Ferber

PROLOGUE: THE COAST AND THE SEA

> . . . sir, don't you hear the sea moaning, as if it knew the hour was at hand when it was to wake up from its sleep!—James Fenimore Cooper, *The Pilot: Tale of the Sea* (1823)

It may surprise some to learn that James Fenimore Cooper's seafaring novel, *The Pilot*, was as widely read in the 1820s as his *Leatherstocking Tales*, which inspired Thomas Cole's wilderness landscapes. The enduring popularity of nineteenth-century American landscape painting as emblematic of the founding myth of continental expansion has, perhaps, obscured the historical fact that the early history and culture of the United States were most closely bound to the sea. The Atlantic frontier loomed largest in colonial life as the barrier separating the Old from the New World and as the vital link that connected colonial subjects to their homelands.[1] The first images of the maritime realm in North America were surely the graphic notations and ornamental cartouches that adorned the nautical charts and maps that guided European mariners and settlers to the eastern coast of the New World.

In the New World, the earliest painted portrayals of the Atlantic Ocean would appear as conventionalized seascapes in the backgrounds of colonial portraits like that painted about 1728 of Joseph Hallett of Hallett's Cove (today Astoria, Queens), whose English family had settled on Long Island about 1655 (fig. 1). Hallett's pose seated before a window and his costume complete with baroque drapery are based on a British mezzotint print after a portrait of the Earl of Exeter by Sir Godfrey Kneller (1646–1723).[2] However, the colonial artist, possibly Gerardus Duyckinck I, departed from his model in ways calculated to signal this particular sitter's connection to the sea. Navigation instruments and a chart lie on a ledge

John Frederick Kensett
Pulpit Rock, Nahant (Nahant Rock and Seashore), 1859
(fig. 59, detail)

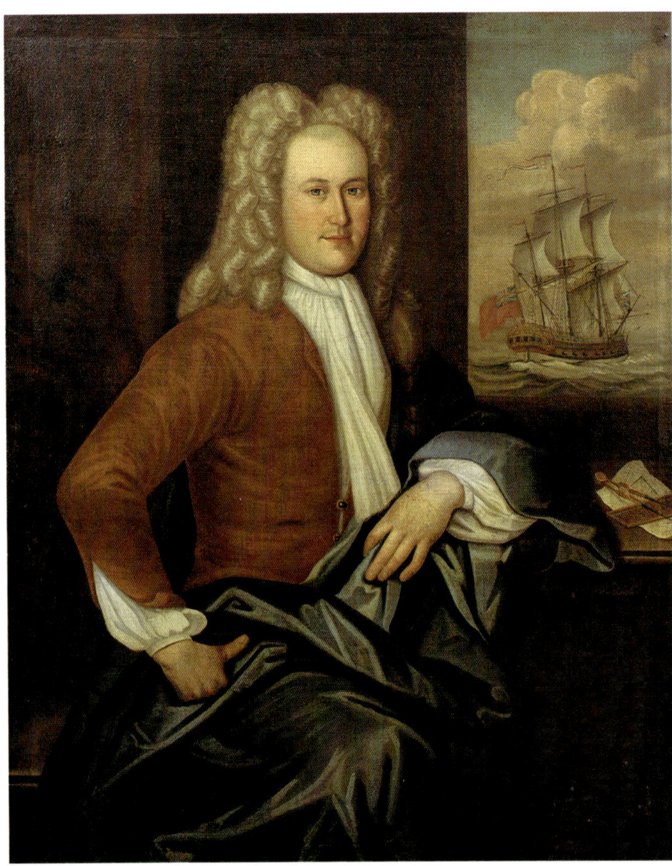

1. Unidentified Artist
Joseph Hallett (1678–1750),
ca. 1728
Oil on canvas, 49½ × 40¼ in.
(125.7 × 102.2 cm)
Bequest of Waldron Phoenix
Belknap Jr., 1950.239

beside Hallett, and the landscape in the print is replaced with a view of a Royal Navy ship of war sailing with open ports and cannons at the ready. These martial elements suggest a military calling as well as mercantile pursuits and were doubtless also lifted from a print source. The presence of such engravings to serve the needs of colonial subjects had a deeper significance than merely providing passive models for local artists. They signaled cultural continuity and familiarity with European portrait and marine painting conventions. Countless future mariners would sit for portraits before such an emblematic seascape (figs. 8, 9, 34, 36, 38, 44), while the pictorial elements of that ocean vista would over time claim the foreground spaces. Sea, ship, and sky would assume the many variations of marine and maritime painting surveyed in this volume.

Thus, the stage was set early on for the rise of a flourishing school of American marine painting, an enterprise whose larger messages in various ways paralleled the agendas expressing national and cultural identity to be found in American landscapes. Many visual motifs of the colonial period were modified after independence to serve a national iconography. His Majesty's ships would become American ships of state with such resonant names as *President*, *United States*, *Congress*, and *Constitution*. Like landscape subjects, paintings of the sea were also vehicles for the expression of cultivated taste, and marine artists worked within the long-established aesthetic hierarchy associated with the picturesque, the beautiful, and especially the sublime.[3]

MARINE PAINTINGS IN THE OLDEST MUSEUM IN NEW YORK

Three seascapes that came into this collection between 1855 and 1862 well embody the maritime picturesque and sublime: one is English, one is French, and one, American. All three have interesting backstories. In 1862 the Society acquired a monumental record of maritime disaster when the bequest of Commodore Uriah Phillips Levy (1792–1862), a fascinating figure, brought a large copy of Théodore Géricault's *Raft of the Medusa* attributed to George Cooke into the collection (fig. 2). About 1830 Cooke, who was a self-taught but highly ambitious American artist living in Paris, painted what was said to be a full-scale copy of Géricault's sensational painting of 1819 already in the Musée du Louvre. He toured the painting in the United States as a moneymaking enterprise, exhibiting it in New York in 1831 and 1840. Cooke painted smaller copies as well, and this one may have been commissioned by Levy, who had been an officer on the rescue ship *Argus* depicted in the painting.[4] Although Géricault's work was based on an actual event, his painting also spoke to those universal meanings in which the storm-tossed boat and the shipwreck function as powerful allegories of the vicissitudes of human existence. Imagine Cooke's large painting hanging in the skylit galleries of the Society in company with those of his friend Cole, in particular Cole's *Course of Empire*, another meditation on human destiny painted in the 1830s.

2. Attributed to George Cooke (1793–1849), after Théodore Géricault (1791–1824)
Raft of the Medusa, ca. 1830
Oil on linen, 51⅜ × 77¼ in. (130.5 × 196.2 cm)
Bequest of Uriah Phillips Levy, 1862.4

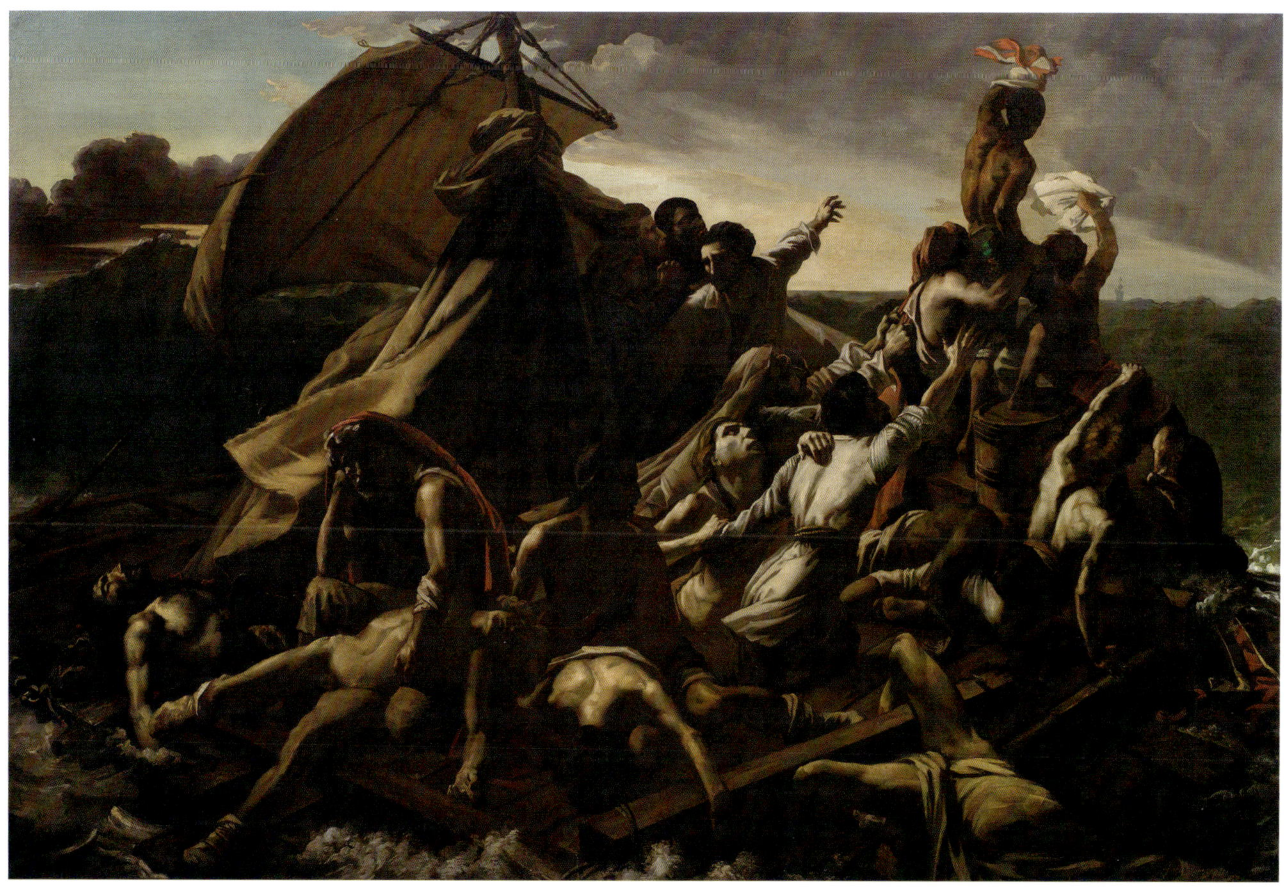

Two less dramatic seascapes—*View of a Seaport*, about 1760, and *Marine View*, 1835—are also among the earliest paintings to come into this museum's collection. The first painting, which may be by a British marine painter, John Cleveley, the Elder, was a gift in 1855 from John MacGregor, a Scottish collector who believed (as did the Society) that the harbor town represented was Dutch New Amsterdam (fig. 3). Cleveley's view of a small port city and shipyards is thought to be an image of Harwich in Essex on the east coast of England. This painting is said to be the first "view," that is, nonportrait to enter the New-York Historical Society's collection, and it did so just before the cornerstone was laid in 1855 for the Society's first permanent home at the intersection of Second Avenue and East Eleventh Street.[5] Thomas Birch's *Marine View* of 1835 was a gift only three years later, in 1858, from the New York Gallery of the Fine Arts as part of the deposit of Luman Reed's great collection at the Society (fig. 4).[6]

3. Unidentified Artist, possibly John Cleveley, the Elder (ca. 1712–1777)
View of a Seaport, ca. 1760
Oil on canvas, 27 × 48 in. (68.6 × 121.9 cm)
Gift of John MacGregor, 1855.1

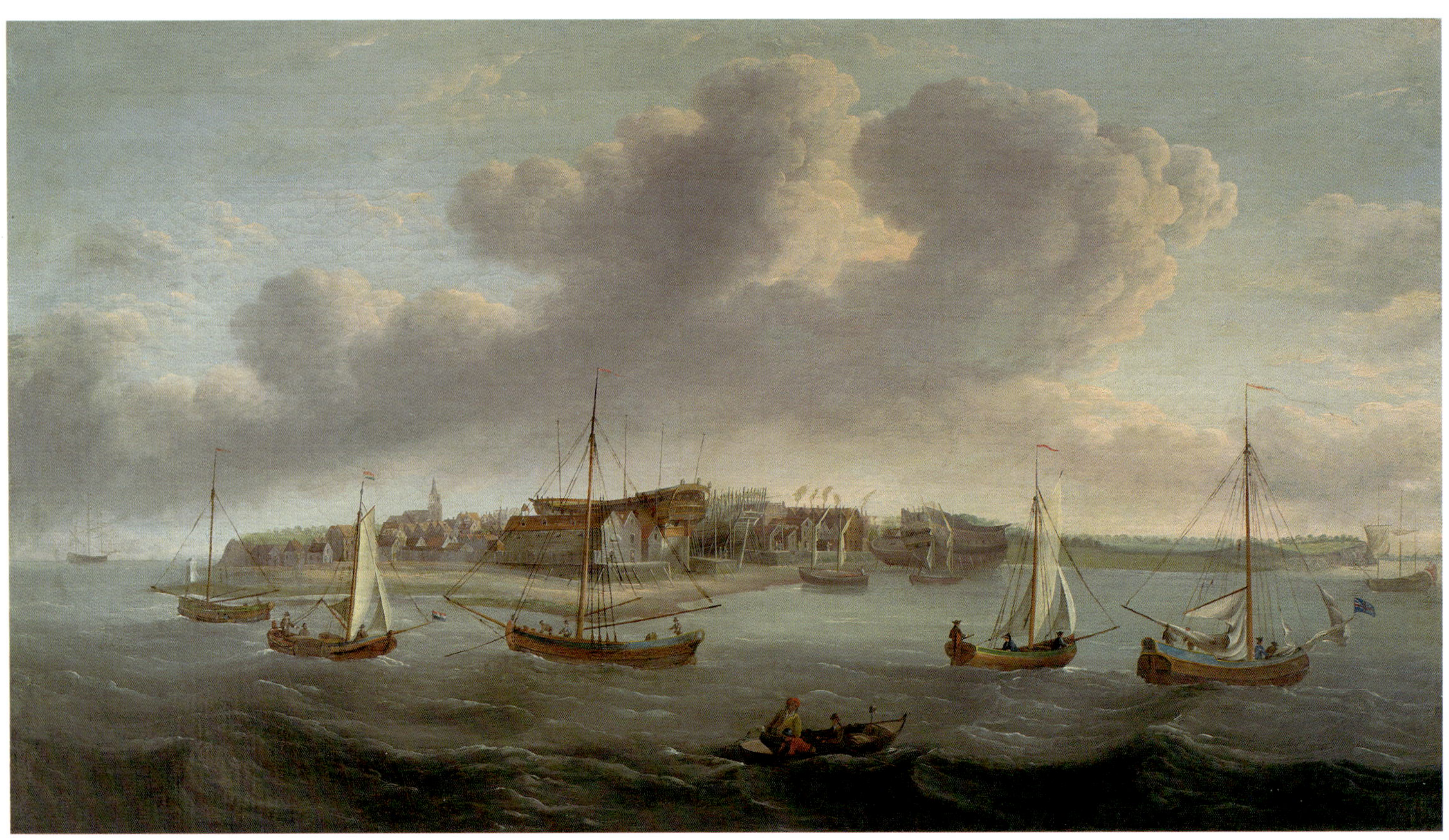

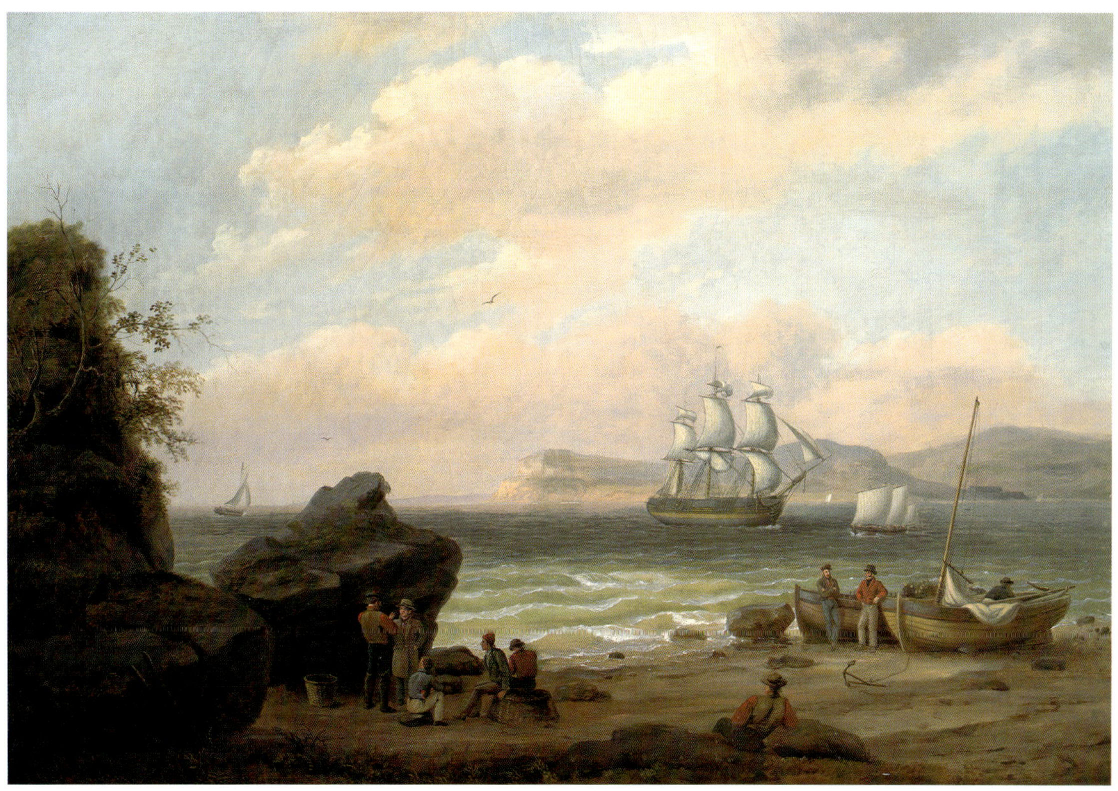

4. Thomas Birch (1779–1851)
Marine View, 1835
Oil on canvas, 25 × 36 in.
(63.5 × 91.2 cm)
Signed and dated lower left:
Tho. Birch / 1835
Gift of The New York Gallery
of the Fine Arts, 1858.13

These two foundational paintings, created some seventy-five years apart—one by a mid-eighteenth-century British maritime specialist and the other by an early nineteenth-century Philadelphia painter of seascapes—also neatly demonstrate the primary traditions that have mediated images of the coast and the sea. The *maritime* tradition placed emphasis on documenting seafaring enterprises on the shore or at sea as sites for human activity. The *marine* tradition, or *seascape*, by contrast, may be said to focus on interpretations in which the coastal and oceanic environment takes center stage. However, these same two works also demonstrate the almost always permeable boundaries between these categories. For example, Cleveley situated his precisely rendered harbor view and shipyard within a convincing envelope of coastal weather conditions. Birch's sweeping marine vista, for its part, includes a foreground filled with carefully rendered maritime paraphernalia and nautical figure types. Both of these visual conventions had been largely invented in seventeenth-century Holland; Dutch maritime masters in turn founded a British school of marine painting in the late seventeenth century that was also transmitted to England's colonies in North America.

THE ANGLO-DUTCH MARINE TRADITION IN COLONIAL AMERICA

Captain John Waddell gazes confidently out of his dignified portrait by the London-trained artist John Wollaston, who depicted the wealthy colonial merchant about 1750 (fig. 5). Portrayed at home bewigged and in elegant dress comprising green coat, wine-colored vest, snowy white tie and cuffs (Wollaston was celebrated for his skillful painting of rich fabrics), Waddell shares the foreground of his portrait with a large globe toward which he gestures, calling our attention to the far-flung voyages of the ships he had built and owned. His right index finger points to the eastern seaboard of North America, indicating the destination of his own voyage to the New World. By 1736 Waddell had settled in New York, where he married and prospered, eventually founding a merchant dynasty in the thriving colonial outpost established by the Dutch a century before and ceded to the English in 1664.[7] By 1749, when Wollaston arrived from England to paint the colony's wealthy mercantile clientele, New York City was a busy port boasting a huge natural harbor and access to a major river estuary that stretched hundreds of miles into the interior.

5. John Wollaston (1710–1775)
Captain John Waddell (1714–1762), ca. 1750
Oil on canvas, 36 × 28 in. (91.4 × 71.1 cm)
Gift of Edmund B. Southwick, 1891.2

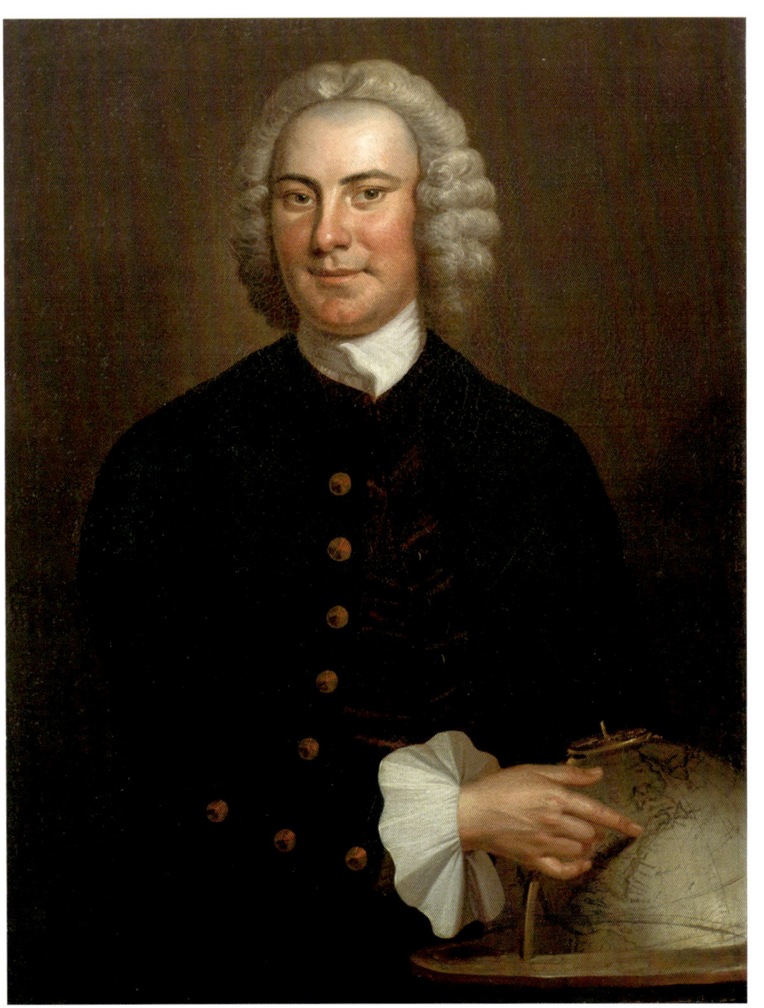

A large, detailed, mid-eighteenth-century view known as *A Southeast Prospect of the City of New York* shows us what New York's skyline and waterfront looked like in Waddell's and Wollaston's day (fig. 6). The painting was said to have once belonged to a prominent British colonial official posted in New York. While the provenance may be apocryphal, we do know that the view was adapted from a famous panoramic print after the British topographical draftsman William Burgis. Painted by a hand far less adept than Cleveley's in producing a convincing portrayal of the atmospheric environment, nevertheless, *A Southeast Prospect* charts the setting of the city's waterfront as well as the busy shipping on

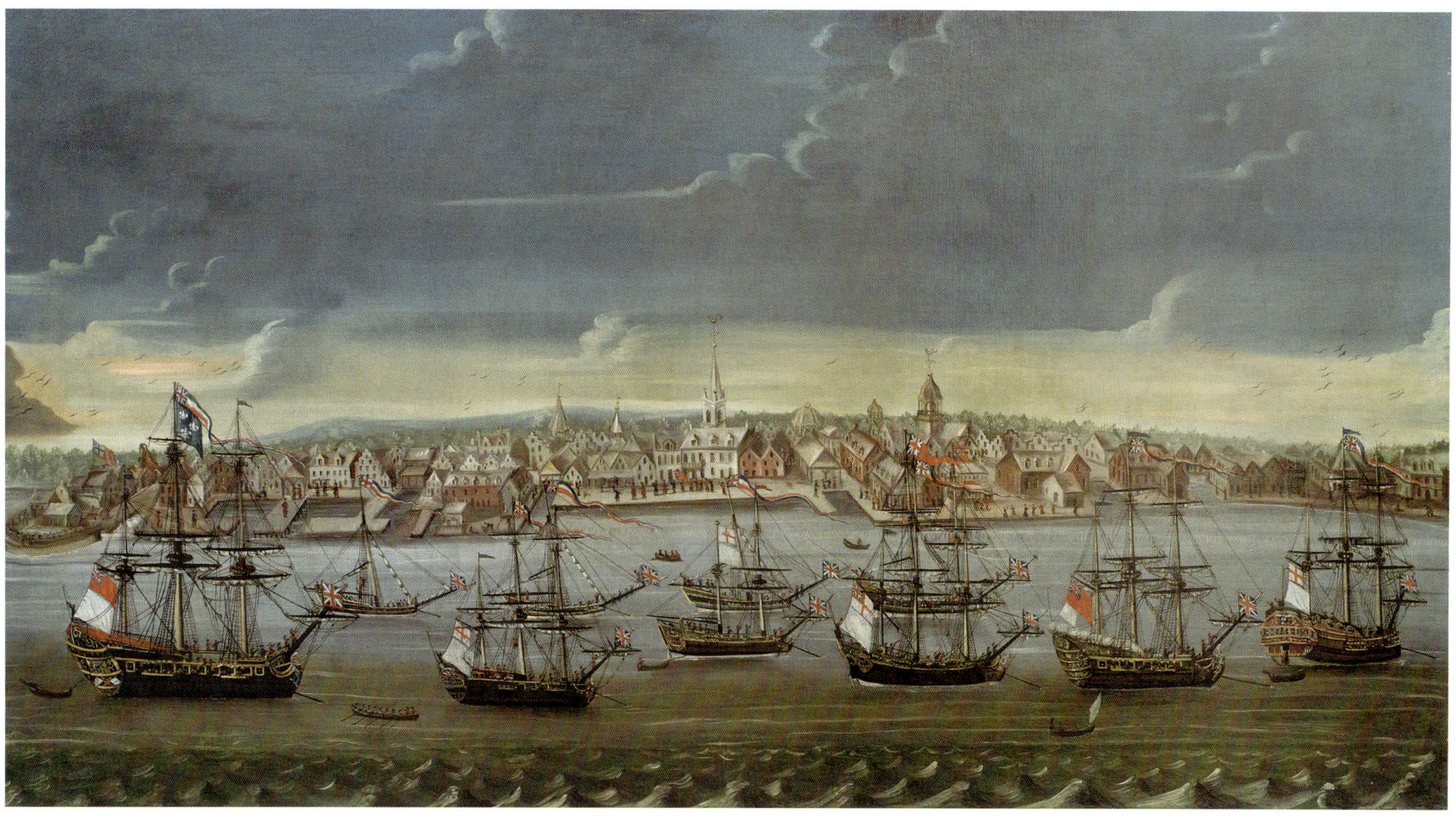

6. Unidentified Artist
A Southeast Prospect of the City of New York, ca. 1756–61
Oil on canvas, 38 × 72½ in.
(96.5 × 184.2 cm)
Gift of Cornelia LeRoy White, in the name of Goldsborough Banyer, 1904.1

the East River. The monumental engraving, known as the *Burgis/Bakewell View* (also in the collection), was conceived in the European topographical tradition of mapping the terrain, waters, and built environment of a specific site. Landmarks include the Battery at the far left and Trinity Church in the center.[8] Tiny figures populate the city and vessels. Most exciting are the magnificent ships anchored in the East River; their presence signals international enterprise as well as the naval might that secured the colonial outpost of New York as part of the British Empire. The bold display of flags and banners flown by this armada also alerts us to the symbolic power of these ships as compelling images of military strength, mercantile prowess, and national patrimony. A work like this one or *View of a Seaport* might well have been displayed in a room of Captain Waddell's fashionable house nearby.

7. William Joy (1803–1867), after Dominic Serres, the Elder (1722–1793)
Forcing the Hudson River Passage, October 9, 1776, ca. 1835
Oil on canvas, 28½ × 46¼ in. (72.4 × 117.5 cm)
Signed lower left: *W. JOY.*
Gift of the Travelers Insurance Company, 1951.69

The captain died as a British subject in 1762 (he and his wife are buried in Trinity Churchyard), but his five children remained to enjoy the fruits of independence after the Continental army and navy successfully challenged the British Empire's dominion on land and sea during the American Revolution. While the patriots would prevail, one of the most dramatic images of naval combat during the Revolutionary War, *Forcing the Hudson River Passage, October 9, 1776*, was commissioned in England to celebrate an important British victory (fig. 7). Dominic Serres, the Elder, a French-born artist associated with the British school who never visited North America, reconstructed the battle based on a sketch or eyewitness account of the engagement on the lower Hudson River early in the war, when British ships broke through the American defenses at what is today Washington Heights to gain command of the critical waterway. This large work, combining elements of marine, landscape, and history painting, shows a British squadron on the New York side of the river. Three frigates, HMS *Tartar*, *Roebuck*, and *Phoenix*, accompanied by two smaller vessels, are pushing their way through wooden barriers set up in the channel. They sail boldly through the billowing smoke, braving the plunging fire from American batteries at Fort Constitution (later renamed Fort Lee) on the summit of the Palisades, in New Jersey, and from Fort Washington on the New York side. In 1778 and 1779, within only a few years of the event, Serres was commissioned to paint a number of versions of this dramatic subject, probably for the commanders of each victorious vessel and others. This work is a careful copy by William Joy, an English artist working in the first half of the nineteenth century, demonstrating the lingering resonance of this episode for the English as a vivid reminder of British naval power in North America.[9]

PATRIOTS, CITIZENS, AND THE SECOND AMERICAN WAR OF INDEPENDENCE

Three lively portraits painted around 1800 by artists of modest training portray confident American citizens of seafaring New York and New England. David Abeel had served as a midshipman on the frigate *Alliance* during the Revolutionary War and later became captain of a merchant vessel. In this old-fashioned but appealing portrait, Abeel is shown before a view of the open sea wearing the dark blue coat with gold buttons typical of a ship's officer (fig. 8). He holds dividers in his right hand while unrolling a chart with his left, as if plotting a course. Behind him sails a three-masted vessel flying an American flag and commissioning pennants.[10] A marine view and nautical attributes served another unidentified artist as the proper setting to record the handsome features of a young man said to be Captain David Bush

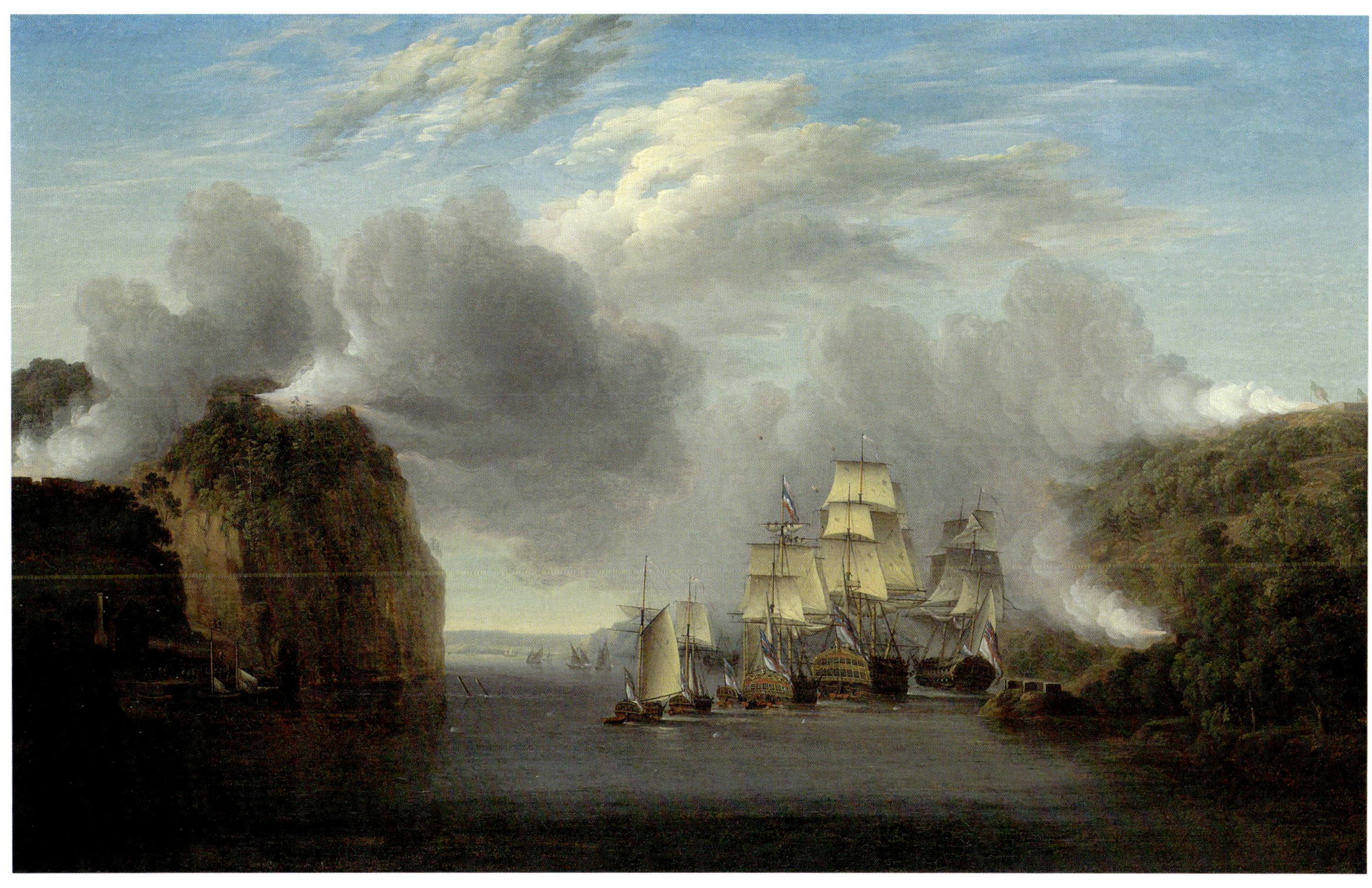

who served in the War of 1812 (fig. 9). He wields a mariner's telescope, or spyglass (fig. 10), while posing before a sprightly seascape to signal maritime enterprises.[11] In marked contrast to these oceanic expanses, Mrs. Truman and her winsome little girl holding flowers embody the domestic side of maritime life (fig. 11). In their portrait attributed to the Connecticut artist Reuben Moulthrop, mother and child are shown at home on Fair Street in New Haven. They are seated near an open door through which we glimpse a tidy garden bounded by a white fence. Beyond lies a distant view of the New Haven harbor with several ships at anchor. The figure standing at the garden gate looking out to sea is said to be her husband, Daniel, who was a ship's captain.[12]

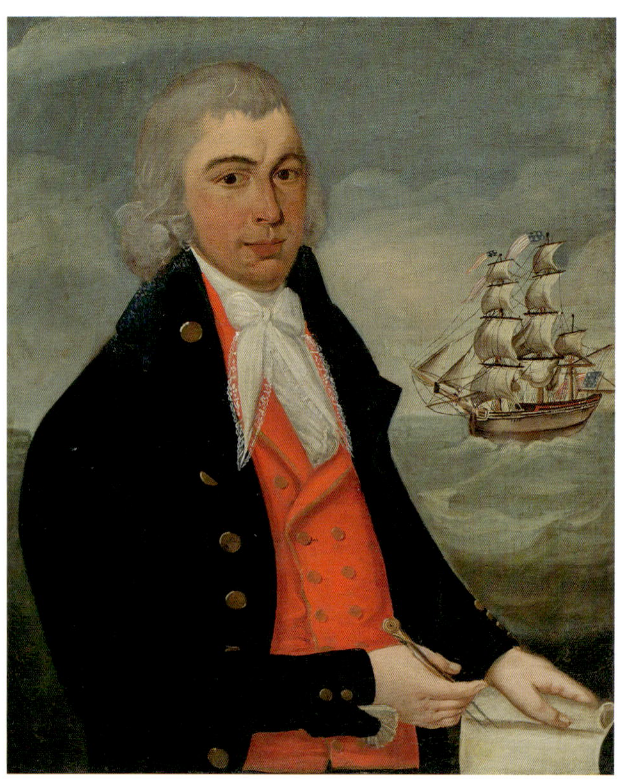

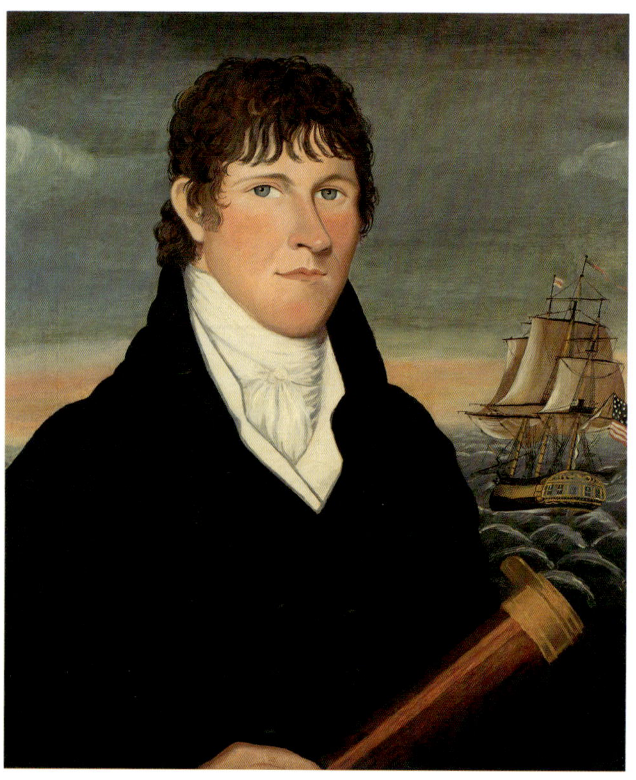

8. Unidentified Artist
David Abeel (1763–1840), ca. 1795–1800
Oil on canvas, 30 × 25 in. (76.2 × 63.5 cm)
Gift of George Abeel, 1896.53

9. Unidentified Artist
Captain David Bush, 1812
Oil on canvas, 26 × 21⅝ in. (66 × 54.9 cm)
Bequest of Irving S. Olds, 1963.48

10. Spencer Browning & Rust (active 1784–1840)
Spyglass, ca. 1800–1810
Brass, wood, glass, 15⅝ × 2½ in. (39.7 × 6.4 cm) (closed), 25⅜ × 2½ in. (64.5 × 6.4 cm) (open)
Engraved on inner cylinder: *Spencer Browning & Rust / LONDON / Day or Night*
Gift of Mrs. Bayard Verplanck, 1956.165

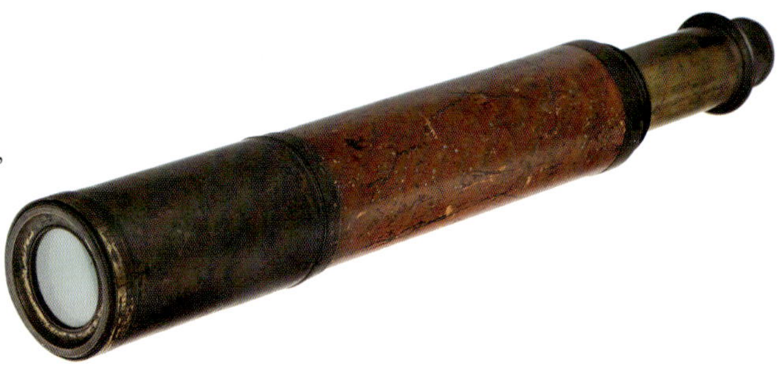

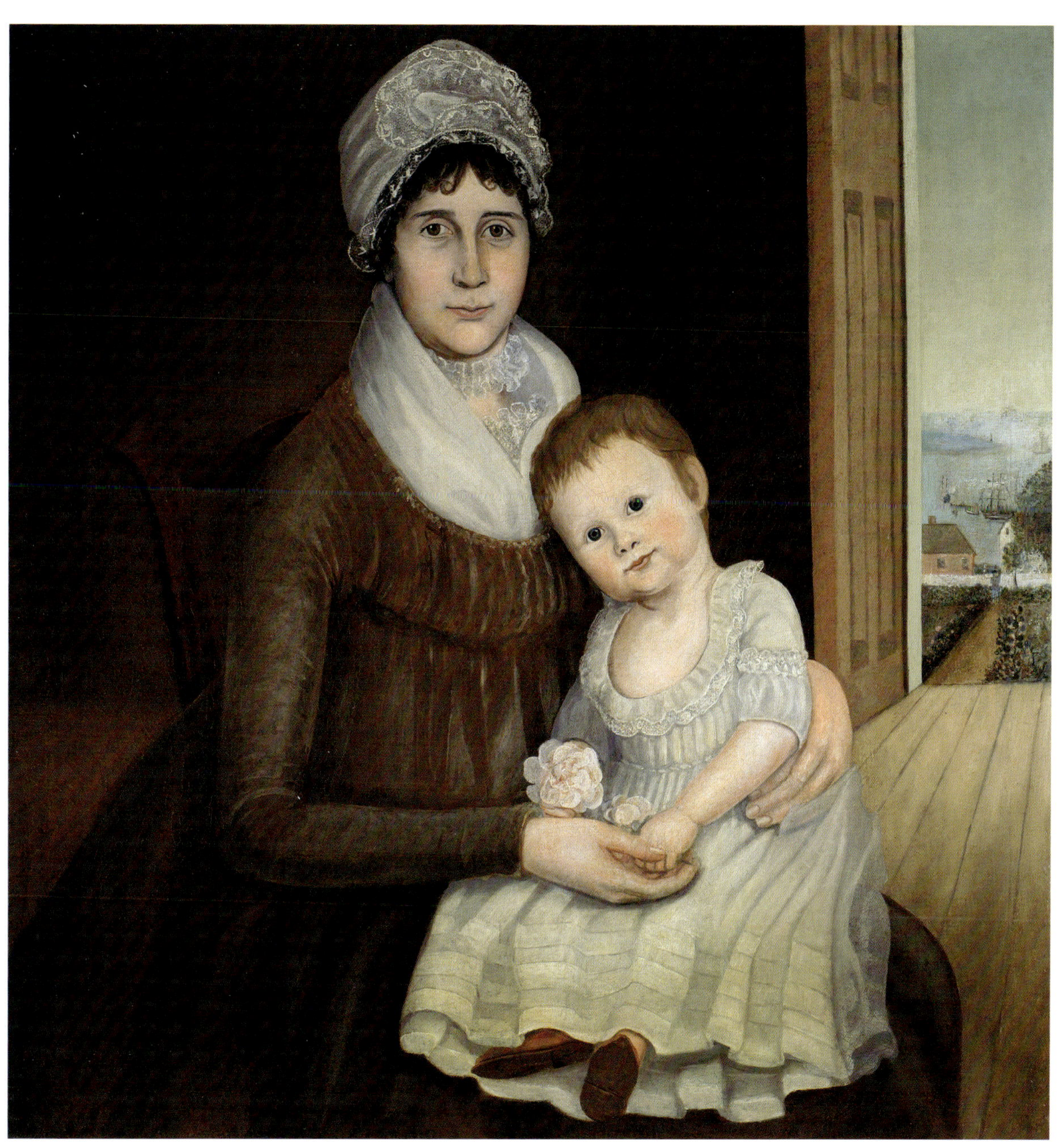

11. Attributed to Reuben Moulthrop (1763–1814)
Mrs. Daniel Truman and Child, ca. 1798–1810
Oil on canvas,
38¾ × 37¼ in.
(98.4 × 94.6 cm)
Purchase, 1952.29

Abeel was a New Yorker and undoubtedly familiar with the city's busy waterfront as it looked about 1818 or 1819, depicted in *Foot of Cortlandt Street* (fig. 12). This important early view, attributed to Johann Heinrich Jenny, a Swiss painter working in New York, shows the Cortlandt Street Ferry with its prominent smokestack docked in the North (or Hudson) River next to sailing ships. On September 7, 1807, Robert Fulton had embarked

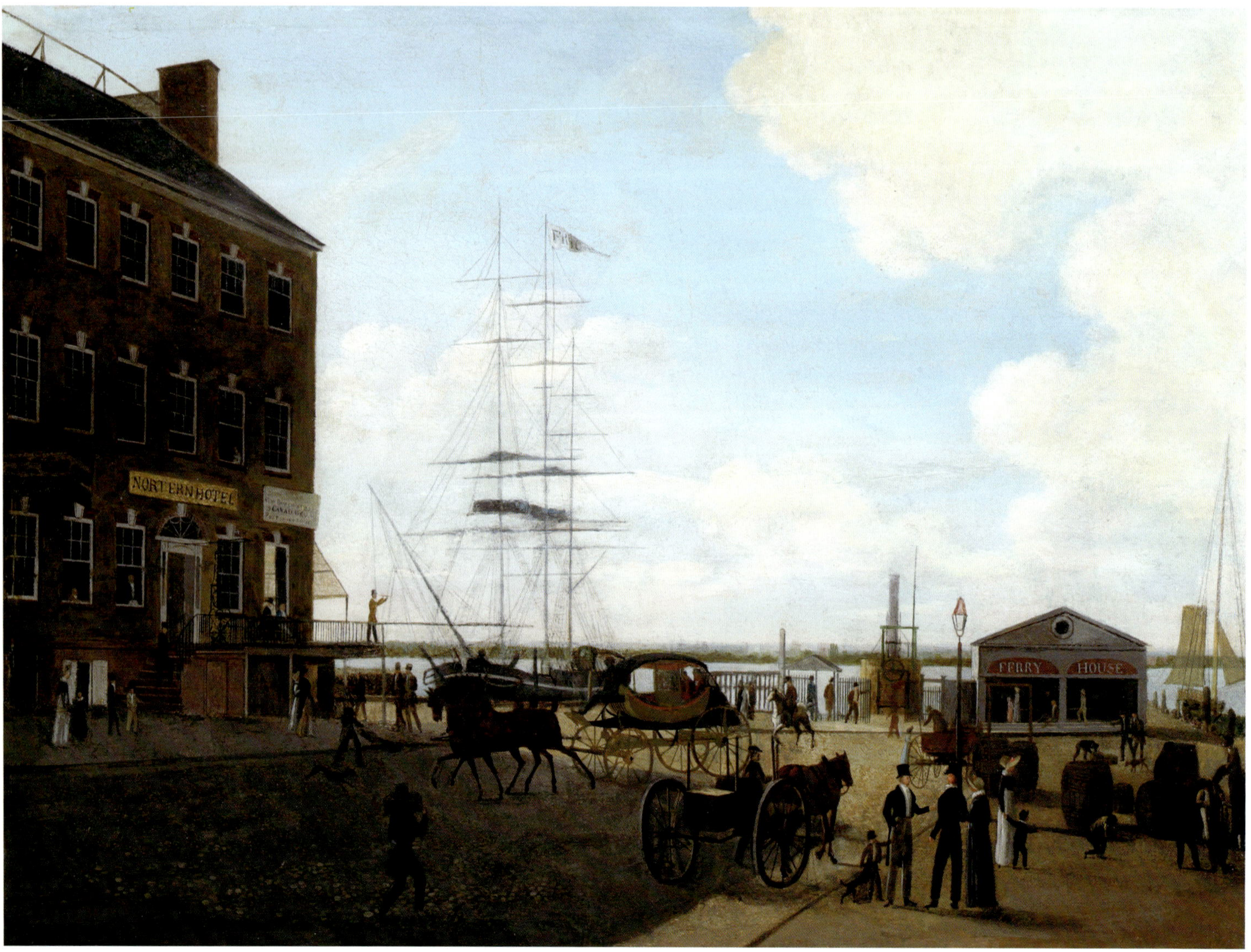

from this spot, then known as Messier's Dock, on the first successful voyage of the steam-driven *Clermont*. The imposing Northern Hotel, a newly opened stagecoach and steamboat hotel, casts a broad shadow across the busy thoroughfare. Jenny has catalogued the bustling waterfront in detail, including the three-masted merchant ship *Frances*, the ferryboat and ferry house, the stagecoach, a fish and oyster peddler's cart, and a distant view of New Jersey. A stagecoach sign on the corner of the hotel displays a route to towns in upstate New York; another advertises a mail coach to Philadelphia, some ninety miles to the south. The rather elegant pedestrians promenading among the commercial activities on Cortlandt Street may be awaiting departures or arrivals at this busy crossroads of ocean, river, and overland traffic.[13] When travelers embarked from Messier's Dock, the harbor waters would have looked much as they do in Thomas Birch's *New York Harbor* (fig. 13). Like Birch's home city of Philadelphia, New York's strategic location on a natural harbor with access to a deep-water river offered twin advantages: spurring commerce and offering picturesque scenery that drew printmakers and painters. Birch used his painterly talents to present an expansive view of the vast harbor as a convincing seascape rather than the staged pageant of maritime activities we saw in *A Southeast Prospect* (see fig. 6). Our nautical vantage point is from a boat out on the waters of the upper bay. Castle Williams, the round fortification on Governor's Island, is seen at the right, and a distant vista of the New York skyline appears at the center. A steamboat and varieties of sailing craft populate the harbor waters along with figures in a small fishing boat, its sail furled, who navigate the choppy waters with oars. Birch skillfully conveyed not only the topographical landmarks of the port but also a convincing sense of atmospherics in a beautifully realized waterscape in which the powers of sky, wind, and weather are experienced in convincing fashion. Flags are flying, sails filled with wind, and whitecaps crest the swells in the foreground. Decades later, Birch would be remembered as an early painter of "marine landscapes" admired for the "freshness of his atmosphere and clearly painted waves."[14]

Since 1794 these waters as well as the American coast and shipping had been protected by the fleet of a newly reestablished United States Navy. Harbor defenses in the major port cities also played an important role in protecting the nation's maritime frontier. These massive military structures in their dramatic settings would become popular scenic landmarks for printmakers and painters; they provided familiar sights that evoked both picturesque and patriotic associations (figs. 46–49, 67). Castle Williams, prominent in Birch's painting, had been built in preparation for the War of 1812; New York City's Battery, the site of Castle Clinton at the southern end of Manhattan Island, had long been fortified. From 1812 to 1815,

12. Attributed to Johann Heinrich Jenny (1786–1854)
Foot of Cortlandt Street, 1818–19
Oil on panel, 13¾ × 19 in. (34.9 × 48.3 cm)
Gift of the members of the Board of Trustees, 1948.576

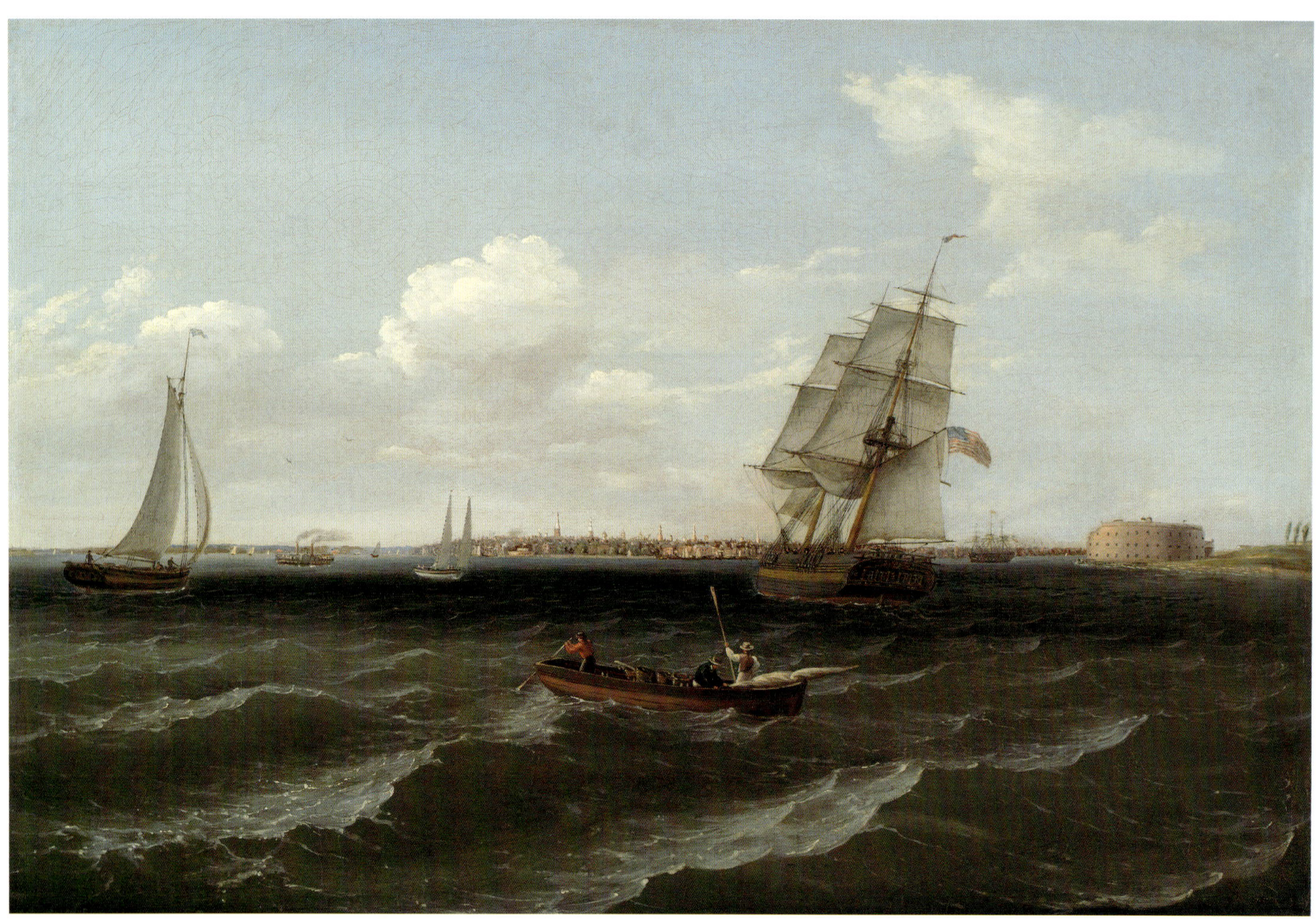

13. Thomas Birch
(1779–1851)
New York Harbor, 1831
Oil on canvas, 20¼ × 30¼ in.
(51.4 × 76.8 cm)
Signed and dated lower right:
Tho. Birch 1831
Gift of Mrs. Ethel McCullough Scott, John G. McCullough, and Mrs. Edith McCullough Heaphy, 1971.118

during the War of 1812, the United States again contested British power. Many battles during America's "Second War of Independence" were fought at sea as well as on land, and celebrated engagements greatly stimulated the production of marine painting in both countries during the war and after. Dramatic naval engagements between the British and American fleets positioned the United States on the world oceanic stage, creating an enduring pantheon of iconic marine battle subjects that vied with the Revolution's battles in their circulation as prints and images on popular tableware.

The original six frigates that formed the U.S. Navy, created by an act of Congress in March 1794 with captains appointed by President George Washington, were especially celebrated

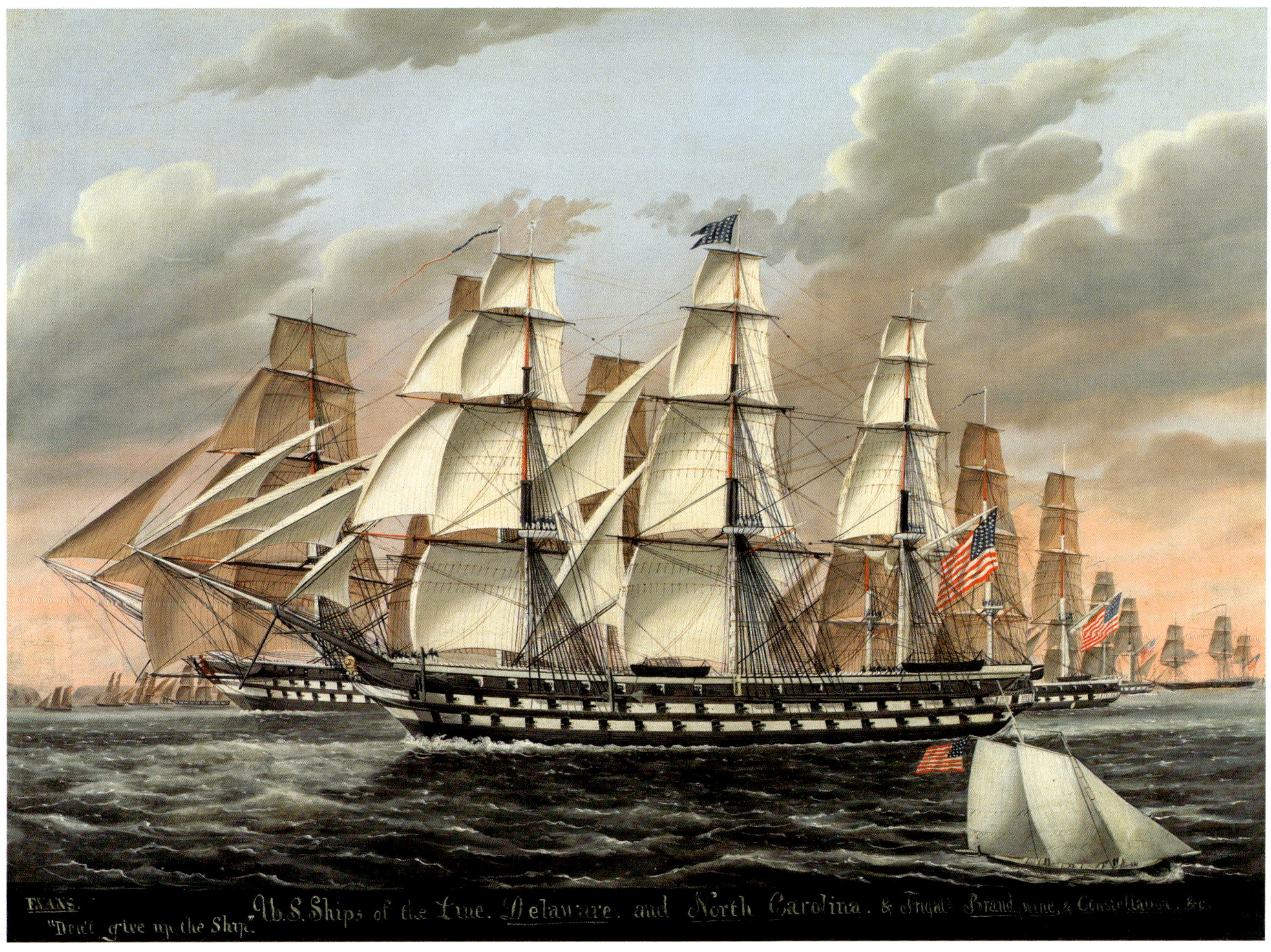

in these paintings and the prints made after them. They were the USS *United States*, *Congress*, *President*, *Chesapeake*, *Constellation*, and *Constitution*. James Guy Evans's splendid *U.S. Ships of the Line "Delaware" and "North Carolina" and Frigates "Brandywine" and "Constellation,"* probably painted sometime between 1835 and 1860, commemorates American military power and national identity in a brilliantly colored maritime pageant recording four warships of the United States Navy under full sail (fig. 14). The *Delaware* and *North Carolina* each mounted seventy-four guns and were ships of the line, so called because their armaments were powerful enough to lie in the line of battle where opposing fleets sailed parallel while firing at each other. The *Brandywine* and *Constellation* were frigates carrying thirty-six and forty-four

14. James Guy Evans (1810–1860)
U.S. Ships of the Line "Delaware" and "North Carolina" and Frigates "Brandywine" and "Constellation," ca. 1835–60
Oil on canvas, 31¾ × 44⅛ in. (80.6 × 112 cm)
Signed lower left: *EVANS*.
Gift of an Anonymous Donor, X.160

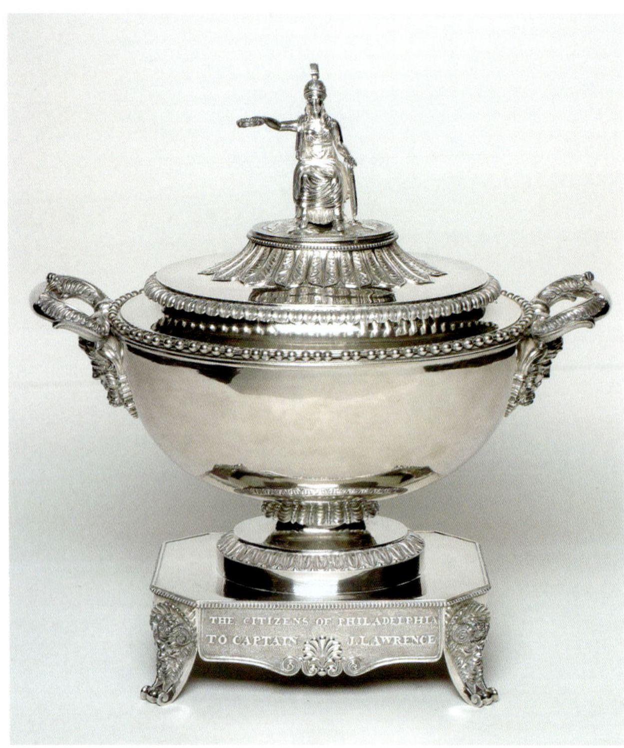

15. Simon Chaudron (1758–1846)
Presentation soup tureen, 1816
Silver, 16½ × 15½ × 8½ in. (41.9 × 39.4 × 21.6 cm)
Engraved on base: *THE CITIZENS OF PHILADELPHIA / TO CAPTAIN JAMES LAWRENCE*
The Eugene H. Pool Collection of Captain James Lawrence, Gift of Dr. Eugene H. Pool, 1942.544ab

guns, respectively. The *Delaware* at the left can be identified by the distinctive figurehead of the Delaware chief Tamenund.[15] A sprightly schooner races across the foreground of the painting, its diminutive size in sharp contrast to the massive scale of these mighty warships assembled on canvas as if parading in a naval review. Evans, who may himself have served in the navy, completed this patriotic tribute by neatly inscribing the names of these vessels embodying the nation's pride, as well as Captain James Lawrence's famous battle cry when mortally wounded while attacking the HMS *Shannon* that became the navy's motto: "Don't give up the Ship." Despite defeat and the British capture of his ship, the *Chesapeake*, Lawrence was hailed as a hero. The citizens of Philadelphia commissioned a set of presentation silver to honor his earlier victory over the *Peacock* when he had commanded the *Hornet*. The captain's widow accepted Philadelphia's tribute of a large soup tureen (fig. 15) and pitcher. A sculptured Athena figure enthroned atop the tureen offers the crown of victory to the fallen hero whose name is inscribed below.[16]

The Americans and British alike had a hearty appetite for maritime paintings that featured the excitement of battles at sea. During the War of 1812 and after, the English marine painter Thomas Buttersworth addressed both audiences with his portrayals of key naval engagements on the high seas between the United States and Great Britain. Said to have served in the British navy, Buttersworth skillfully conceived battle subjects that gained their widest currency in America as prints, after which many copies were painted by other artists. However, the command with which the artist represented the powerful drama of heroic ships in combat at sea is best appreciated in two brilliant little battle paintings whose small scale in no way diminishes their impact. Buttersworth cleverly chose daring naval exploits that would engage audiences on both sides of the Atlantic, regardless of nationality. One work depicts the first naval action of the War of 1812, and the other records one of the last. Moreover, both paintings chronicle exploits of the USS *President*, one of the original six and a vessel whose very name evoked the American republic for friend and foe alike. *Escape of HMS "Belvidera" from the U.S. Frigate "President"* portrays the American navy on the attack (fig. 16). Three days after war was declared on June 18, 1812, an American squadron of five vessels under Commodore

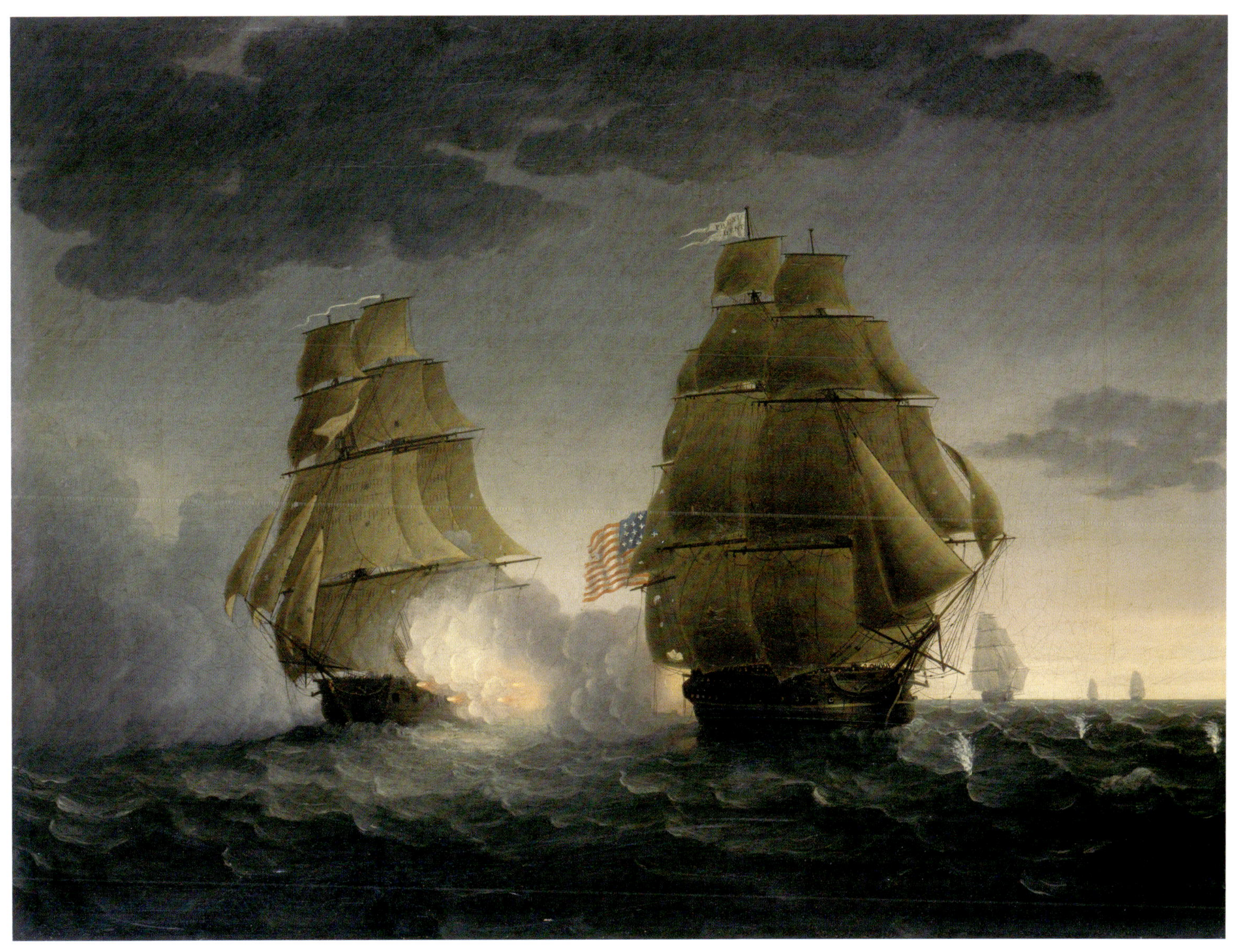

16. Thomas Buttersworth (1768–1842)
Escape of HMS "Belvidera" from the U.S. Frigate "President," ca. 1815
Oil on canvas, 16 × 22 in. (40.6 × 55.9 cm)
Signed lower left: *T. Buttersworth*
Bequest of Irving S. Olds, 1963.58

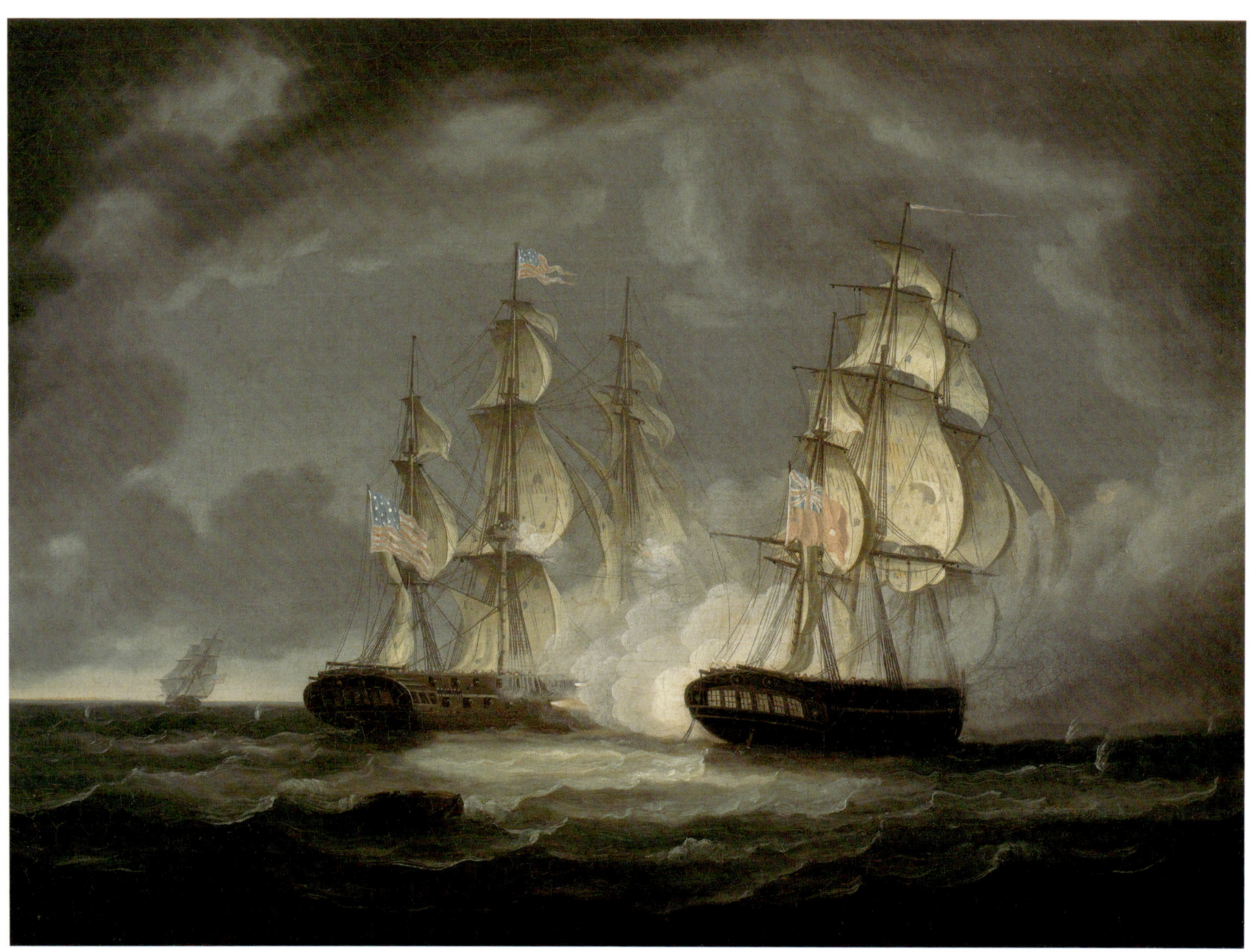

John Rodgers put to sea from New York. On June 23 they sighted the British frigate *Belvidera*, with thirty-six guns and Captain Richard Byron at the helm. Rodgers gave chase in his forty-four-gun flagship, *President*, and a long, running fight ensued before the *Belvidera* eventually escaped. The American squadron continued on its cruise of ninety days as far as the coast of Spain before returning to Boston. In Buttersworth's painting, the *President* is seen at the right exchanging fire with the *Belvidera*; other ships of the pursuing American squadron are in the distance. The darkening sky enhances the drama of cannon fire and billowing smoke of battle as the two ships fire broadsides at each other and cannonballs splash into the sea.[17]

Buttersworth's *Running Action between the U.S. Frigate "President" and HMS "Endymion"* is a nocturnal work of the same size conceived as a pendant and records the British capture of the *President* several years later, when it was under the command of Captain Stephen Decatur (fig. 17). On the night of January 14, 1815, the *President* slipped out of New York Harbor intending to rendezvous with three other American vessels in the South Atlantic and then cruise the Indian Ocean against enemy shipping. Early the next morning she encountered four vessels of a blockading British squadron under Captain John Haynes. Haynes gave chase, but by late afternoon Decatur managed to outdistance his enemies, except for the frigate *Endymion*. Unable to break clear, Decatur turned and engaged his pursuer at dusk, and we see the ships exchanging fire under an evening sky. After a two-and-a-half-hour fight, the badly damaged *Endymion* dropped out of the battle as the other British vessels hove into view. Decatur again attempted to escape. Around midnight, however, the British vessels overtook him, and he was compelled to surrender on January 16, and the American prize was taken to Bermuda. However, the war had ended, and Decatur was later released. Prints after Buttersworth's renditions of these dramatic encounters were published in London some months later.[18]

The American demand for naval images from the War of 1812 would secure Thomas Birch's reputation as the first homegrown marine specialist. Birch had immigrated as a youth from England to Philadelphia with his father, William Birch, from whom he learned the rudiments of maritime and marine painting. His subsequent mastery of the Anglo-Dutch marine tradition was demonstrated in spirited portrayals of successful American naval engagements such as the daring escape of the USS *Constitution* from the British fleet early in the War of 1812 (fig. 18). One of the original six and named by George Washington, the *Constitution* sailed out of Chesapeake Bay in July 1812 shortly after the outbreak of war en route from Annapolis to New York. On July 17, off the New Jersey shore, Captain Isaac Hull encountered a British squadron, which gave chase. With skillful seamanship, Hull kept the *Constitution* ahead of the

17. Thomas Buttersworth
(1768–1842)
Running Action between the U.S. Frigate "President" and HMS "Endymion," 1815
Oil on canvas, 16 × 22 in.
(40.6 × 55.9 cm)
Signed lower left:
T. Buttersworth
Bequest of Irving S. Olds,
1963.59

British for two days, even towing his ship after the breeze died down. Toward sundown on July 19, a favorable wind enabled Hull to slip away from his pursuers, and the *Constitution* reached Boston on July 26. Birch documented Hull's daring naval maneuvers by showing a trio of American longboats, the leader bearing the kedge anchor used to tow the massive ship while exchanging fire with the British in close pursuit. The artist's equal skills as a painter of splendid seascapes are also demonstrated here by the luminous atmosphere of water, light, and sky in which the dramatic chase takes place. The most famous of the original six, the *Constitution*'s later battles earned her the nickname "Old Ironsides," especially her victories against the *Guerriere* and the *Java* (figs. 64–66). Sometime before 1838, the *Constitution*'s retired commander commissioned this work from Birch to commemorate the famous escape of 1812. His decision to do so may well have been inspired by the national campaign in the 1830s to save the ship from being decommissioned and scrapped. This rumor had also inspired Oliver Wendell Holmes Sr. to write the poem "Old Ironsides" in 1830.[19]

Birch portrayed another famous naval exploit in one of his most celebrated battle subjects: *Capture of HMS "Macedonian" by the U.S. Frigate "United States."* Birch treated the subject several times in nearly identical painted versions. His interpretation became the iconic version when a print was published after one of these in Philadelphia in 1813 on the first anniversary of the famous victory, and another was issued in 1815 at the conclusion of the war (fig. 19). These widely circulated engravings provided models for copies in oil by other artists (fig. 20). This unsigned painting is slightly larger than Birch's originals, and the artist has taken certain liberties by introducing figures clinging to wreckage afloat in the foreground as well as ships in the distance. The work is undoubtedly modeled on the engraving and, although painted by a lesser hand, demonstrates the enduring popularity of these stirring battle subjects. The painting depicts the capture early in the war of the thirty-eight-gun British frigate *Macedonian*, with Captain John S. Carden, by the *United States*, with forty-four guns, one of the original six commanded by Captain Stephen Decatur. The ninety-minute action between the two vessels took place in the Atlantic Ocean several hundred miles west of the Canary Islands on October 25, 1812. The British prize was transported to Newport, Rhode Island, early in December 1812 and a few weeks later moved to New York. The *Macedonian* was the first British frigate captured in the War of 1812 that was taken to the United States; this was a cause for patriotic celebration that also confirmed Decatur as a national hero.[20]

The War of 1812 expanded the Revolutionary portrait pantheon as well, and a new generation of American heroes joined the founding fathers and patriots of the Revolution.

18. Thomas Birch
(1779–1851)
Escape of the U.S. Frigate "Constitution," 1838
Oil on canvas, 25⅛ × 35¾ in.
(63.8 × 90.8 cm)
Signed and dated lower right:
Thos Birch / 1838
Bequest of Matilda Wolfe Bruce, 1908.5

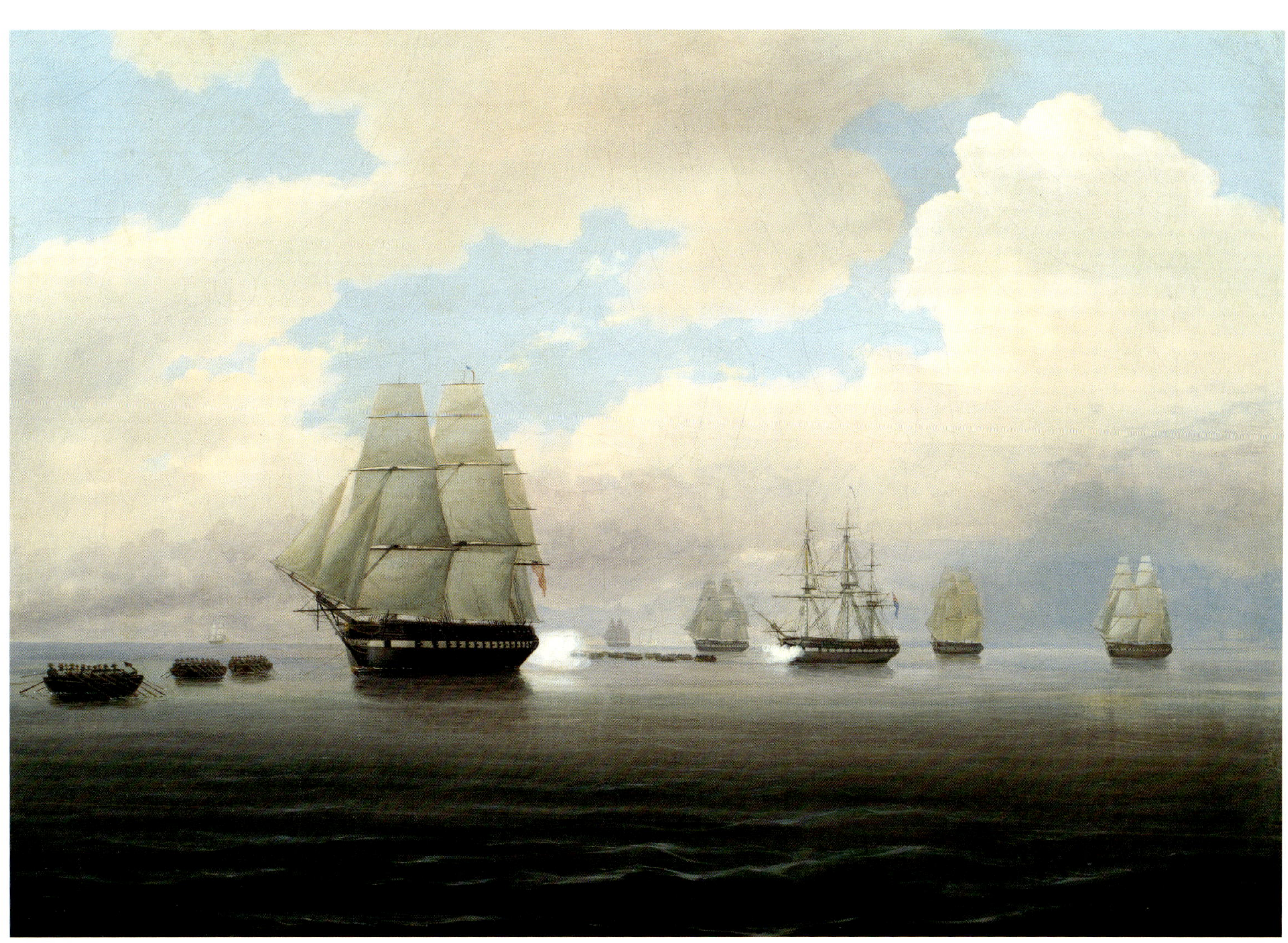

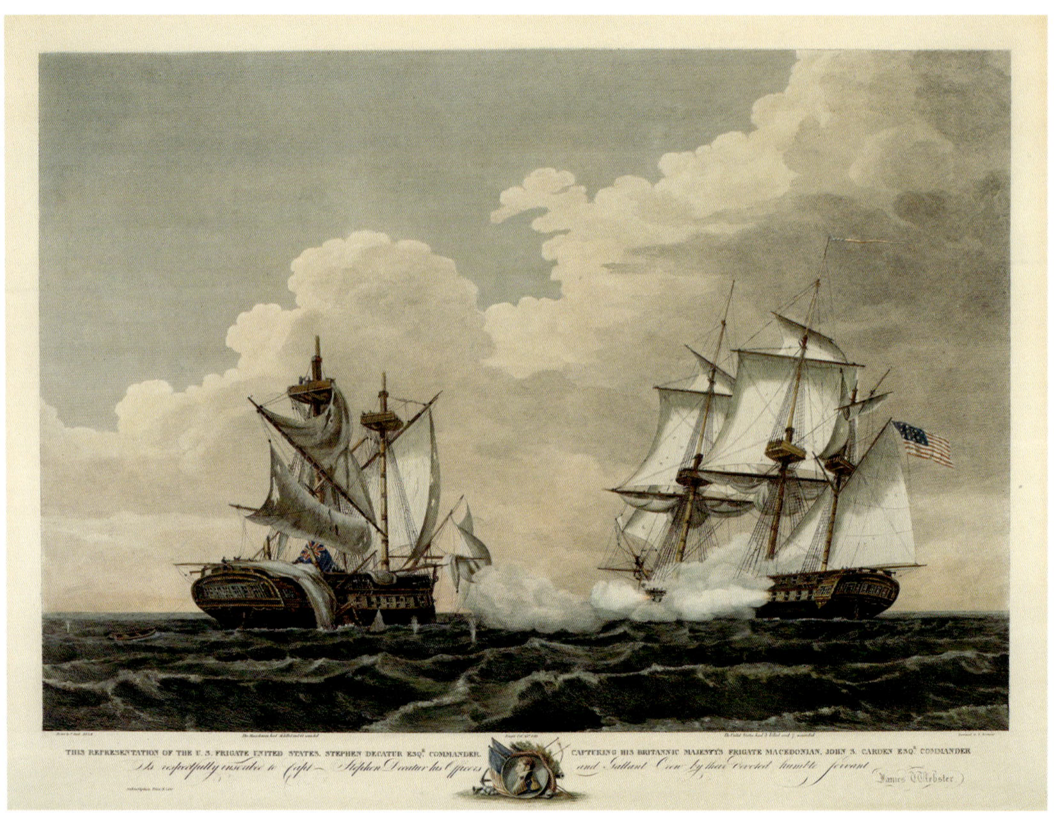

19. Samuel Seymour (active 1796–1823), hand-colored engraving after Thomas Birch (1779–1851)
Capture of HMS "Macedonian" by the U.S. Frigate "United States," 1815
Hand-colored engraving, 21⅜ × 28 7/16 in. (54 × 72 cm)
New-York Historical Society, Department of Prints, Photographs, and Architectural Collections

Portraits of naval commanders were in demand, as were paintings of their ships and battles. Their likenesses were also often replicated in popular prints and as images on ceramics. Rembrandt Peale, whose father Charles Willson Peale had portrayed the founding fathers, painted a series of naval heroes including Commodore Stephen Decatur (fig. 21). Peale's romantic bust-length portrait, originally among the portraits of prominent men in the collection of the Peale Museum in Philadelphia, presents the naval hero as both a dashing figure and a commanding martial presence. Gazing into the distance, resplendent in his dress uniform, Decatur is posed in a timeless setting before a stormy sky whose dramatic clouds also evoke the smoke and turbulence of battle. Decatur's popular celebrity inspired mass replication of images of his likeness and his victories, seen here in miniature as applied to snuffboxes (figs. 22, 23).[21]

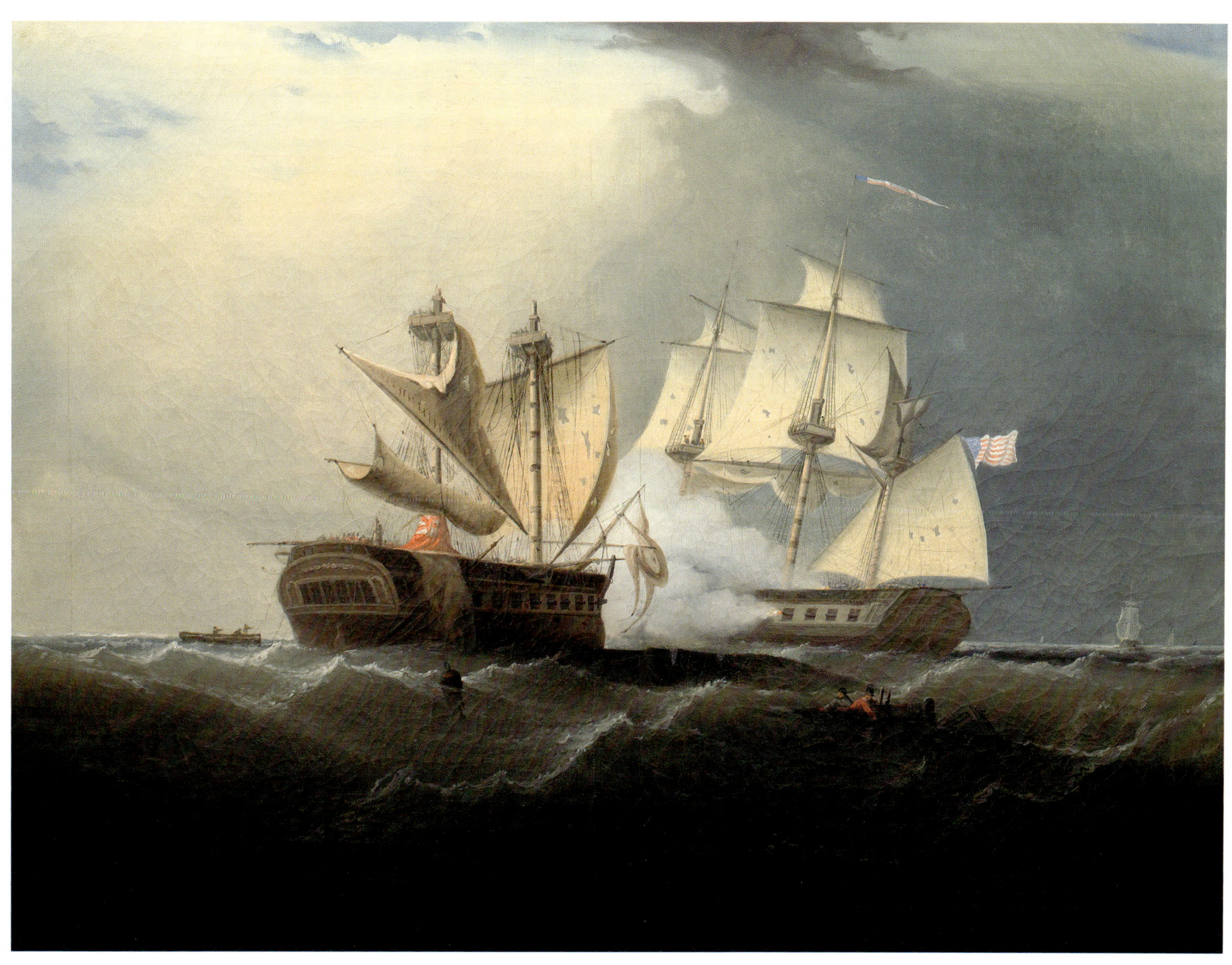

20. Unidentified Artist, after Thomas Birch (1779–1851)
Capture of HMS "Macedonian" by the U.S. Frigate "United States," ca. 1813
Oil on canvas, 34⅜ × 45½ in. (87.3 × 115.6 cm)
Gift of Naval History Society Collection, 1925.112

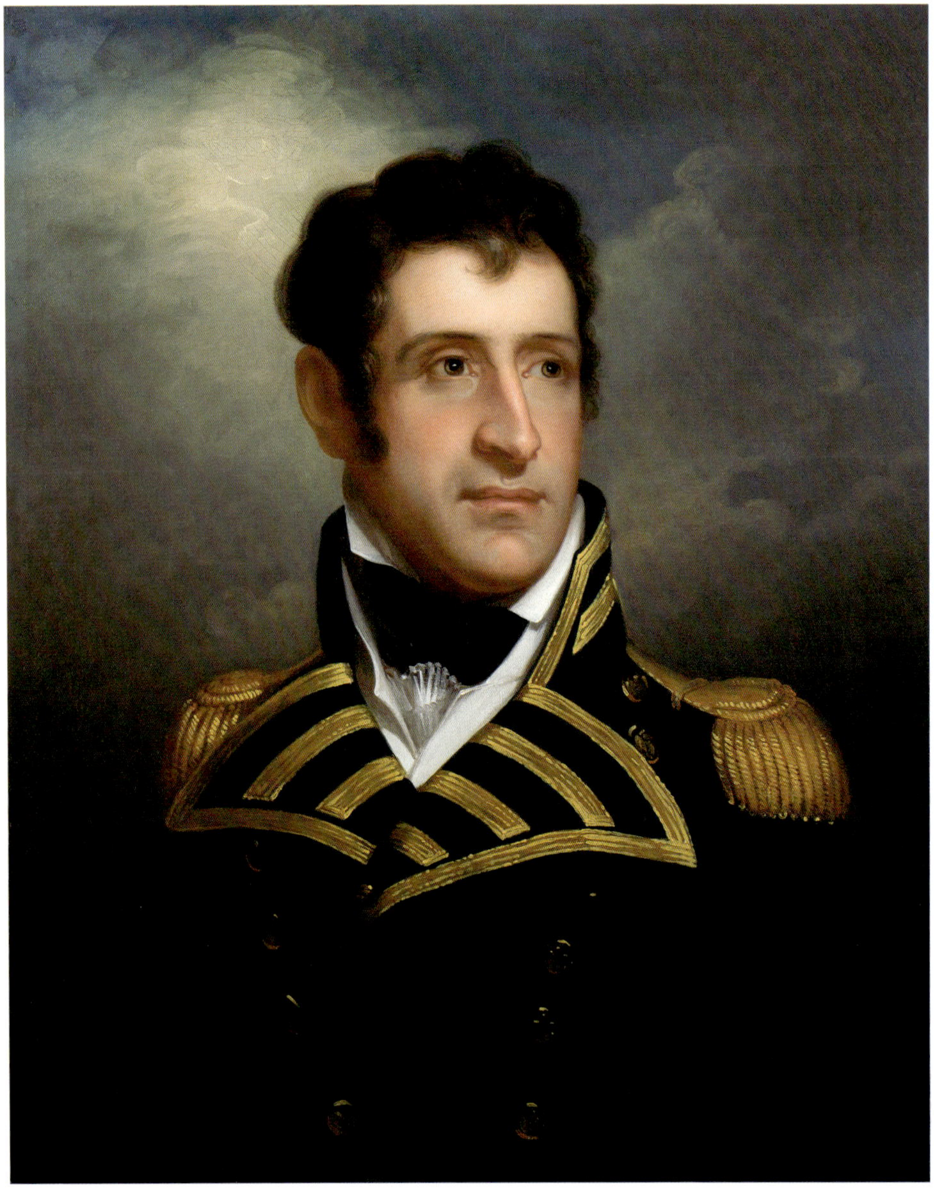

21. Rembrandt Peale (1778–1860)
Stephen Decatur (1779–1820), ca. 1815–20
Oil on canvas, 29 × 23⅝ in. (73.7 × 60 cm)
Gift of Thomas Jefferson Bryan, 1867.309

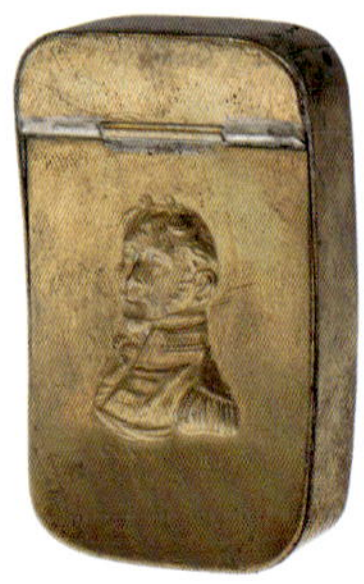

22. Unidentified Maker
Snuffbox, 1816
Brass, tin, 2¾ × 1½ × ½ in.
(7 × 3.8 × 1.3 cm)
Engraved on lid:
COMMODORE / DECATUR / 1816
Gift of Bernard Cone,
1937.66

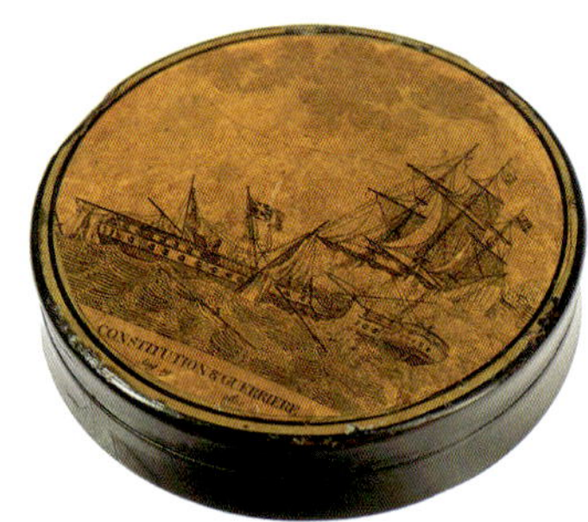

23. Unidentified Maker
Snuffbox, 1812–30
Papier-mâché, paint,
H. ¾ × Diam. 3⅜ in.
(1.9 × 8.6 cm)
Printed on lid:
CONSTITUTION & GUERRIERE / Aug–19 1812
Z.1851ab

ADVENTURE AND ALLEGORY: THE ROMANTIC SEASCAPE

The proud vessels enacting Buttersworth's and Birch's spirited naval adventures, doing battle as military adversaries on the high seas, also carried symbolic freight as patriotic emblems—ships of state—with names like *United States*, *President*, and *Constitution* bestowed on them to inspire national pride. Another realm of maritime contest offered even greater challenges and adventure. There, the adversary was not man but nature, and shipwreck was no less terrible and sometimes far worse than defeat in battle. In these paintings, the boat or ship in stormy seas off dangerous coasts is the actor in a marine theater of the sublime engaged in a battle against fate in the form of natural forces. In this context, shipwreck serves as a symbol of life's trials and vicissitudes. Spectacular shipwrecks were international news by the early nineteenth century, as demonstrated by the enduring popular fascination with the tragedy of the *Medusa* that inspired Cooke's copy after Géricault (see fig. 2).

On a much more modest scale, both Thomas Cole's drawing *Shipwreck Scene (Allegory of Fortune/Hope)*, 1828, and Birch's *Ship in a Storm*, 1841, present humanity helpless before the forces of nature and fate. The tragic saga of the *Medusa*'s wreck was famous, and Cole in New York and Birch in Philadelphia may have known prints after Géricault's masterpiece, but they surely knew engravings or, perhaps, copies after the works of the earlier French master of the maritime sublime Claude-Joseph Vernet (fig. 24). Birch also knew Vernet's paintings in the local collection of Joseph Bonaparte, which were often lent to and eventually acquired by the Pennsylvania Academy of the Fine Arts. Vernet's dramatic paintings of shipwrecks and storms at sea offered powerful models for romantic seascapes in the sublime mode. Cole's small drawing is ambitious despite its size, an exercise in the sublime that employs the motif of a shipwreck survivor's plight to visualize an allegory of human destiny (fig. 25). A rocky promontory rising unexpectedly in mid-ocean has caused a ship to founder and sink. A lone survivor atop the rock waves a flag as a distress signal, as does the figure in Géricault's painting, hoping to attract the attention of a distant passing ship. The curving menace of an ocean swell breaking against the massive rock brings up a shattered mast from the sunken ship with a pennant still attached, bearing the unlucky vessel's name, *Fortune*.[22]

Cole only occasionally painted seascapes, whereas Birch advanced in a career as America's best-known early marine painter, able to portray a wide range of maritime subject matter, as we have already seen. He moved easily from ship portraits and harbor views to romantic seascapes like *Ship in a Storm* that explore the perils of the sea exemplified in the struggles of the unseen crew of a brig to maintain control of their ship, perhaps already aground in the

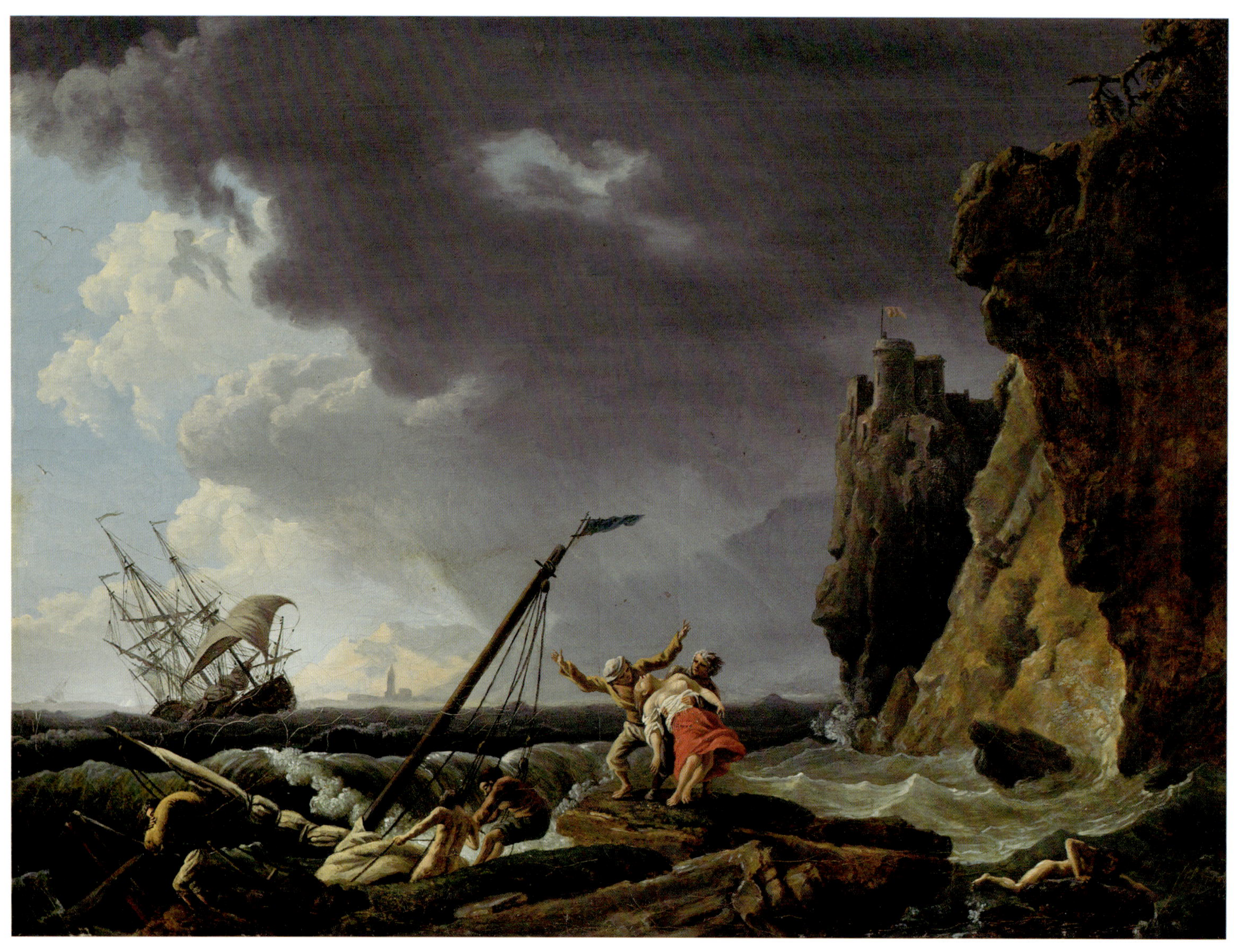

24. Unidentified Artist in the manner of Claude-Joseph Vernet (1714–1789)
Shipwreck off a Rocky Coast, ca. 1800
Oil on canvas, 16 × 22 in. (40.6 × 55.9 cm)
Gift of Livingston Goodhue, 1950.376

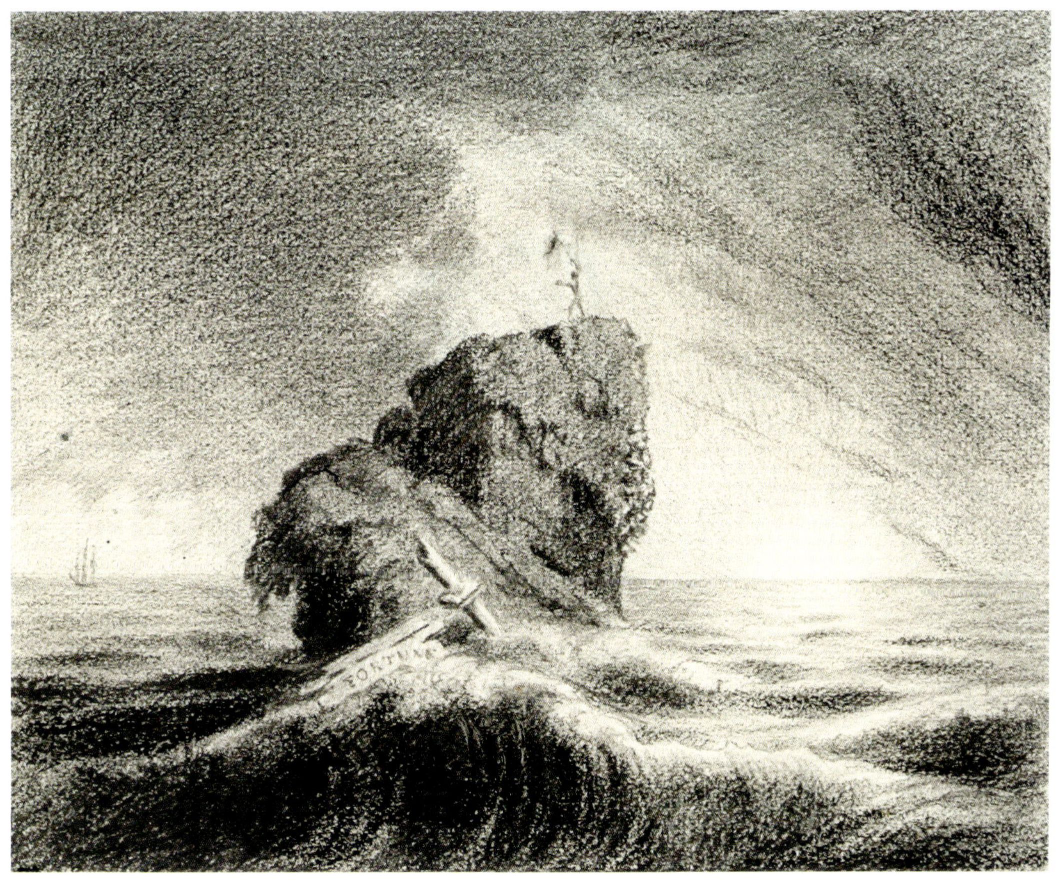

heavy-weather gale that drives the rough sea to break in huge waves against massive boulders and hidden ledges of the lee shore (fig. 26). Unlike Cole's drawing, no figures can be seen here; the ship itself is the major actor in a drama of the elements. Nature is the adversary. Ominous clouds, powerful waves, and looming rocks in the foreground create a menacing yet somehow thrilling environment that epitomizes the sublime, a contest in which the fate of the distant vessel is uncertain. The artist himself is symbolically threatened as the waves creep higher and higher on the rocky shore, where Birch has inscribed his signature. Works like *Ship in a Storm* were admired for vivid portrayals of maritime peril: "His brig in distress is so faithfully painted that we could almost imagine him to have been one of those in the boat which he exhibits."[23]

25. Thomas Cole (1801–1848)
Shipwreck Scene (Allegory of Fortune/Hope), Folio 11 in the John Ludlow Morton Album, 1828
Conté crayon and graphite on paper, 3 5/16 × 4 1/8 in. (8.4 × 10.4 cm)
Bequest of Emily Ellison Post, 1944.376

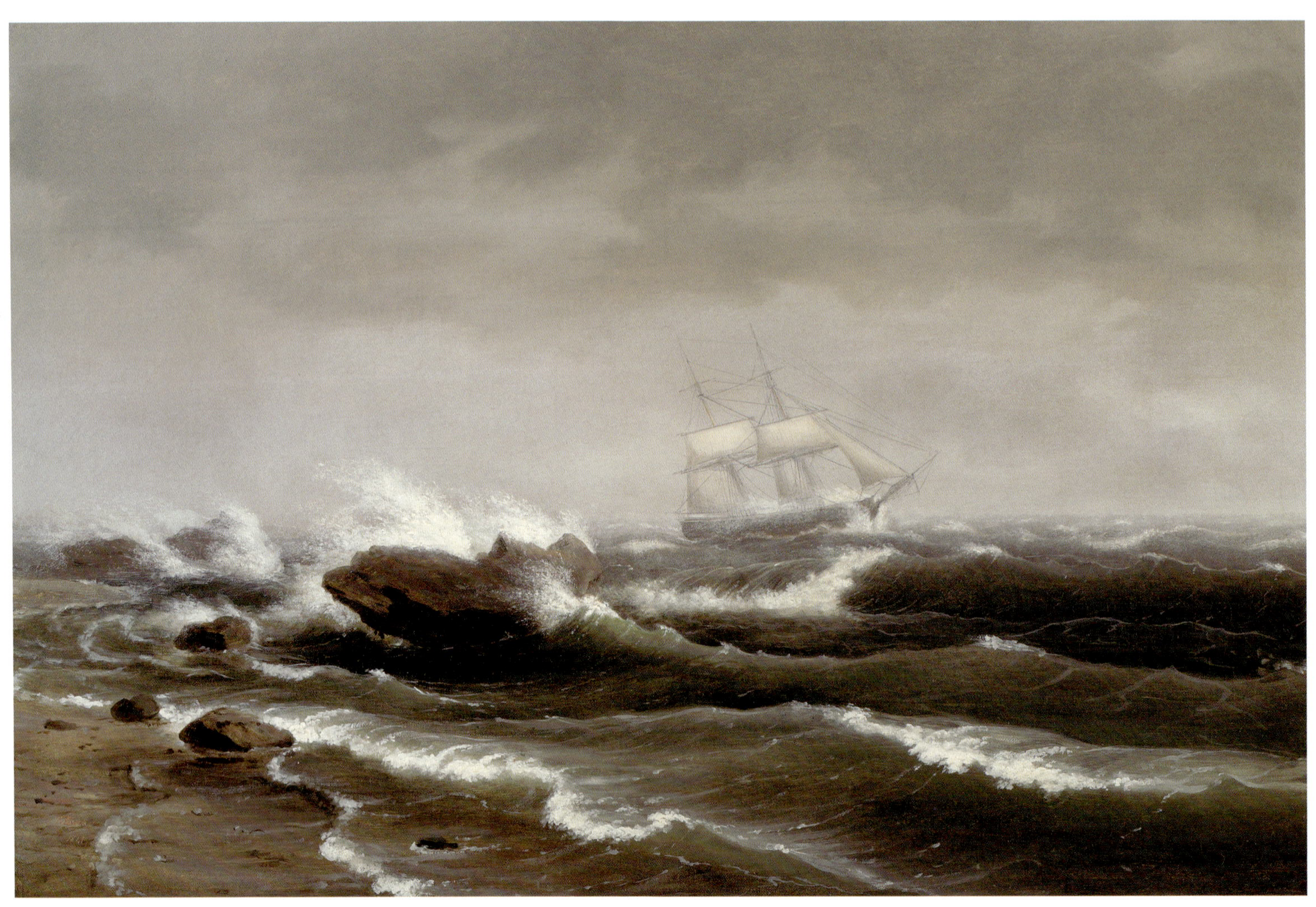

26. Thomas Birch (1779–1851)
Ship in a Storm, 1841
Oil on canvas, 18 × 27⅛ in. (45.7 × 68.9 cm)
Signed and dated lower left: *T. Birch / 1841*
Gift of Mrs. Louis A. Gillet, 1945.451

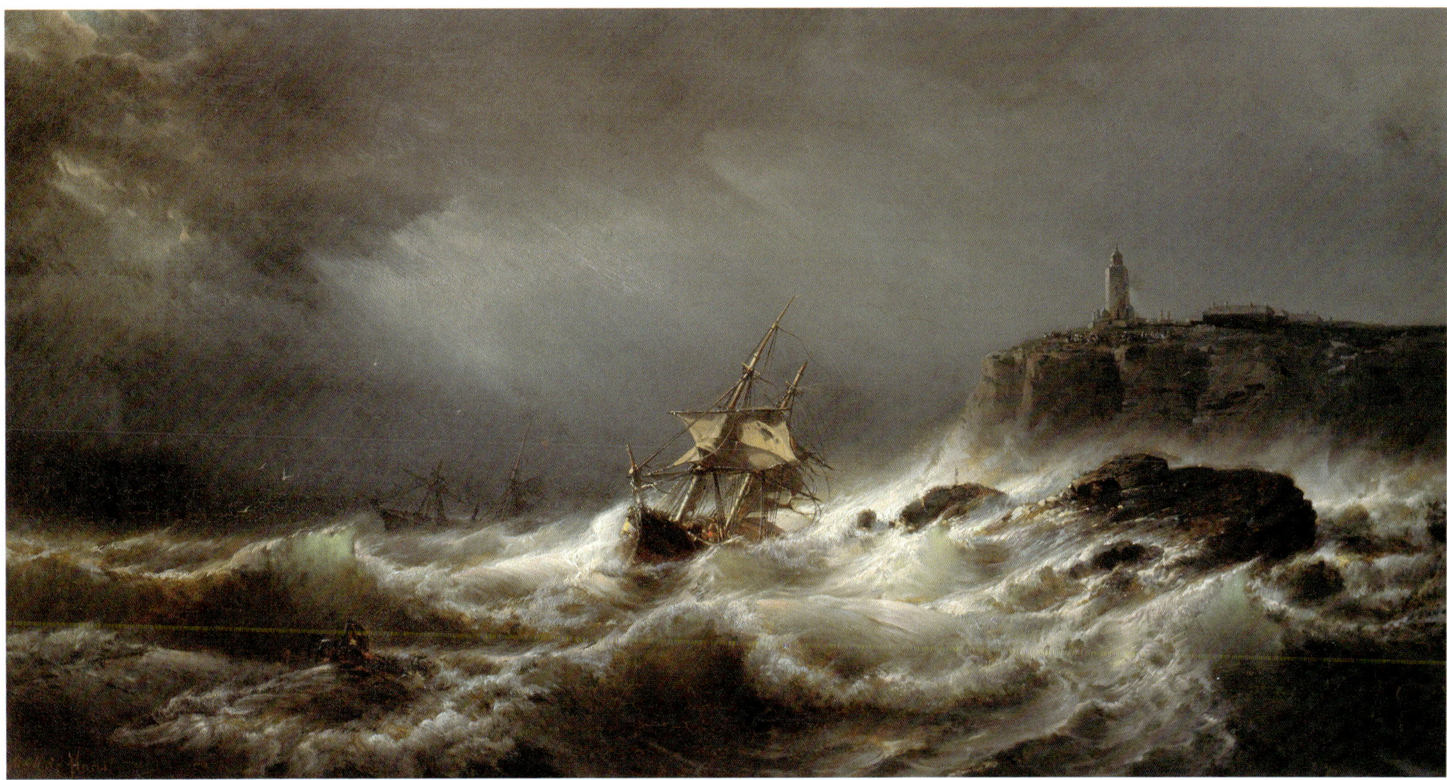

Human actors play a subordinate role as the powerless observers of Mauritz Frederick Hendrick De Haas's stirring *Wreck on the Isle of Jersey* painted some twenty years later (fig. 27). Born and trained in Holland, De Haas enjoyed great success as a maritime painter with an artist's commission in the Dutch navy, until the American ambassador, August Belmont, persuaded him to emigrate to the United States in 1859.[24] Settling in New York, De Haas repeated his success, and his painterly skills are evident in this portrayal of the most dreaded of maritime disasters unfolding within sight of the lighthouse that should be a beacon of safety in this dangerous passage. Peering closely, we are able to discern crowds clustered near the lighthouse on the cliffs above the channel, all helpless witnesses as huge storm-driven waves overwhelm the struggling vessels foundering on the rocks below. De Haas's own experience as a mariner in these waters may have inflected the subject as well. His somber palette and painterly touch create a surface in which storm clouds and rough seas seem to merge into a boiling mass of vapors and waves. Errant beams of light break through the clouds to highlight the sails and foaming waves in the foreground, a bit of aerial stagecraft that reinforces the

27. Mauritz Frederick Hendrick De Haas (1832–1895)
Wreck on the Isle of Jersey, ca. 1862
Oil on canvas, 17 × 32 in. (43.2 × 81.3 cm)
Signed lower left: *M.F.H. de Haas*
The Robert L. Stuart Collection, S-89
(detail overleaf)

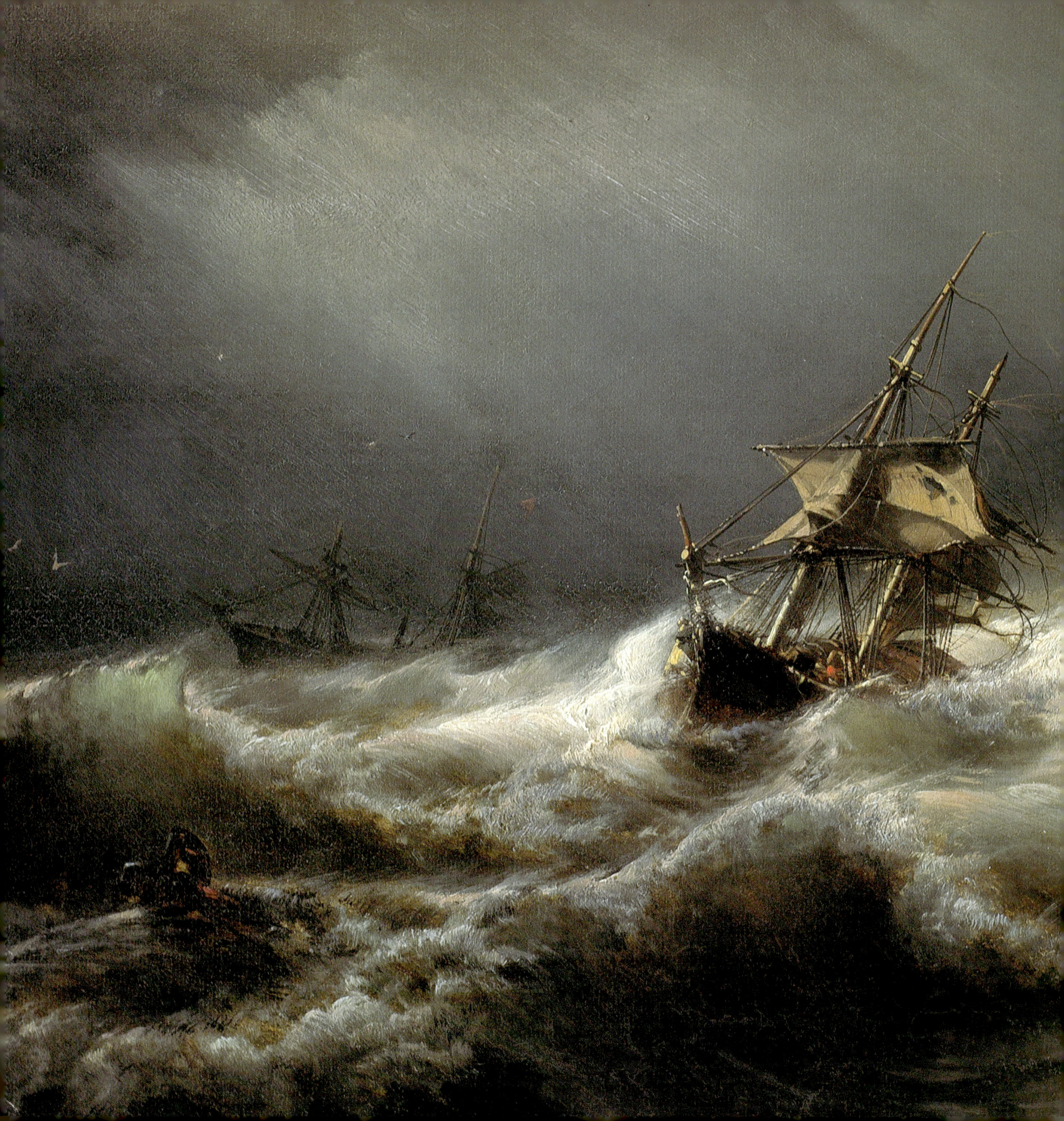

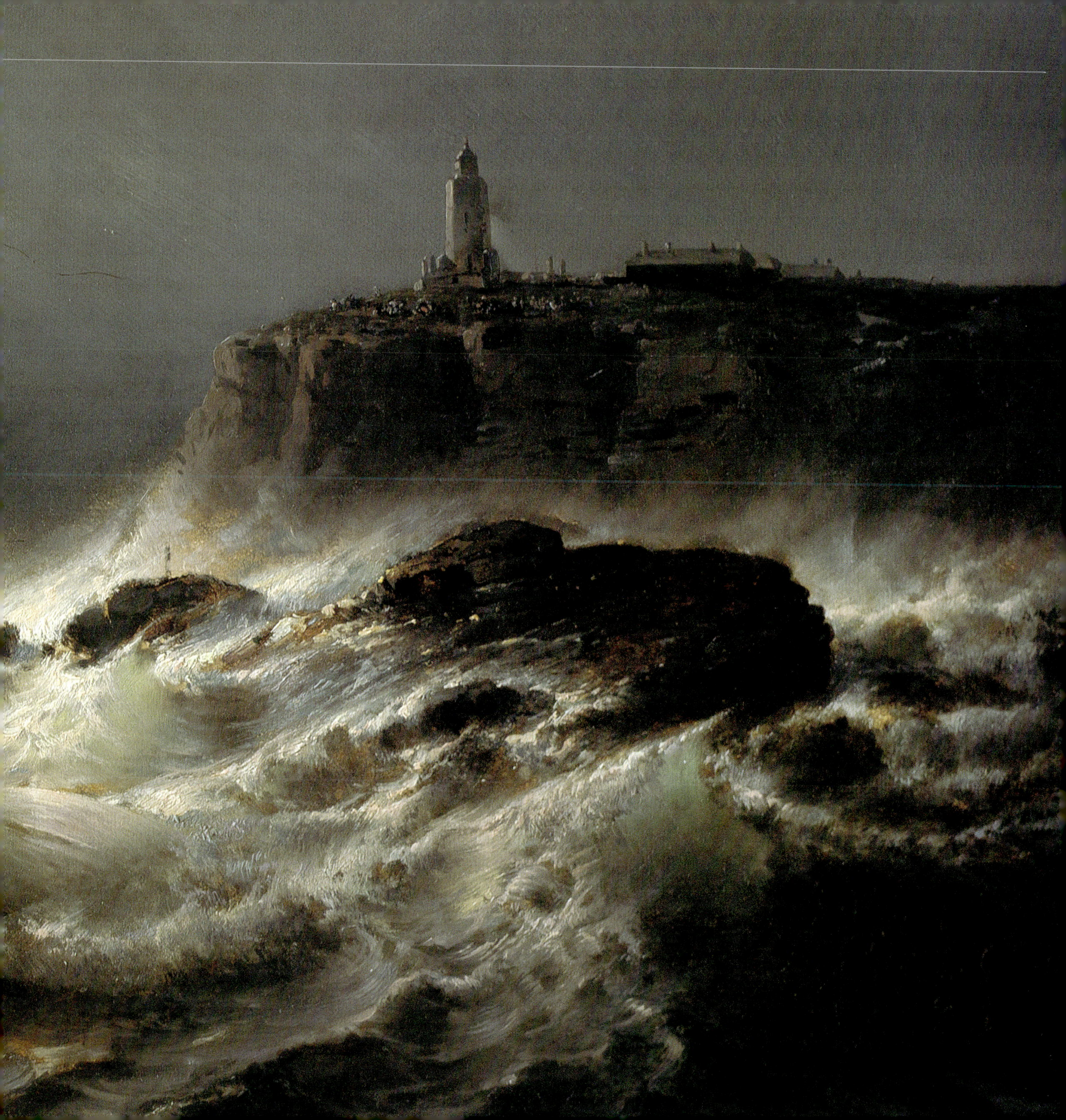

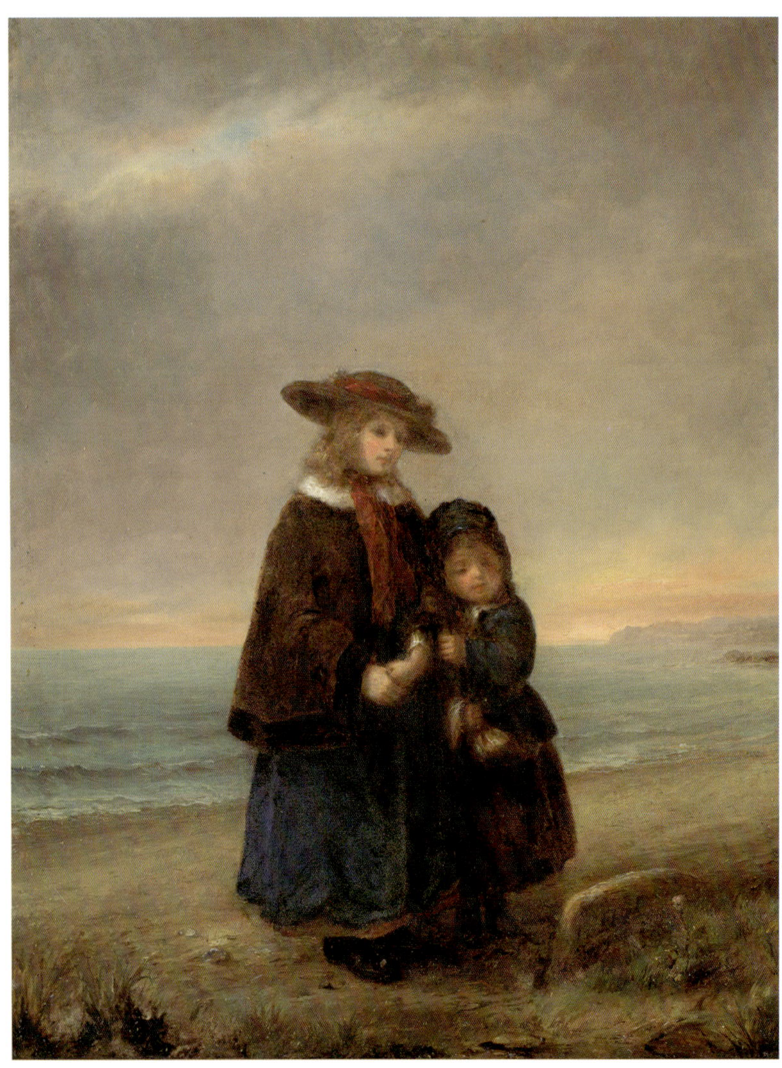

28. Richard Morrell Staigg (1817–1881)
The Sailor's Grave, ca. 1862
Oil on board, 14 × 10⅜ in. (35.6 × 26.4 cm)
The Robert L. Stuart Collection, S-38

tragic drama playing out below. Richard Staigg's *The Sailor's Grave* presents the aftermath of loss at sea (fig. 28). The storm has passed and a mood of quiet melancholy pervades this modestly scaled but poignant little figure painting that shows two young girls on the seashore mourning at the grave marker of a father or brother as the very waves that may have claimed him roll in behind them. *The Sailor's Grave* is a touching reminder of the tragic consequences of such marine disasters. The title evokes a popular poem of the 1820s, reminding us again of the rich seafaring literature that parallels these paintings.[25]

The pervasive theme of shipwreck not only embodied the thrill of the sublime but also mirrored the awful reality of frequent disasters at sea. Reports of such catastrophes abounded in the news. In 1813 the beautiful Theodosia Alston, Aaron Burr's adored and accomplished daughter, shown here in John Vanderlyn's portrait of 1802, had perished in a storm off Cape Hatteras on a voyage from Charleston to New York (fig. 29). Years later, Winslow Homer's dramatic illustration for *Harper's Weekly,* "The Wreck of the Atlantic—Cast Up by the Sea," documented another such victim (fig. 30). This anonymous beauty was one of 562 drowned in a catastrophic wreck in 1873, when the steamship *Atlantic* foundered on rocks in the middle of the night near Halifax. The half-submerged vessel is seen in the distance.[26] Homer worked between the worlds of journalism and fine art, as did another New England–born marine painter, Wesley Webber. Webber is little known today, but his dramatic painting *Sinking of the "Ville du Havre," November 22, 1873* graphically details the shipboard horror of another marine calamity that same year (fig. 31). En route from New York to France in the early hours of November 22, the steamship collided with the Scottish iron clipper *Loch Earn*, sinking in twelve minutes with the loss of 226 lives. Only 87 survivors were rescued by the *Loch Earn*, which was itself badly damaged by the crash and would sink after all aboard had been rescued by an American cargo ship. Webber undoubtedly made use of extensive newspaper reports and images in the illustrated press to aid him in an effort to re-create a highly detailed bird's-eye view to present accurate visual reportage of the final minutes of the *Ville du Havre* and many of her passengers.[27] The painting is moderate in scale but depicts the vast nocturnal mid-Atlantic under a starry sky. The dark ocean is illuminated only by the catastrophe itself, as flames from the stacks of the doomed ship cast a lurid glow over crowds of passengers struggling amid the wreckage on the decks and in the dark waters near the half-submerged ship. The clipper appears at the left as a dark silhouette. A lifeboat from the *Loch Earn* approaches the sinking ship, while another, filled with survivors, labors to avoid fallen spars and rigging at the right. Webber spares us no discomfiting detail of the ship's destruction and the passengers' afflictions.

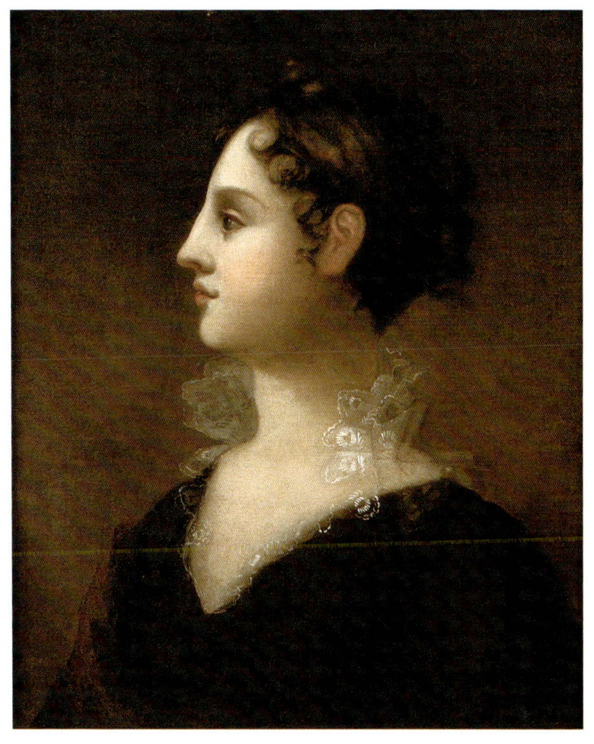

29. John Vanderlyn (1775–1852)
Theodosia Burr (Mrs. Joseph Alston) (1783–1813), 1802
Oil on canvas, 22 × 18¾ in. (55.9 × 47.6 cm)
Gift of Dr. John E. Stillwell, 1931.60

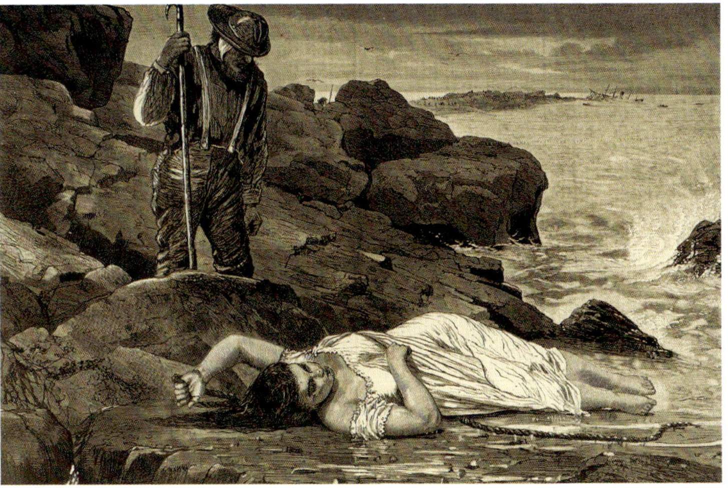

30. Winslow Homer (1836–1910)
"The Wreck of the Atlantic—Cast Up by the Sea."
Harper's Weekly, April 26, 1873, 345
New-York Historical Society Library

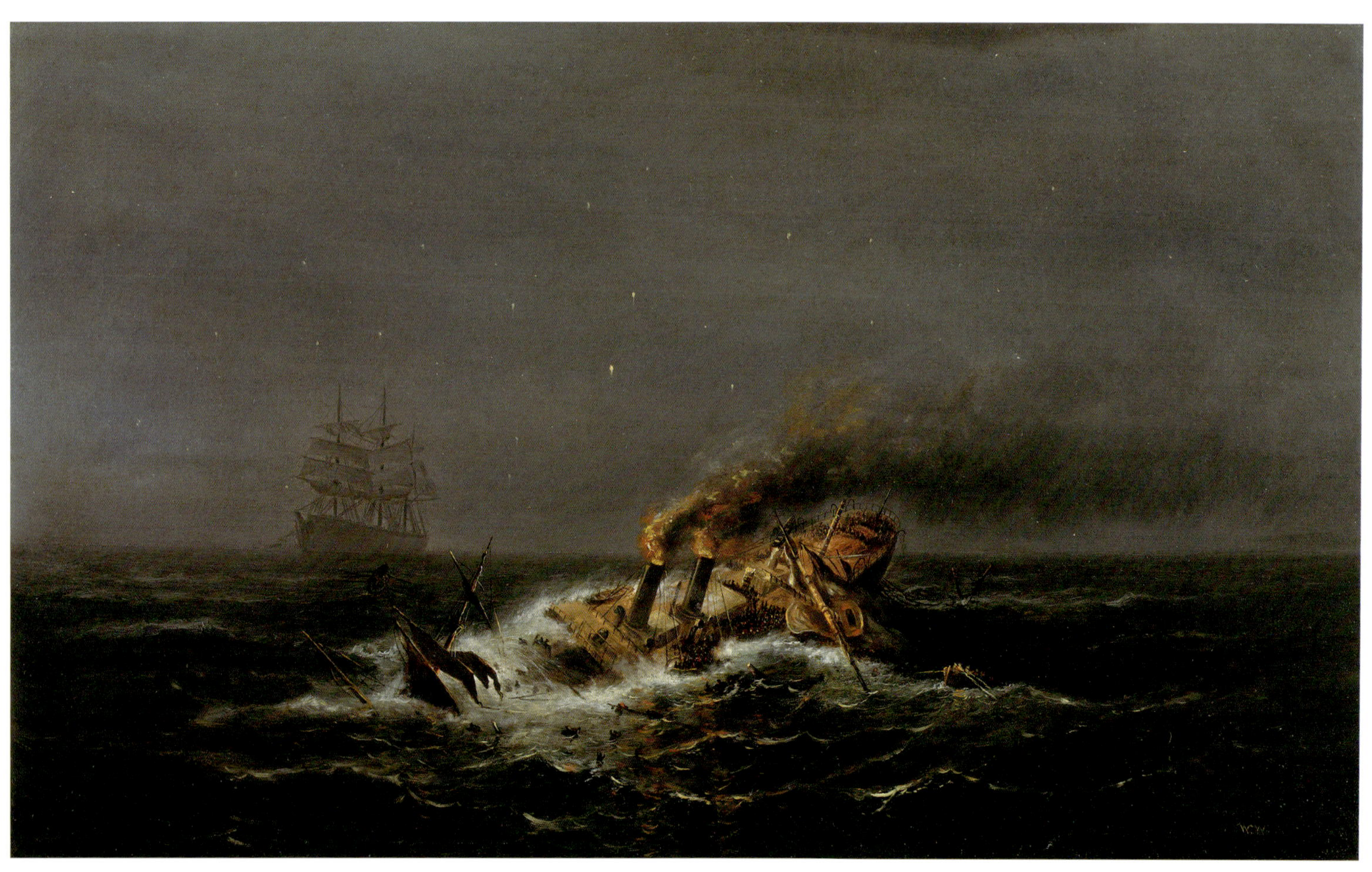

31. Wesley Webber (1841–1914)
Sinking of the "Ville du Havre," November 22, 1873, ca. 1874
Oil on canvas, 24 × 40 in. (61 × 101.6 cm)
Signed lower left: *W. Webber*
Purchase, 1938.437

While one wonders who would have welcomed such a work on their walls, both wrecks were immortalized in popular prints issued by Currier and Ives that same year. These disasters and others highlighted the inadequacies of maritime safety practices. The United States Life-Saving Service would be reorganized and modern lifesaving technology introduced. Beginning in the 1850s, medals were struck by the United States Mint to recognize those who saved the lives of shipwrecked mariners, honoring both individual and collective acts of bravery (fig. 32). Efforts to develop better lifesaving equipment were also recognized. The bronze Joseph Francis lifesaving medallion was modeled after the Congressional Gold Medal awarded to Francis in 1890 for his endeavors. The reverse of the medal portrays a shipwreck with Francis's most famous invention in operation. His metallic life-car, credited with saving thousands of lives, is shown transporting the passengers and crew to safety from a stranded vessel foundering offshore (fig. 33).[28]

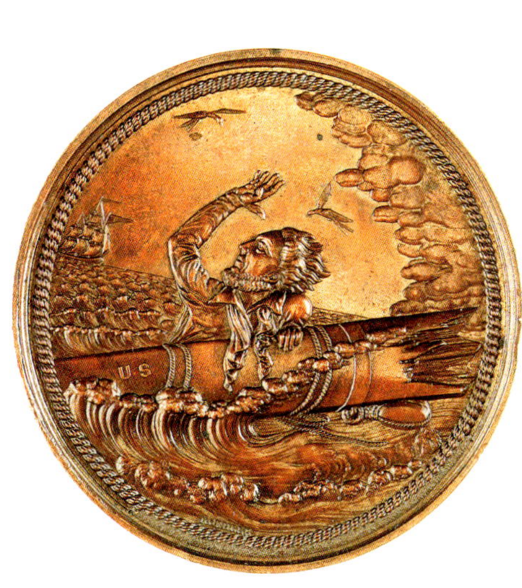

32. Francis X. Koehler (1818–1886)
State Department lifesaving medal (obverse), 1862
Bronze, Diam. 2½ in. (6.4 cm)
Signed bottom obverse: *KOEHLER*
Gift of the Naval History Society, 1925, 2008.42.368

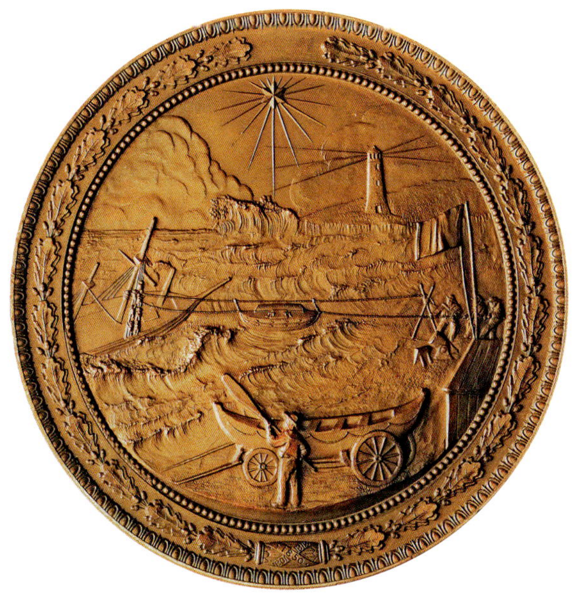

33. Louis St. Gaudens (1854–1913)
Joseph Francis lifesaving medallion (reverse), 1890
Bronze, Diam. 4 in. (10.2 cm)
Gift of the Naval History Society, 1925, 2008.42.370

SEAFARING ENTERPRISE: MIDCENTURY PORTRAITS OF MERCHANTS, MARINERS, AND SPORTSMEN

True to his name, Preserved Fish, who was descended from early New Englanders, found his career on the sea, a memoir of which is included in this attractive, although unattributed, portrait of the gray-haired gentleman (fig. 34). By age twenty-one, he had been master of his own whaling ship and soon after established a successful whale oil business in New Bedford, Massachusetts. By 1815 Fish had relocated and was well established as a leading merchant in New York City. In this occupational portrait, he is seated in a handsomely furnished chamber with the implements of his trade. Holding a telescope with which to watch his many ships coming into New York Harbor, Fish rests his left hand on a marine chart. Through the window is a maritime vista of two ships in pursuit of a spouting whale, a testimonial to the original source of his wealth. When at leisure, the crews aboard Fish's whaling ships probably crafted scrimshaw, carving or incising lively drawings and decorations into the jawbones or teeth of their prey.[29] This fine example chronicles the saga of whaling played out in episodes that document the voyage and the hunt on one side and, on the other, a scene of crew members cutting-in a carcass (fig. 35).

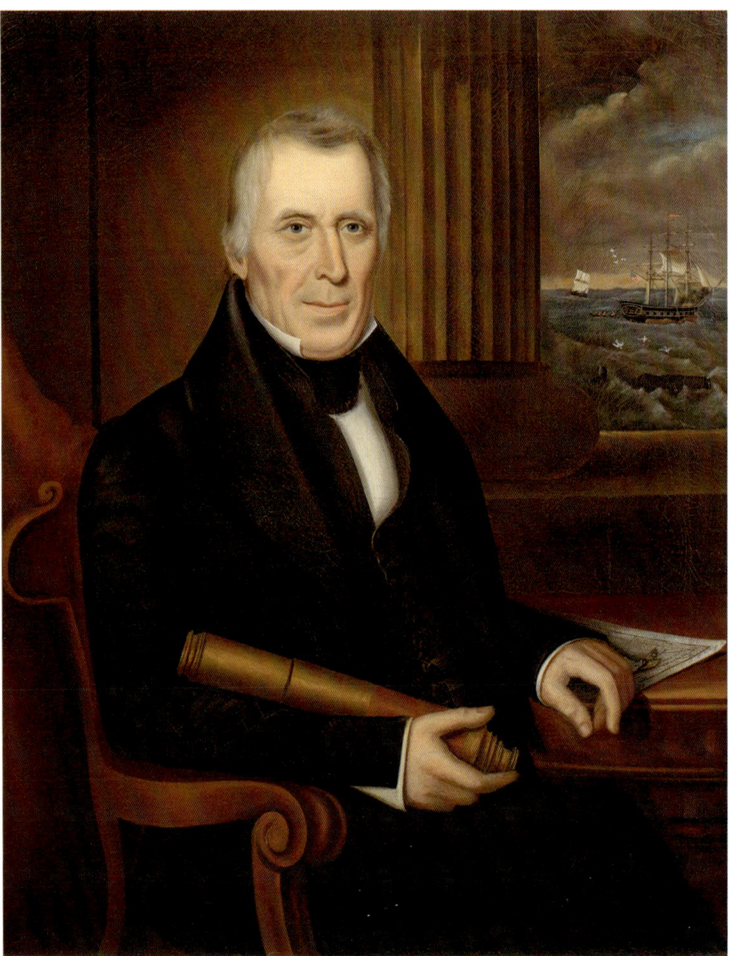

34. Unidentified Artist
Preserved Fish (1766–1846), ca. 1830
Oil on canvas, 41¼ × 33¼ in. (104.8 × 84.5 cm)
Gift of the Tradesmen's Bank of New York, 1900.4

One of Fish's business partners had been Henry Grinnell who, when he retired in 1850, pursued a passion for polar exploration by providing the ships for two important American Arctic expeditions. Their mission was to find Sir John Franklin's party of explorers who were lost in 1845 on their quest to complete the traverse of the Northwest Passage, a series of Arctic waterways connecting the Atlantic and Pacific Oceans sought for centuries by European and American explorers as a possible trade route to Asia. Dr. Elisha Kent Kane, a Philadelphian who had led a seafaring life as a naval surgeon, joined the first Grinnell expedition of 1850 as senior medical officer

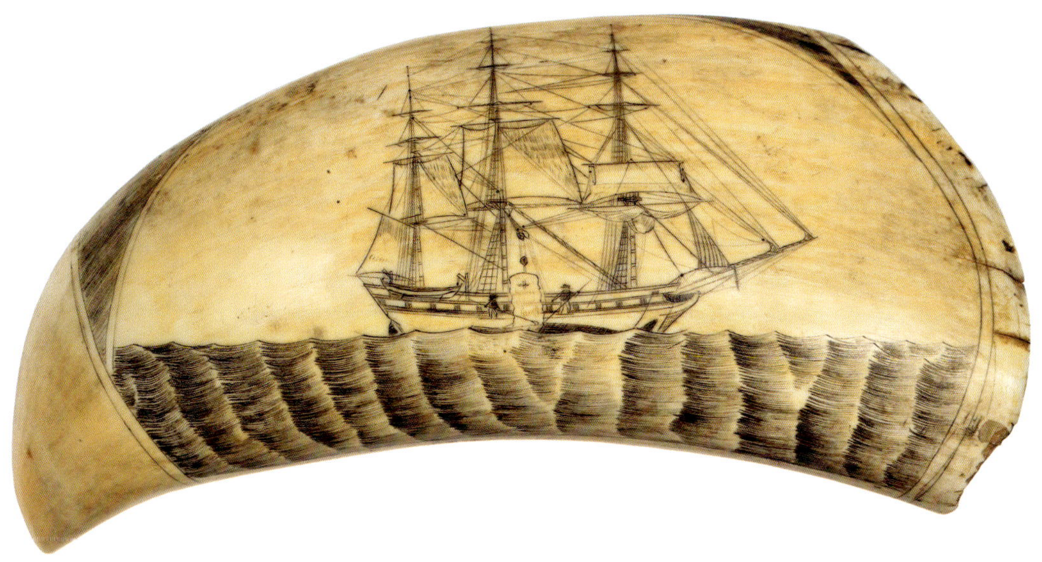

35. Unidentified Maker. Whale's tooth, scrimshaw, 1840–60
Ivory, black ink, 3⅛ × 7¼ × 2¼ in. (7.9 × 18.4 × 5.7 cm)
Gift of Colonel Henry O. Havemeyer, 1981.33[dup]

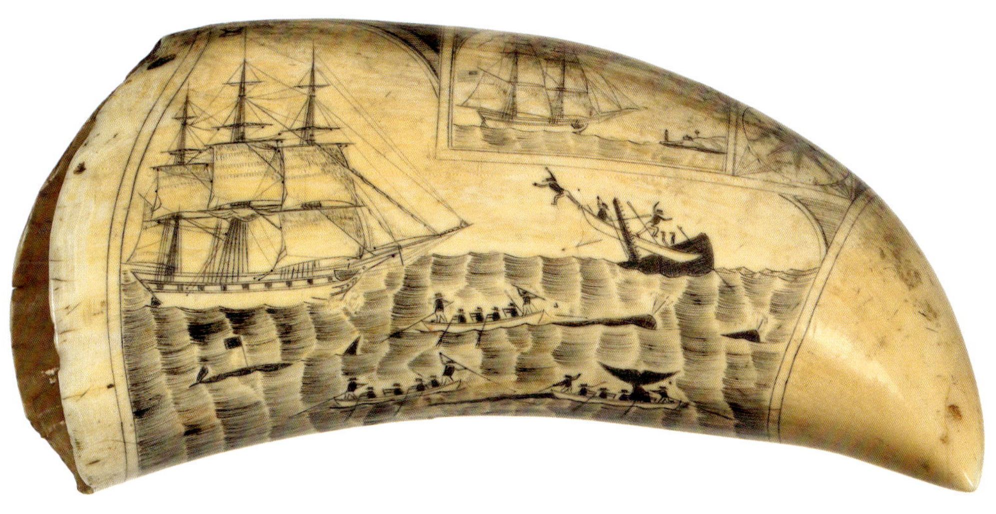

(fig. 36). He led the second voyage from 1853 to 1855 during which his ship, the *Advance*, was trapped in ice for twenty-one months. Abandoning ship, Kane led his party on a perilous overland journey to safety, a feat for which he was hailed as a hero. Kane's popular celebrity was based on two best-selling memoirs about the Arctic adventure (1854, 1856), illustrated by the Philadelphia marine painter James Hamilton after Kane's own sketches. Drawn from his journals, Kane's narrative deftly combined the modes of the travelogue with a seafaring exploration adventure narrative. Sadly, hardships borne on the expedition had ruined Kane's health, and he died at thirty-seven in 1857 at the height of his fame. Within a few years, Thomas Hicks had painted several memorial portraits of the explorer, in each basing Kane's features on widely published daguerreotypes.[30] The likeness presented to the Society in 1859 by "several ladies of New York" portrays a clean-shaven Kane in profile: a thoughtful, scholarly figure dressed as he might have appeared at the lecture podium. He looks up from his work, pen in hand and seated before a window opening on to a twilit ocean view with a vessel anchored in the distance with sails furled. The ship and a globe refer to Kane's far-flung voyages, while the table covered with books, charts, and documents signifies his role as both the leader and official historian of the expedition.

Popular fascination with the polar region extended to contemporary American landscape painters like Frederic Church and William Bradford. Inspired by Kane's adventures, Bradford would specialize in Arctic subjects, making seven expeditions to the region between 1861 and 1869 to capture "the terrible aspects of the Frigid Zone."[31] His large painting *Summer in the Land of the Midnight Sun* portrays the perils of a voyage to the Arctic regions, where waters were open to navigation for only one or two months of the year (fig. 37). Perhaps recalling Kane's narrative, and probably aided by photographs from his own publication, *The Arctic Regions: Illustrated with Photographs Taken on an Art Expedition to Greenland* (1873), Bradford captures the drama of vessels trapped in a vast and barren landscape of vividly colored glacial peaks. In the foreground, the ship's crew struggles to salvage supplies and equipment under the eerie light of the midnight sun.

Even though the Northwest Passage proved to be elusive, the China trade flourished, creating a vast commercial maritime network between certain Chinese ports and the West. The United States established trade relations with China in 1784, when the first American merchant vessel, *Empress of China*, sailed from New York to Canton. These contacts also generated schools of Chinese artists who served the demand by foreign mariners for images of themselves and their vessels. A modestly scaled portrait records the features of Hevlyn Benson who,

36. Thomas Hicks (1816–1890)
Elisha Kent Kane, M.D. (1820–1857), 1858
Oil on canvas, 42 × 51 in. (106.7 × 129.5 cm)
Signed and dated lower left: *T. Hicks / 1858*
Gift of several ladies of New York, 1859.1

conducted his business in the foreigners' district of Canton, the so-called Thirteen Factories, or hongs, as the Chinese called them, documented along with the Anglican church in a small, carefully painted view (fig. 39). The large two- and three-story buildings on the waterfront were called factories, but they did not actually manufacture goods. Instead, they served as the sites for international commerce, providing both residences and trading quarters for Western merchants. Flags of five nations are on display, indicating Canton's importance in the global maritime commerce of the mid-nineteenth century. A medley of exotic Chinese vessels passes by on the Pearl River before the factories including, at the far right, one of the famous Canton floating brothels called "flower boats." Western sailing ships and steamboats ply the waters in a matching panoramic vista of Hong Kong harbor viewed from Kowloon. By 1850 this busy port was already a British Crown Colony (fig. 40).[34]

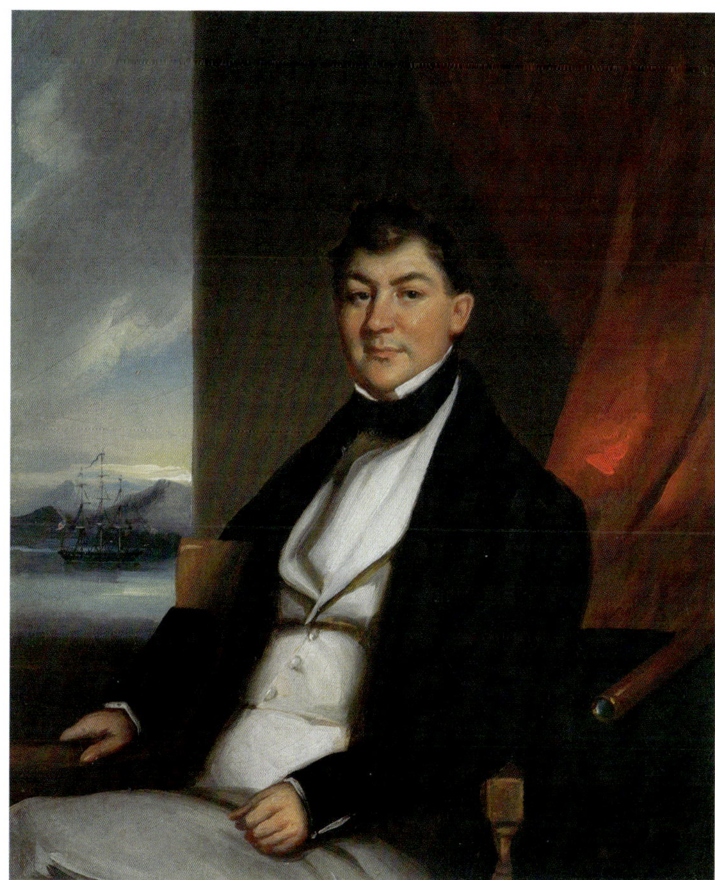

38. Attributed to Lamqua (1801–1860)
Hevlyn Benson (1805–1858), ca. 1840–45
Oil on canvas, 11½ × 9½ in. (29.2 × 24.1 cm)
Gift of Hevlyn D. Benson, 1933.2

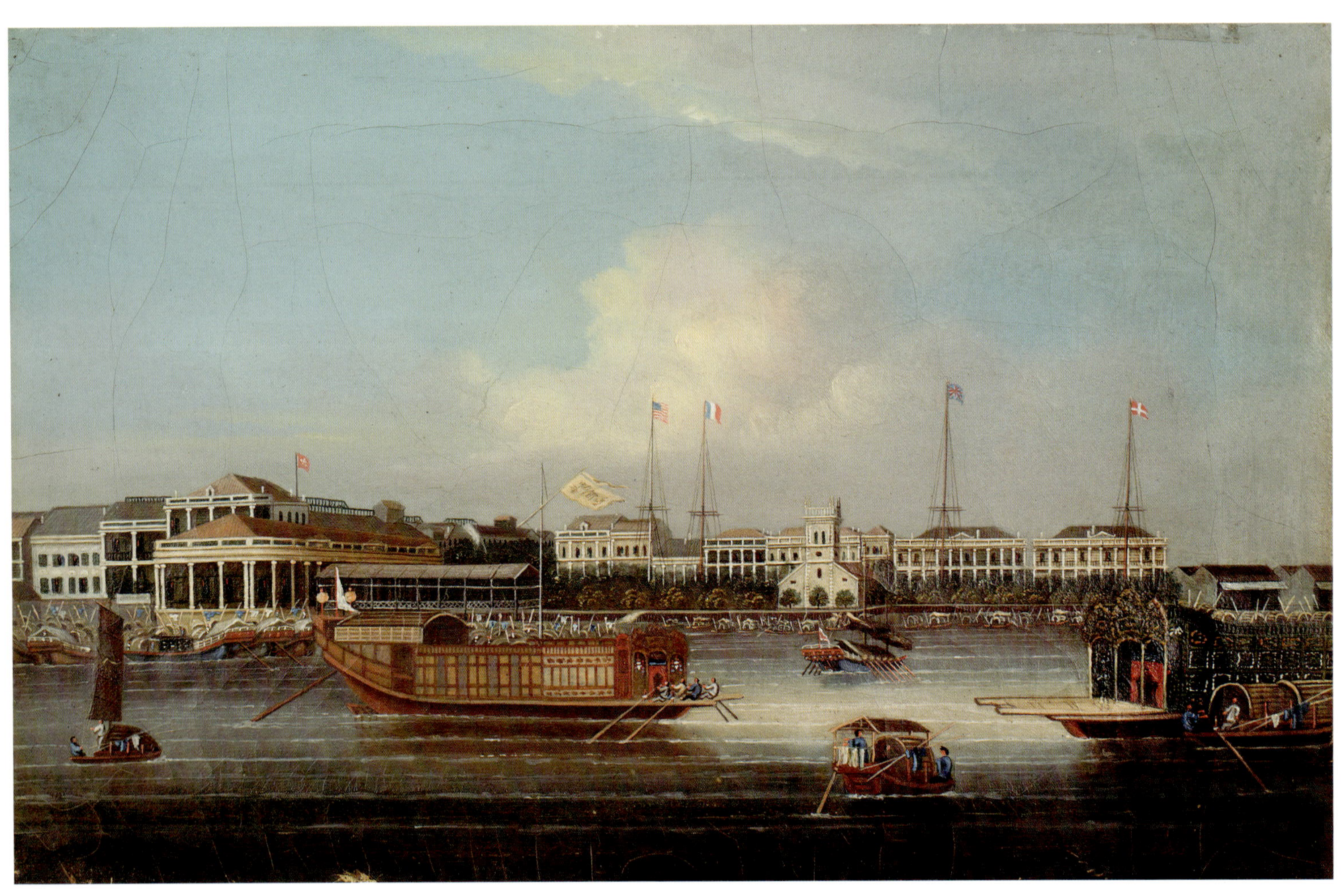

39. Unidentified Artist
Factories at Canton (from the Harbor), China, 1850
Oil on canvas, 6⅞ × 10¾ in. (17.5 × 27.3 cm)
Gift of Miss Alice Temple Parkin, 1946.82

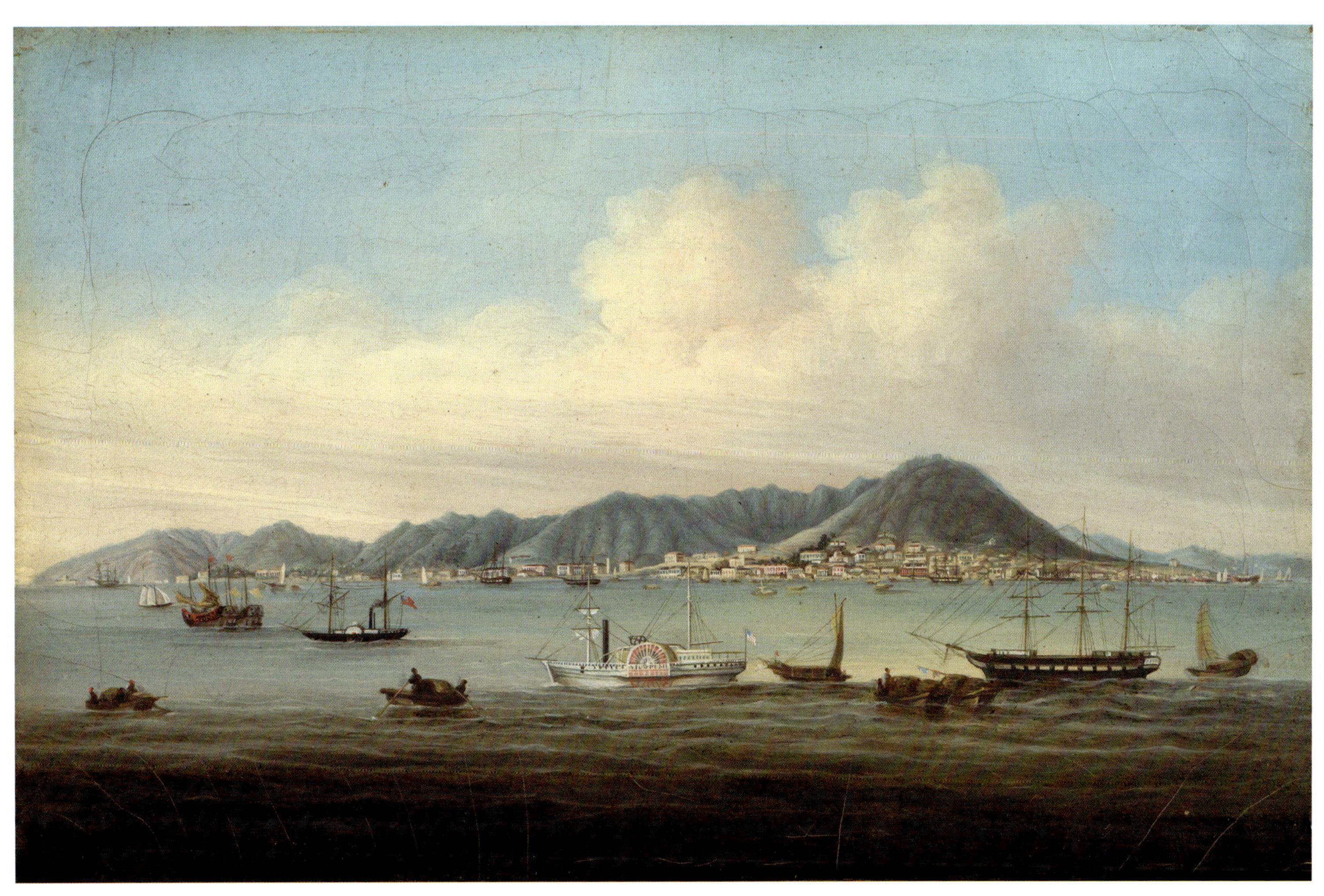

40. Unidentified Artist
Hong Kong Island, Victoria Peak and the Harbor, Painted from Kowloon, 1850
Oil on canvas, 7 × 10¾ in. (17.8 × 27.3 cm)
Gift of Alice Temple Parkin, 1946.80

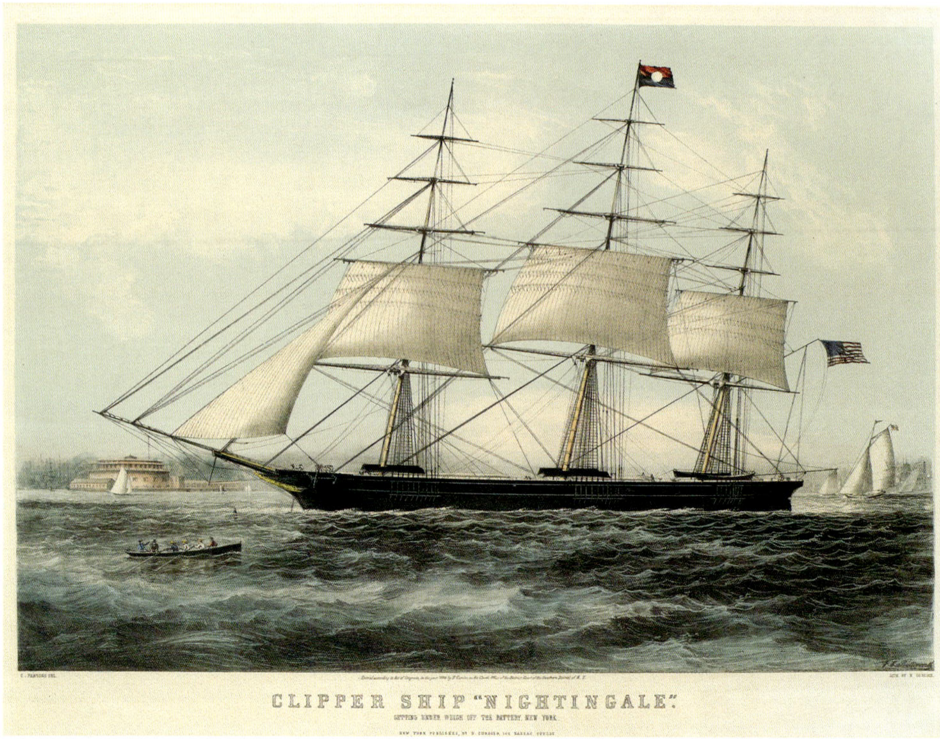

41. Charles Parsons (1821–1910), after James Edward Buttersworth (1817–1894)
Clipper Ship "Nightingale," 1854
Hand-colored lithograph published by Currier and Ives, $21^{13}/_{16} \times 28$ in. (55.3×71 cm)
New-York Historical Society, Department of Prints, Photographs, and Architectural Collections

We get a closer look at a classic clipper ship in a hand-colored print published by Currier and Ives based on a painting by James E. Buttersworth of the *Nightingale* (fig. 41), an extreme clipper launched in 1851 and named in honor of Jenny Lind, whose likeness as a figurehead graced her bow. The beautiful ship is shown before Castle Garden on the Battery, where the Swedish Nightingale had made her American debut the year before. Clippers were cargo ships built for speed with three or more masts and were renowned for long voyages completed in record time. British- and American-built clippers sailed all over the world, primarily on trade routes between China, in the transatlantic trade, and on the route from New York to San Francisco around Cape Horn during the California gold rush. Boom years for clippers during the mid-nineteenth century were stimulated by the demand for rapid delivery of tea from China, the opium trade, and the discovery of gold in California (1848) and Australia (1851). The clipper trade would decline with the rise of steam shipping and the opening of the Suez

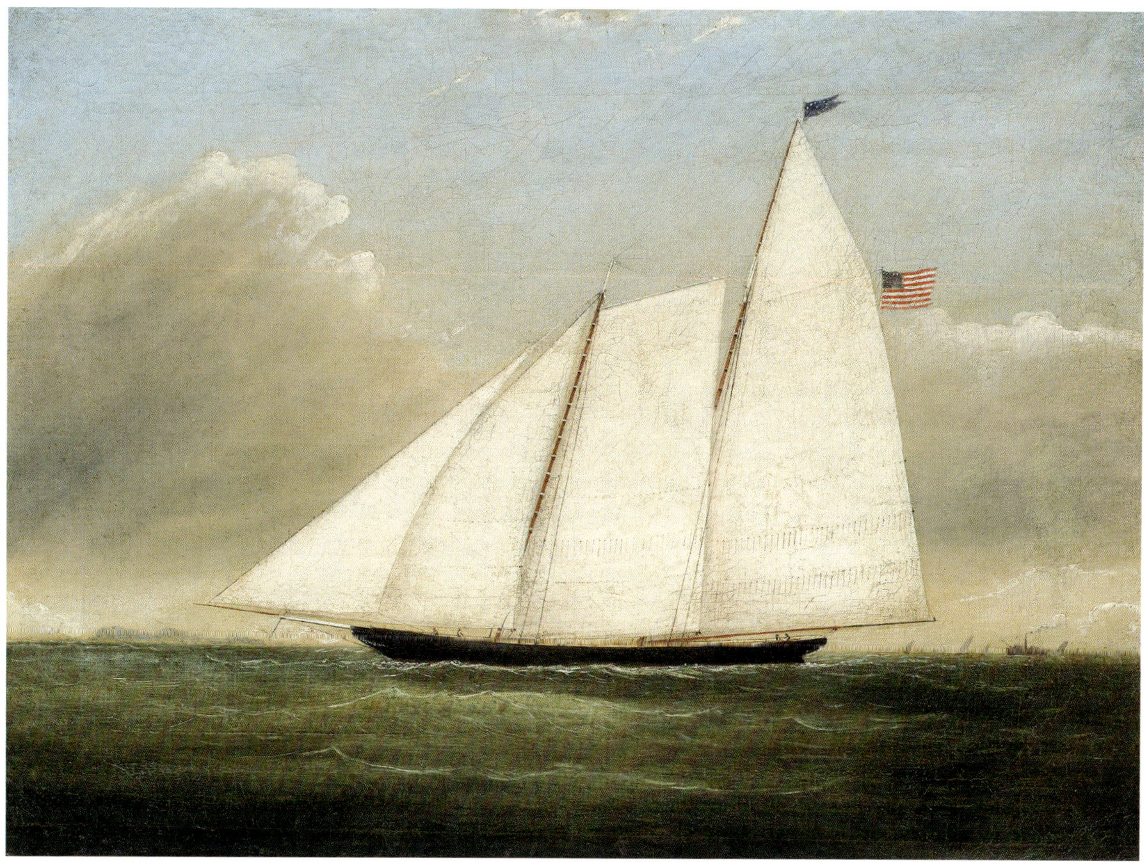

42. Unidentified Artist
Yacht "America," 1851
Oil on canvas, 22⅛ × 30⅛ in.
(56.2 × 76.5 cm)
Gift of Henry O. Havemeyer, 1949.47

Canal in 1869. Yet during their heyday, when clippers vied to break records for sailing time between ports, their exciting races on the high seas were covered by the press and captured the public's attention. Soon after her launch, the *Nightingale* had twice run such "tea races" from Shanghai to London against a British clipper, *Challenger*, for very high stakes.[35]

As the era of swift clipper ships waned and steam power came to dominate maritime commerce (and warfare), yacht racing emerged as a major international sport in contests of nautical skills that continue today. Thus, speed under sail would continue to play an important role in maritime realms but now was driven more by sporting competition than by commercial gain. A spirited portrait by an unknown artist portrays the famous racing yacht *America* that first captured the British Royal Yacht Squadron's trophy in 1851 (fig. 42). Afterward known as the America's Cup, the trophy was in the keeping of the New York Yacht Club from 1851 until 1983. The *America* and other yachts were widely celebrated in paintings and prints as

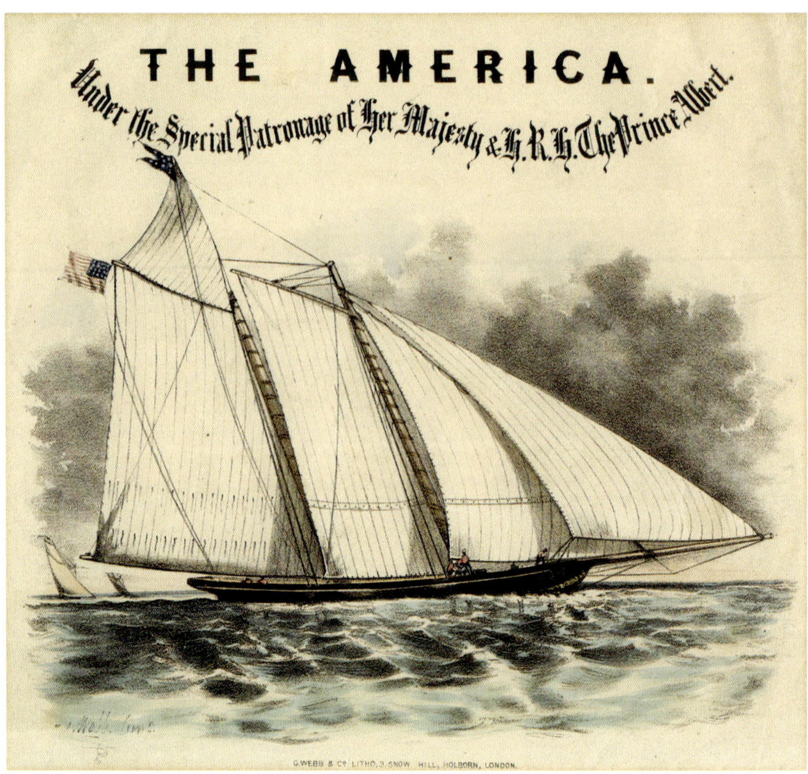

43. G. Webb & Co. (active 1846–55)
"The America," ca. 1850
Hand-colored lithograph, 9 9/16 × 10 1/2 in. (24.3 × 26.5 cm)
New-York Historical Society, Department of Prints, Photographs, and Architectural Collections

emblems of the nation's achievement in building and racing superior sailing vessels (fig. 43).[36] These enterprises were championed and financed by wealthy sportsmen like James Gordon Bennett Jr., shown here in a fashionable nautical portrait of 1867 painted in Paris, perhaps to mark his election that year as vice commodore of the New York Yacht Club (fig. 44). In 1867 Bennett also took over as publisher of the *New York Herald* when his father retired. The elegant young man is in naval uniform (he had served during the Civil War), seated before an expanse of sea and sky on the open deck of his yacht, *Henrietta*, in which he had won a celebrated transatlantic race just the year before. Flamboyant and eccentric, Bennett enjoyed a successful and, at times, notorious career as an international newspaper publisher, continuing to pursue his lifelong passion for sailing.[37] Years later Julius LeBlanc Stewart (1855–1919) would portray the publisher and his guests aboard Bennett's most famous vessel in the painting *On the Yacht "Namouna," Venice* (1890; Wadsworth Atheneum Museum of Art, Hartford, Conn.).

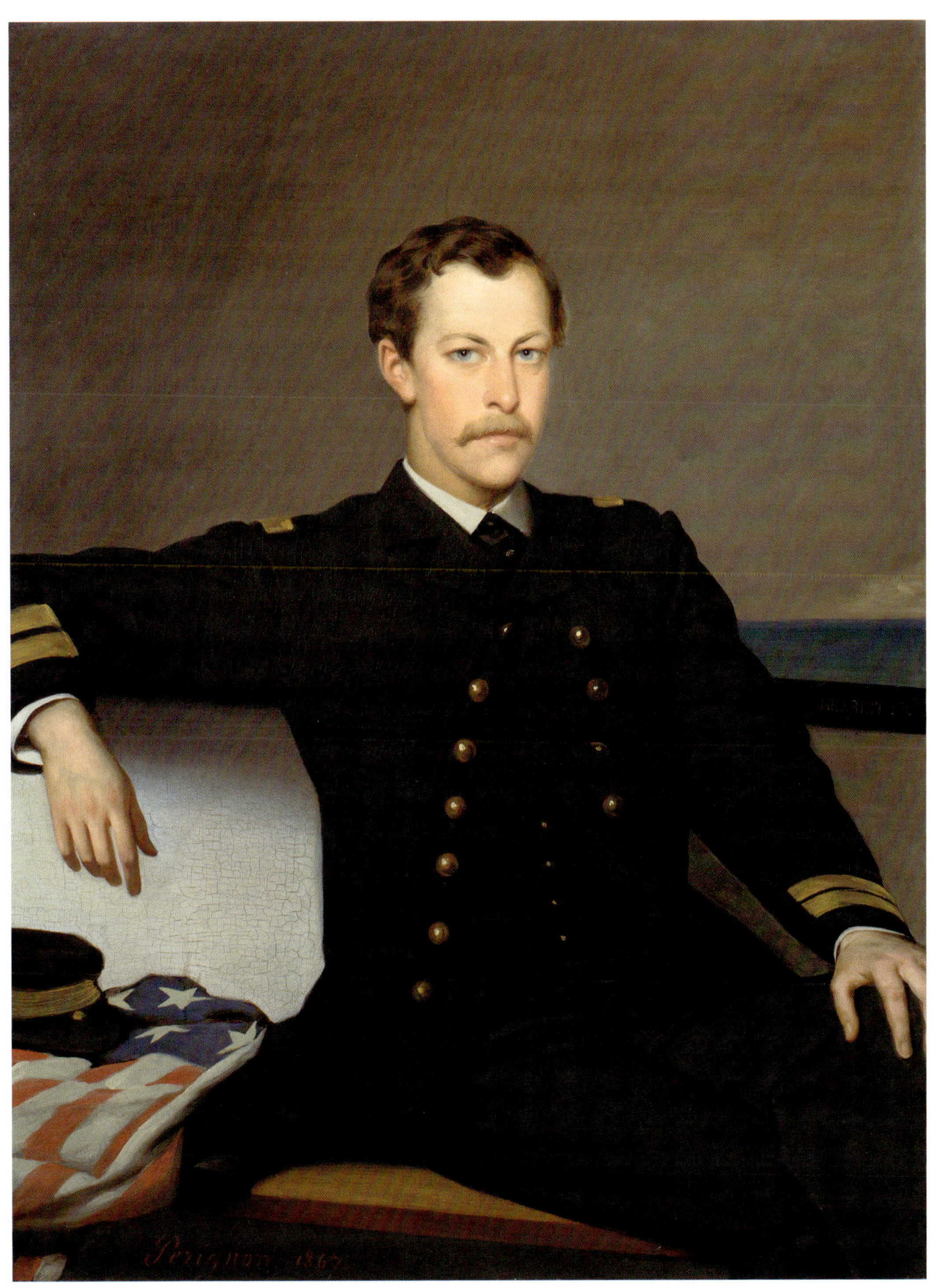

44. Alexis-Joseph Pérignon
(1806–1882)
James Gordon Bennett Jr.
(1841–1918), 1867
Oil on canvas,
51¼ × 38¼ in.
(130.2 × 97.2 cm)
Signed and dated lower
left: *Perignon 1867*
Gift of Mrs. Arthur S.
Grossman, 1957.80

45. Junius Brutus Stearns (1810–1885)
Fishing in a Catboat in Great South Bay, 1871
Oil on canvas, 29 × 39¼ in. (73.7 × 99.7 cm)
Signed and dated in circular monogram stamp on sail of boat at center right: *J.B. STEARNS 1871*
Gift of C. Otto von Kienbusch, 1964.21

Marine recreation of a more modest sort is recorded in Junius Brutus Stearns's delightful group portrait—an American conversation piece to be precise—*Fishing in a Catboat in Great South Bay*, 1871 (fig. 45). Stearns skillfully combined genre, sporting subjects, and portrait painting in a series of fishing pictures in which male subjects angle along rocky trout streams. Two works in this sequence portray saltwater fishing expeditions, and ours is the only one in which ladies join the outing.[38] The subjects do not turn to face the painter and pose but are instead portrayed as if fully engaged with deploying their fishing lines and the duties of a fishing party. Costume differentiates the local mariner who pilots the catboat from the more fashionable day-trippers who fill his boat. The gently humorous episode (could the seasick fellow in the bow be a self-portrait of the artist?) evokes the popularity of seaside leisure in the latter decades of the nineteenth century. Distinguishing this particular work is the brilliance with which Stearns also captures the light and atmosphere of open water off the southern shore of Long Island, rendered here with as much conviction as he does the smart little sailboat that provides a maritime setting for his charming narrative.

A CITY IN THE "ARMS OF THE SEA"

> [T]hose large arms of the sea which embrace Manhattan Island render its situation, in regard to health and pleasure, as well as to the convenience of commerce, peculiarly felicitous.—Thomas A. Janvier, "The Evolution of New York," 1893

The vast coastal environs of New York Harbor were also "peculiarly felicitous" for the artist, presenting infinite opportunities to portray diverse topographies that were alternately maritime and terrestrial and whose multiplicity exceeded that of other great port cities of the Atlantic seaboard. In fact, those "arms of the sea" had swallowed the ancient Hudson River thousands of years before, when glaciers melted and the sea level rose, flooding the prehistoric coastal plain. In the process, one of the world's great natural harbors was formed, as was the estuary that we know today as the Hudson River that carries the Atlantic's tides some 153 miles into the interior. Such rich permutations of seascape and landscape might well be called waterscapes, and they have inspired printmakers, painters, and poets for more than two hundred years. The vast, protected harbor at the mouth of the Hudson River established New York City as a great port and the nation's commercial and shipping capital during the nineteenth century. Just as historic sites and the varied terrain along the course of the Hudson would be co-opted into a landscape vision embraced as national patrimony, so the unique

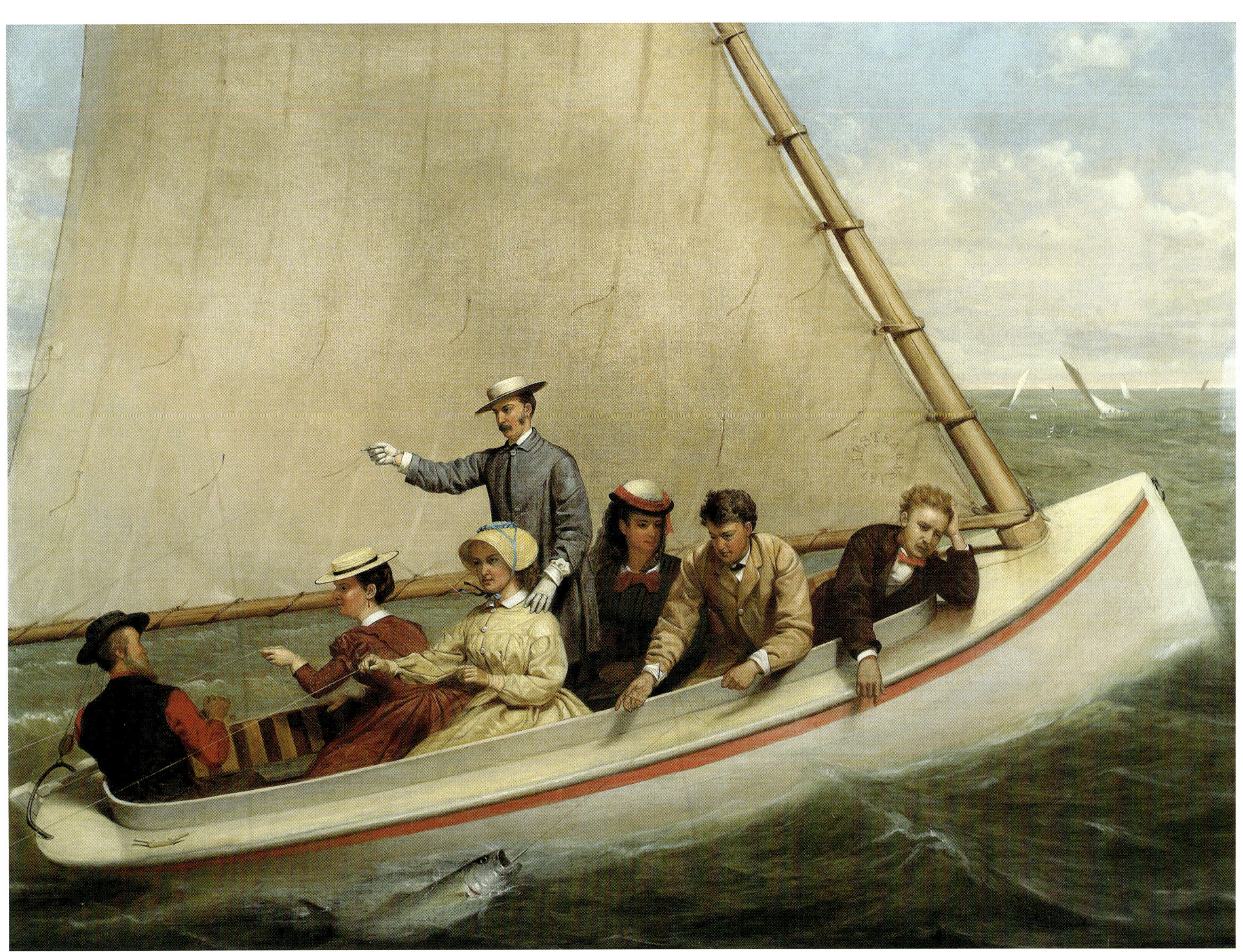

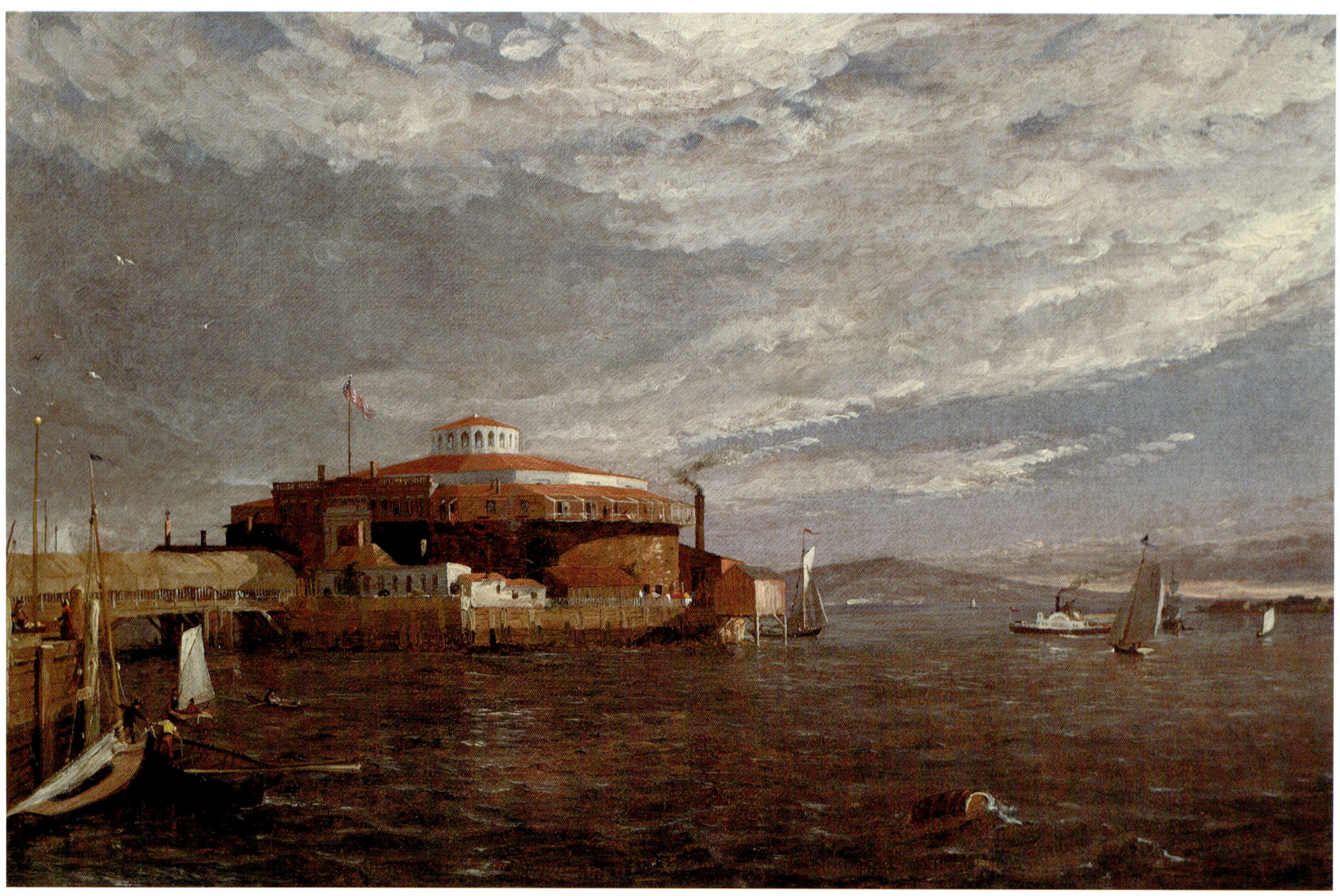

46. Jasper Francis Cropsey (1823–1900)
A Sketch of Castle Garden, 1851
Oil on canvas, 10½ × 16⅜ in. (26.7 × 41.6 cm)
Signed lower right: *J F Cropsey*
Inscribed in ink on reverse in artist's hand: *A sketch of Castle Garden / for M[lle]* [illegible] / *Jenny Lind / with the best wishes of the Artist / J. F. C.*
Thomas Jefferson Bryan Fund, 1977.76

setting of the city at the river's mouth offered myriad opportunities for artists to combine seemingly endless configurations of land and sea, city and ships, re-created for international audiences on canvas, as prints, and as images on popular tableware.

The massive structures of early harbor defenses also functioned as historic relics and picturesque landmarks. Thomas Birch's earlier sweeping harbor view had featured Castle William to signal that his seascape depicted the port of New York (see fig. 13). Castle Clinton had also originally been constructed as a neighboring fortification on the Battery in preparation for the War of 1812 and then turned into a place of public entertainment in 1824 and renamed Castle Garden. The marquis de Lafayette, the French hero of the American Revolution, was honored there during his visit to the United States. On a breezy May day in 1851, Jasper Francis Cropsey, who was trained as an architect, made a careful drawing of

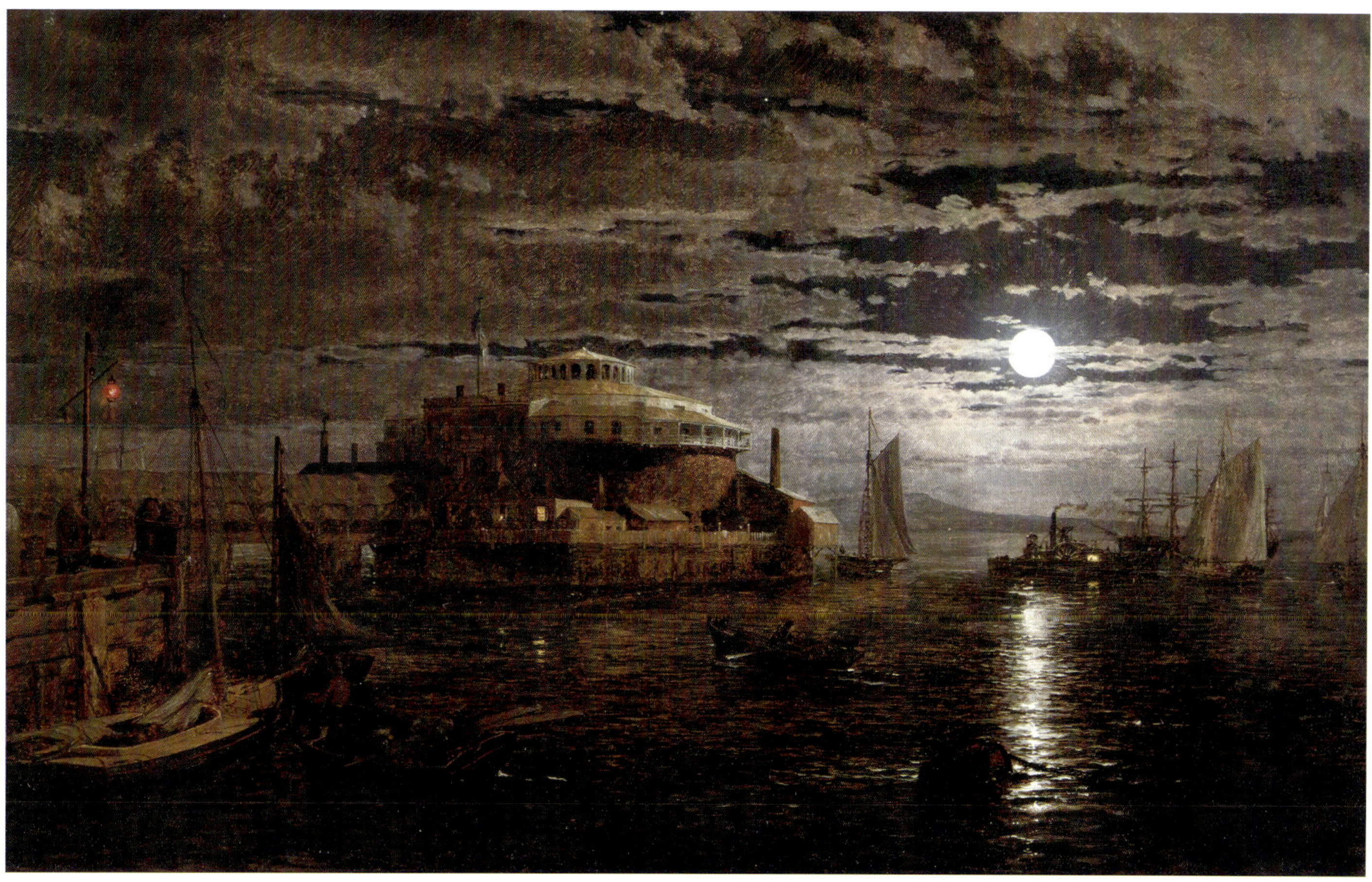

Castle Garden, keenly observing the intricacies of the actual structure and the siting. Cropsey used that study as the basis for a series of daytime and nocturnal views of Castle Garden painted over a decade, which exploited the picturesque possibilities of the fortress's situation at the southernmost tip of Manhattan Island.[39] New York's Battery with spectacular views of both upper and lower harbor was long a popular public promenade. In 1850 P. T. Barnum chose the locale for the debut performance of Swedish soprano Jenny Lind's American concert tour. Cropsey's fluidly painted portrayal of the former fortress now converted to a theater and connected to the Battery via a covered walkway also exploits a dramatic view of an expansive sky and harbor busy with traffic surrounding the pavilion (fig. 46). Cropsey carefully delineated the original structure's masonry walls with the later addition of a roof and clerestory that created a pavilion. He also recorded the motley cluster of outbuildings

47. Jasper Francis Cropsey (1823–1900)
Castle Garden, New York, 1859
Oil on canvas, 15⅛ × 24¼ in. (38.4 × 61.6 cm)
Signed and dated lower middle: *J F Cropsey / 1859*.
Inscribed in pencil on wood backing panel: *Castle Garden, New York / J. F. Cropsey— London—1859*
Thomas Jefferson Bryan Fund, 1972.13

that hug the massive fort's perimeter. This version was said to have been presented as a gift to the Swedish Nightingale herself. Cropsey returned to the subject some years later in a larger painting, based on the same study but showing the theater at night (fig. 47). Sunshine is replaced by the nocturnal drama of a cloudy night sky with the full moon illuminating the waters that are still thronged with boats. Cold moonlight and contrasting lantern glow and shadowy vessels and walkways lend an aura of romantic mystery as the hulking mass of the fortress looms above the dark waters. Cropsey's picturesque pendants document a city and a port open both day and night for business and entertainment.

The landscape and genre painter Andrew Melrose portrayed the landmark in 1885 as a prominent feature of his *New York Harbor and the Battery*, an animated view of the park on the Battery and the busy port beyond (fig. 48). By then, landfill had connected the formerly water-bound structure to Manhattan Island, and Castle Garden had been used for several decades as an immigration center. Appropriately sited right on the harbor, it received the ships carrying new and growing populations. The foreground promenade provides a sunny stage for a diverse urban demographic that includes fashionable New Yorkers out for a stroll as well as recent arrivals to Castle Garden with their bundles and boxes. Those looking down the harbor in 1885 would have seen the pedestal for the Statue of Liberty under construction on Bedloe's Island. Castle Garden would be turned over to New York City in 1890 and reopened as an aquarium in 1896. Today a national historic site, the fort has been restored as Castle Clinton.[40]

Samuel Colman, known for his landscapes and port scenes, painted a sweeping view of the Narrows, the channel at the mouth of New York Harbor, looking west from the Long Island (Brooklyn) shore at Fort Hamilton (fig. 49). In the far left distance, Fort Wadsworth on the shore of Staten Island can be seen. However, the massive walls of Fort Lafayette, built on a small island and originally called Fort Diamond, dominate the center of the painting. Colman and his viewers would have remembered that, during the Civil War, the fort had been notorious as the "American Bastille" used to house Confederate prisoners of war and political prisoners. When Colman painted the scene in 1868, the last prisoner of war had been released only two years earlier; the sight of soldiers assembling at the fort and cannons on the dock would have been reminders of recent history. The mood, nevertheless, is mellow. Two boats are moored with a fishing party aboard, suggesting excursionists. A man and woman on the shore are about to step into a boat and join them. Two artists observe the passing scene from the banks; one sketches while the other reclines with closed umbrella and portfolio beside him. Majestic merchant vessels are drifting before Fort Wadsworth, carried by the tide

48. Andrew Melrose
(1836–1901)
New York Harbor and the Battery,
1885
Oil on canvas, 22 × 36 in.
(55.9 × 91.4 cm)
Signed and dated lower left:
Andrew Melrose / 85
James B. Wilbur Fund,
1939.585

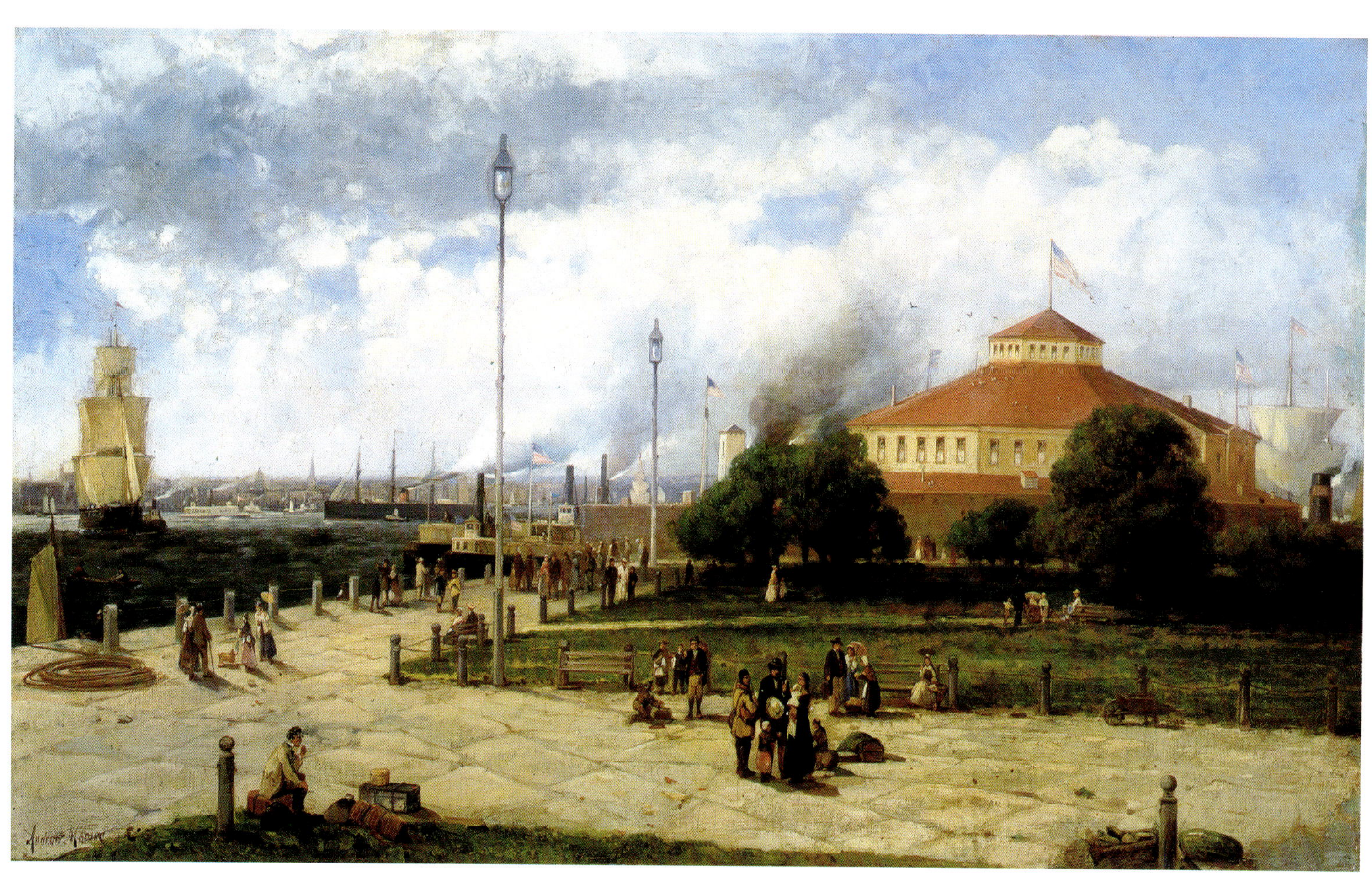

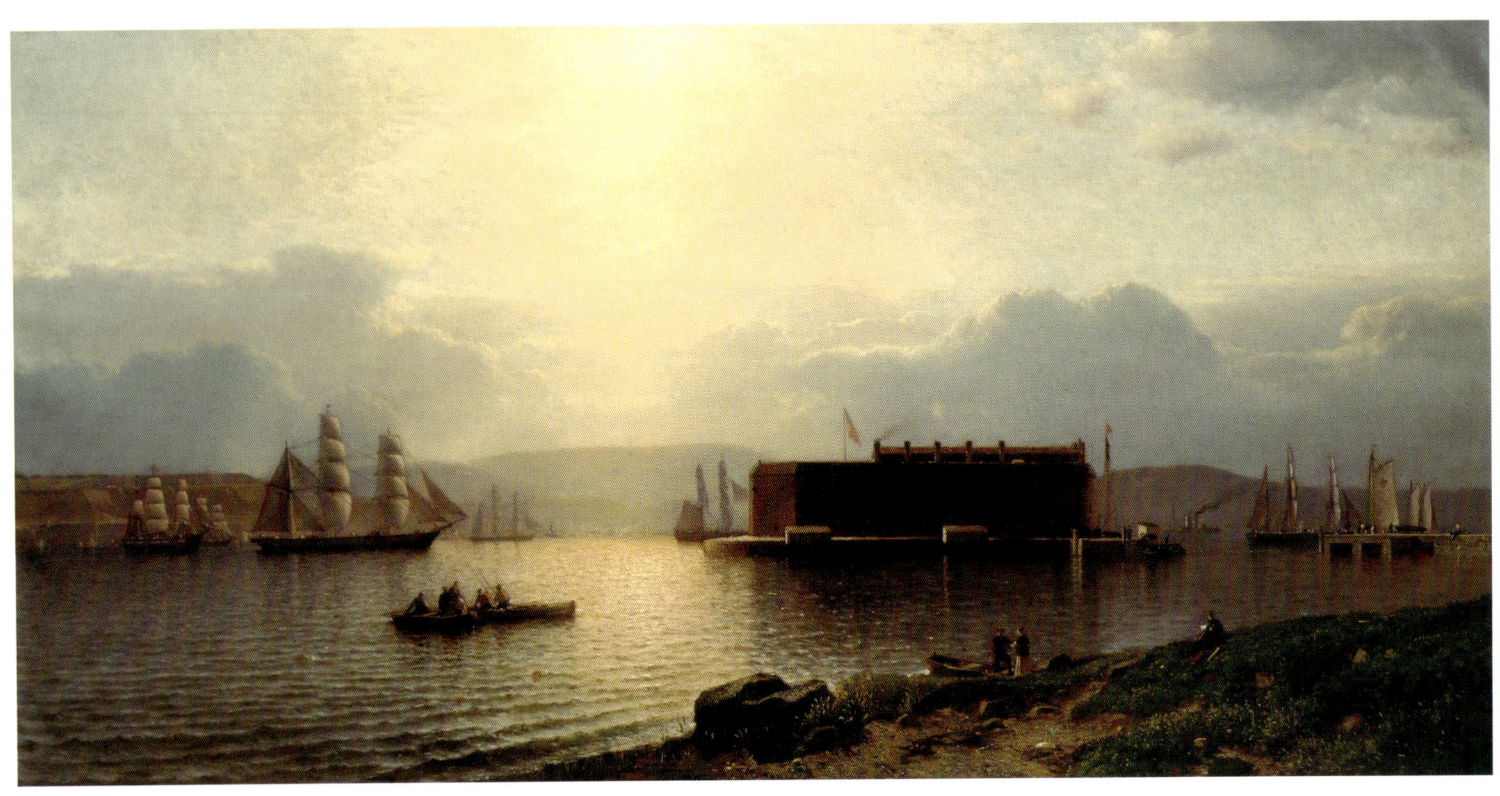

49. Samuel Colman (1832–1920)
The Narrows and Fort Lafayette, Ships Coming into Port, 1868
Oil on canvas, 30 × 60 in. (76.2 × 152.4 cm)
Signed lower left: *Sam. Colman.*
The Watson Fund, 1976.2
(detail overleaf)

into the harbor. Colman paints into the sun, bathing the scene in a golden afternoon glow, conferring an aura of nostalgia that co-opts historical landmarks into picturesque touring destinations. Fort Lafayette was later demolished to make way for the Brooklyn anchorage of the Verrazano-Narrows Bridge.[41]

Francis Augustus Silva would also circumnavigate the maze of interconnected waterways in and around the harbor to find the subjects for his luminous waterscapes. In *New York Harbor*, 1880, Silva transforms the busy port into a romantic vista by portraying the expanse of water radiant with sunset's glow (fig. 50). On the left, sails, masts, pilings, and docks seem to stretch as far as the eye can see, indicating the waterfront and a city unseen, while open waters at the right fade away into evening mists, suggesting limitless horizons. At the center, a husky tugboat steams toward us in a businesslike fashion; its homely profile is in sharp contrast to the graceful vessels nearby. Three sloops and a schooner coming into port at twilight are poised on the shining water like birds in a line of flight that recedes into the distance, drawing our eye to the luminous twilight and the open waters beyond and the poetry of empty spaces.[42]

Perhaps they might be sailing away into the romantic alternative universe of De Haas's *Tropical Sunset at Sea*, existing in another twilight in another harbor at the other end of the world (fig. 51). Here a splendid vessel under the American flag is guided into a huge harbor by a small steam vessel. The tall ship is dramatically silhouetted against a spectacular sunset. The disk of the setting sun throws the tower of sail into sharp profile against the glow of the sunset sky. Distant waters are darkened by cloud cover on the horizon, and the sun tints the edges of clouds whose soaring masses echo the ship in the foreground. The romantic title resonates with suggestions of sultry climates in exotic ports of call, evoking the thrill of seafaring adventure in faraway places.

If Silva calls up universal responses with the poetry of sunsets and narratives of the voyage and De Haas conjures the calm harbors of his seventeenth-century Dutch models, Edward Moran and Arthur Quartley eschew poetry for a vigorous plein air painterliness that grounds their harborscapes in time and place by adding the skyline of modern New York to the narratives of their briskly painted urban marines. Each artist adopts a somewhat distant view taken from out on the harbor waters that are heavily populated with all kinds of craft. Nearby vessels in the foreground bring us into the pictures at water level. Moran, who relished marine paining, was from a Philadelphia family of long-lived artists who worshipped the most famous sea painter of the nineteenth century, J. M. W. Turner.[43] Hailed as an artist of great promise, Quartley died in 1889 after a short career of only little more than a decade.[44]

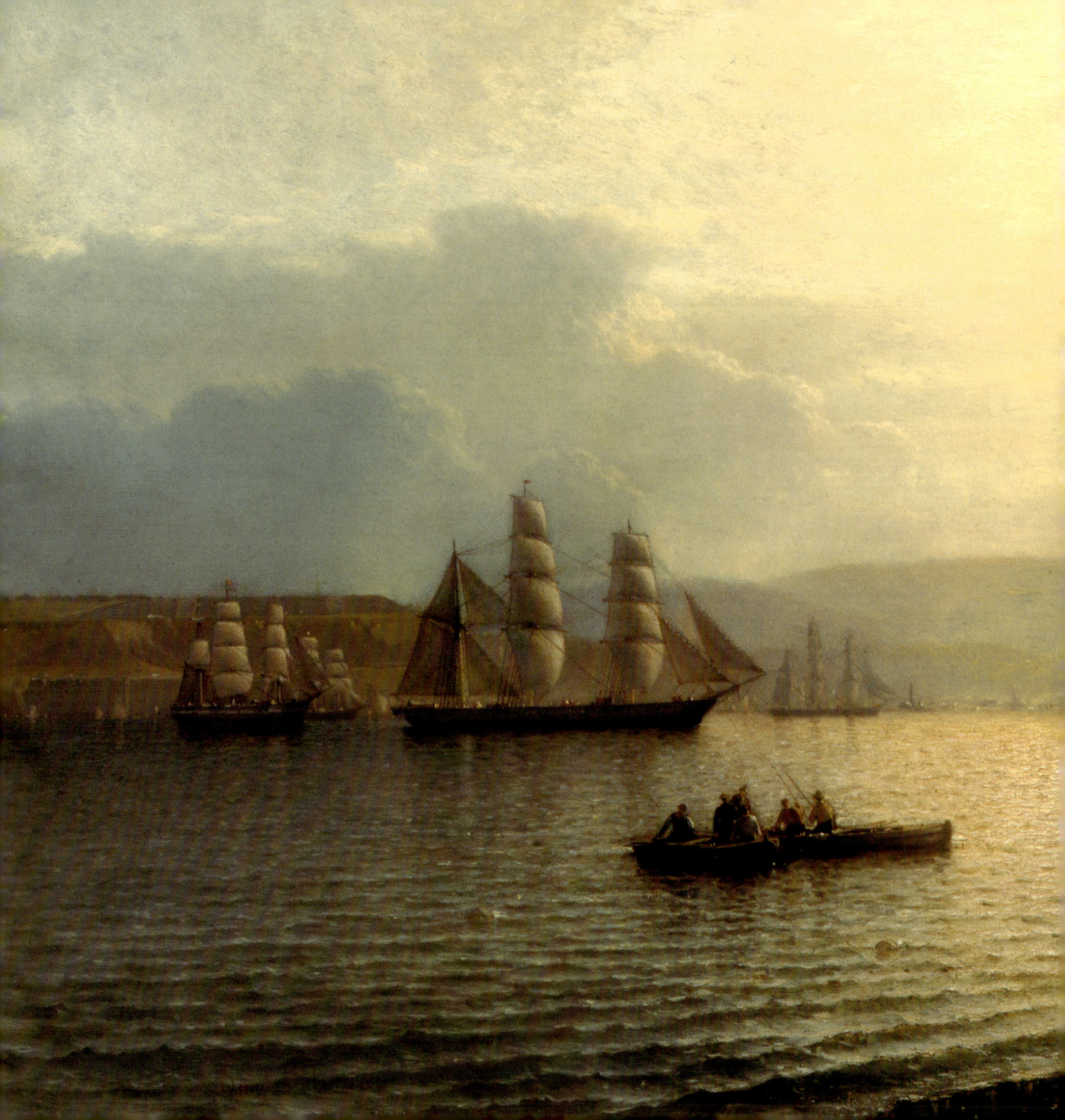

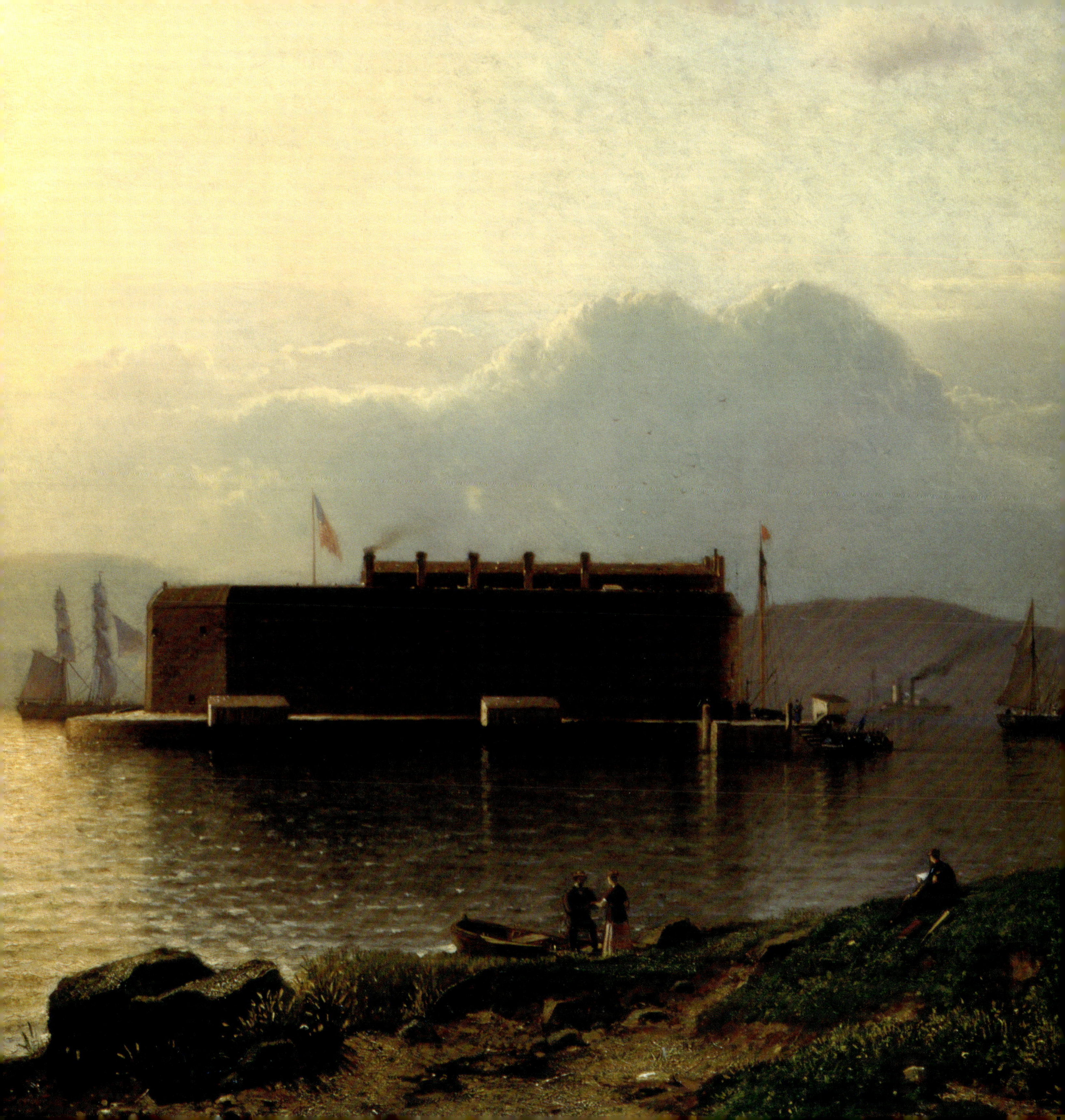

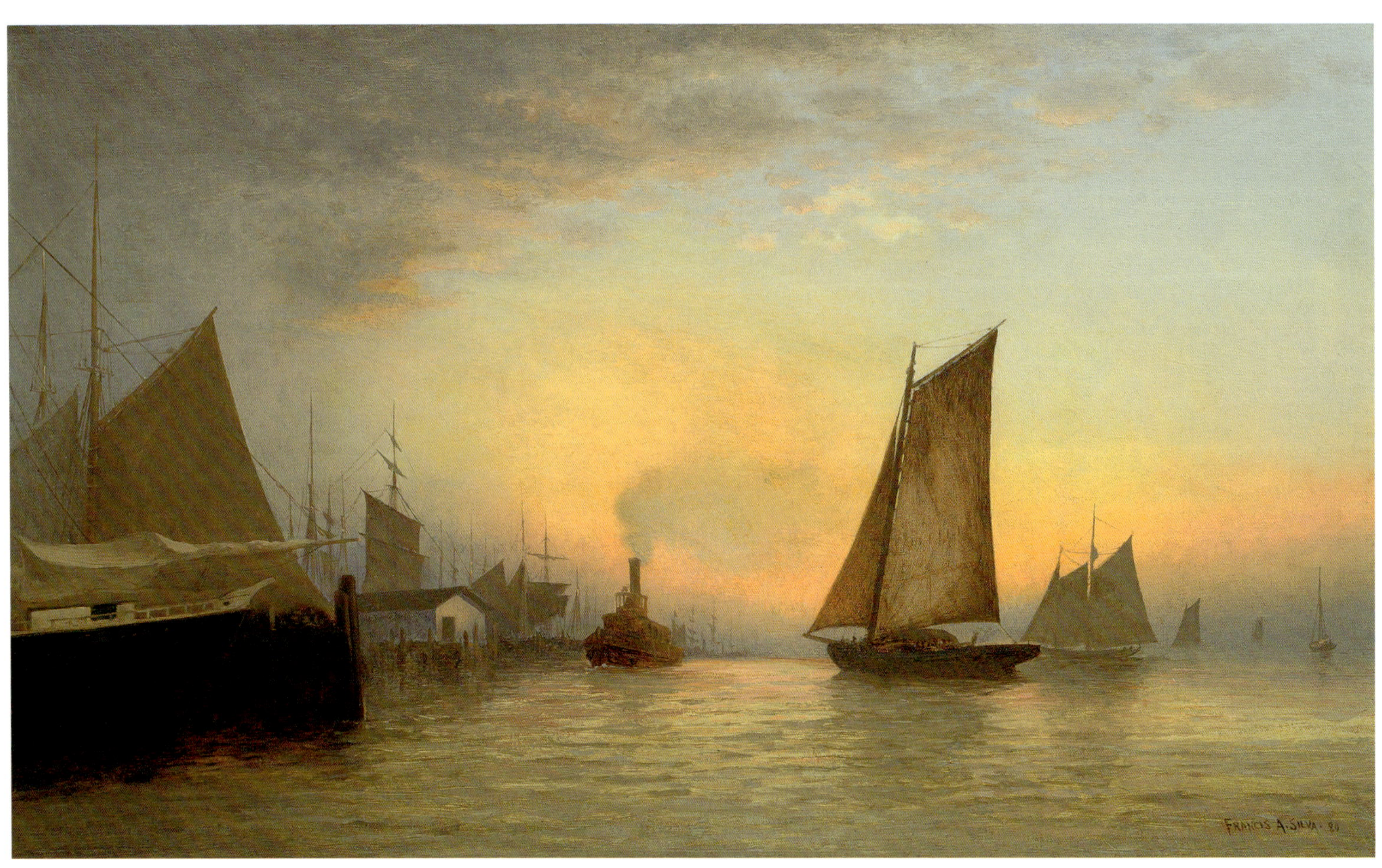

50. Francis Augustus Silva (1835–1886)
New York Harbor, 1880
Oil on canvas, 12 × 20 in. (30.5 × 50.8 cm)
Signed and dated lower right: *FRANCIS A. SILVA. 80*.
Gift of the Pintard Fellows, 1975.29

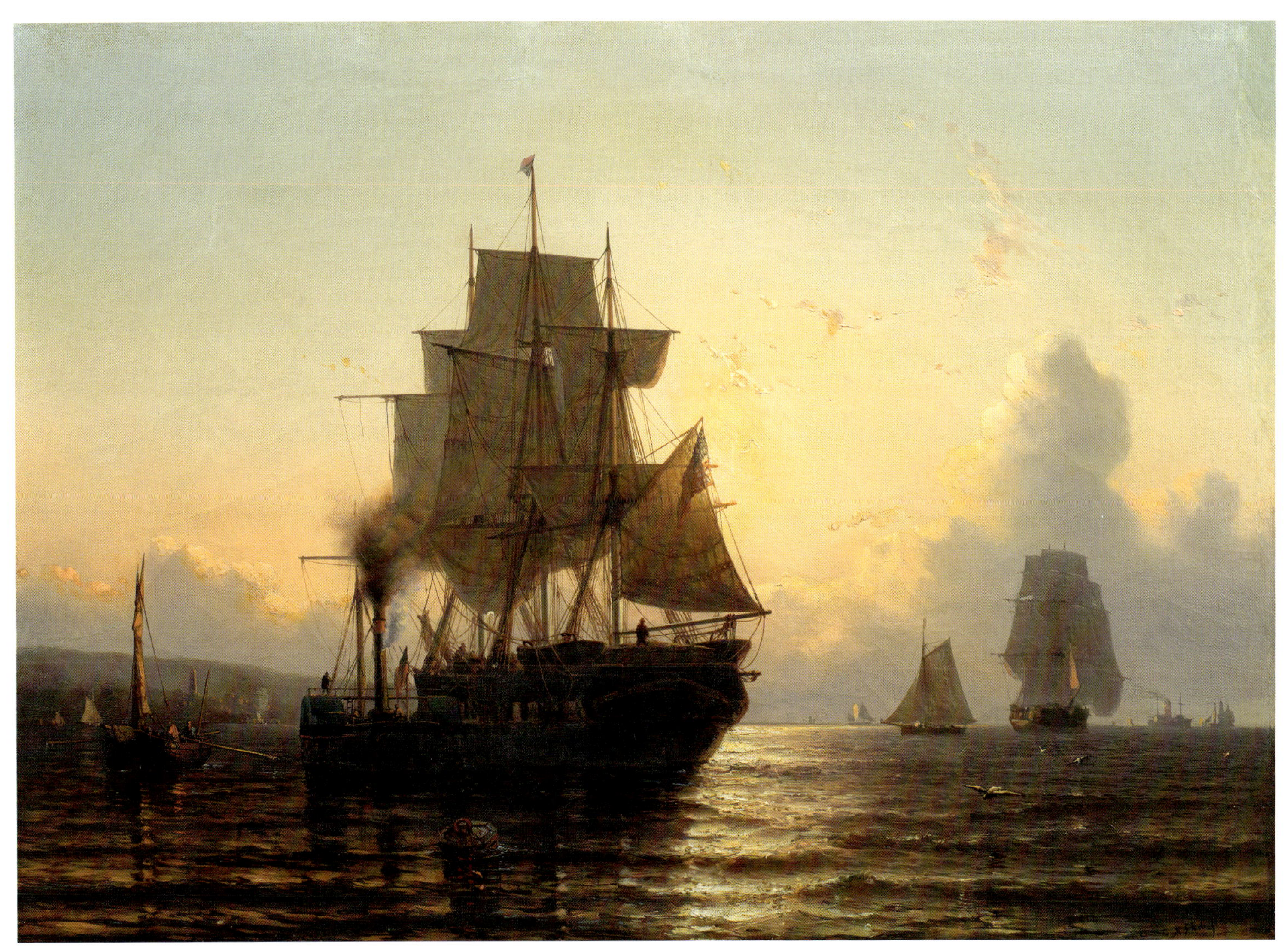

51. Mauritz Frederick Hendrick De Haas (1832–1895)
Tropical Sunset at Sea, ca. 1862
Oil on canvas, 24 × 34 in. (61 × 86.4 cm)
Signed lower right: *M.F.H. de Haas*
The Robert L. Stuart Collection, S-109

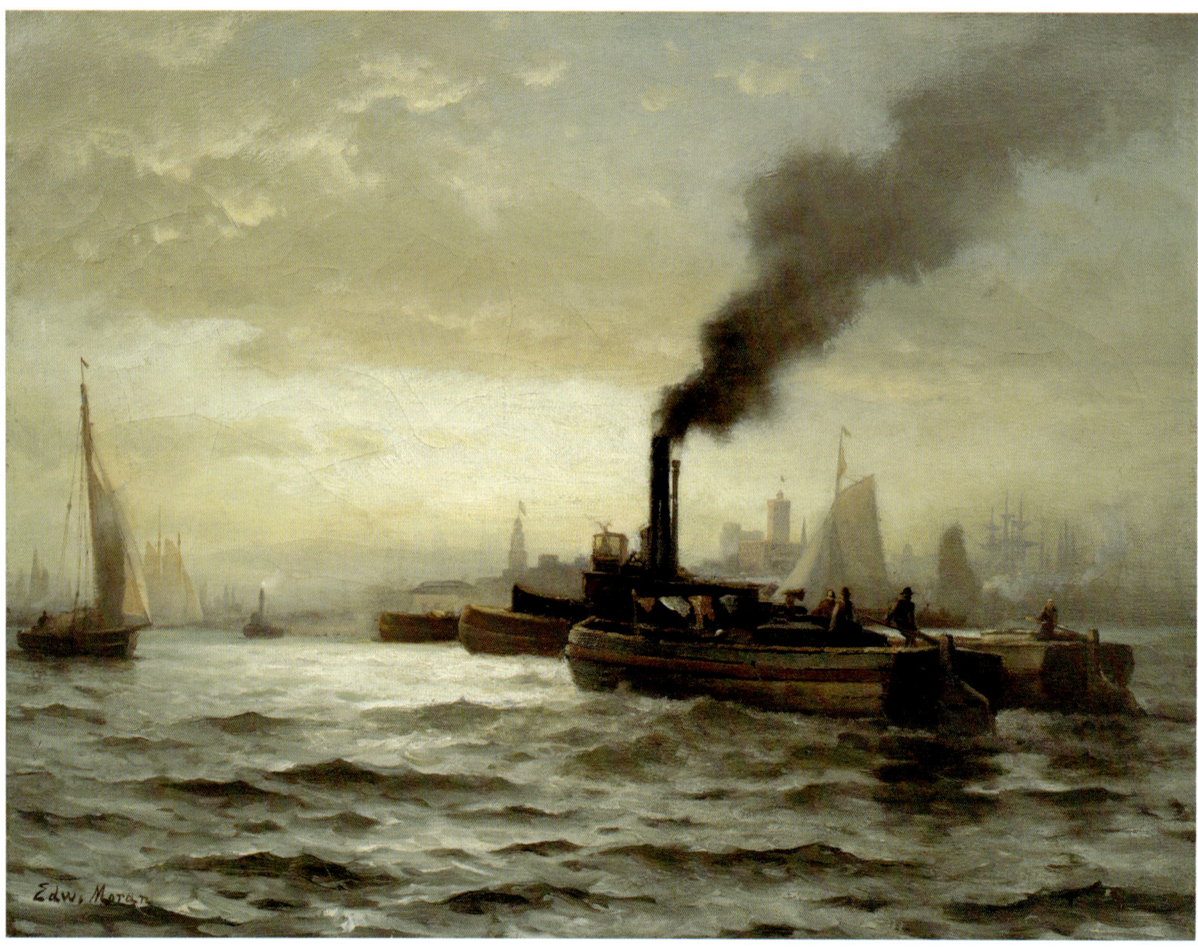

52. Edward Moran (1829–1901)
New York Harbor, ca. 1880
Oil on canvas, 18 × 24 in. (45.7 × 61 cm)
Signed lower left: *EDW. MORAN*
Purchase, 1935.71

Moran's *New York Harbor* looks north toward the Battery, capturing the bustle of the harbor, as steamships, tugboats, fishing trawlers, and pleasure boats appear to collide in their attempt to share the crowded water of the upper bay (fig. 52). The tugboat in the foreground tows a pair of lighters, or barges, freed of their cargo; drying laundry on one adds a picturesque domestic note. An empty swath of harbor waters forms the immediate foreground, demonstrating Moran's acclaimed skill in depicting the mass and motion of these ever-changing reflective surfaces. "The forms of the water are exquisitely chiseled," wrote a contemporary critic, "so sharp and yet so fleeting and painted all with two colors, the local color of the water and its shadow color."[45] Quartley's *An April Day, New York* (fig. 53), with its lively brushwork and silvery gray tonalities, was much admired when displayed at the 1881

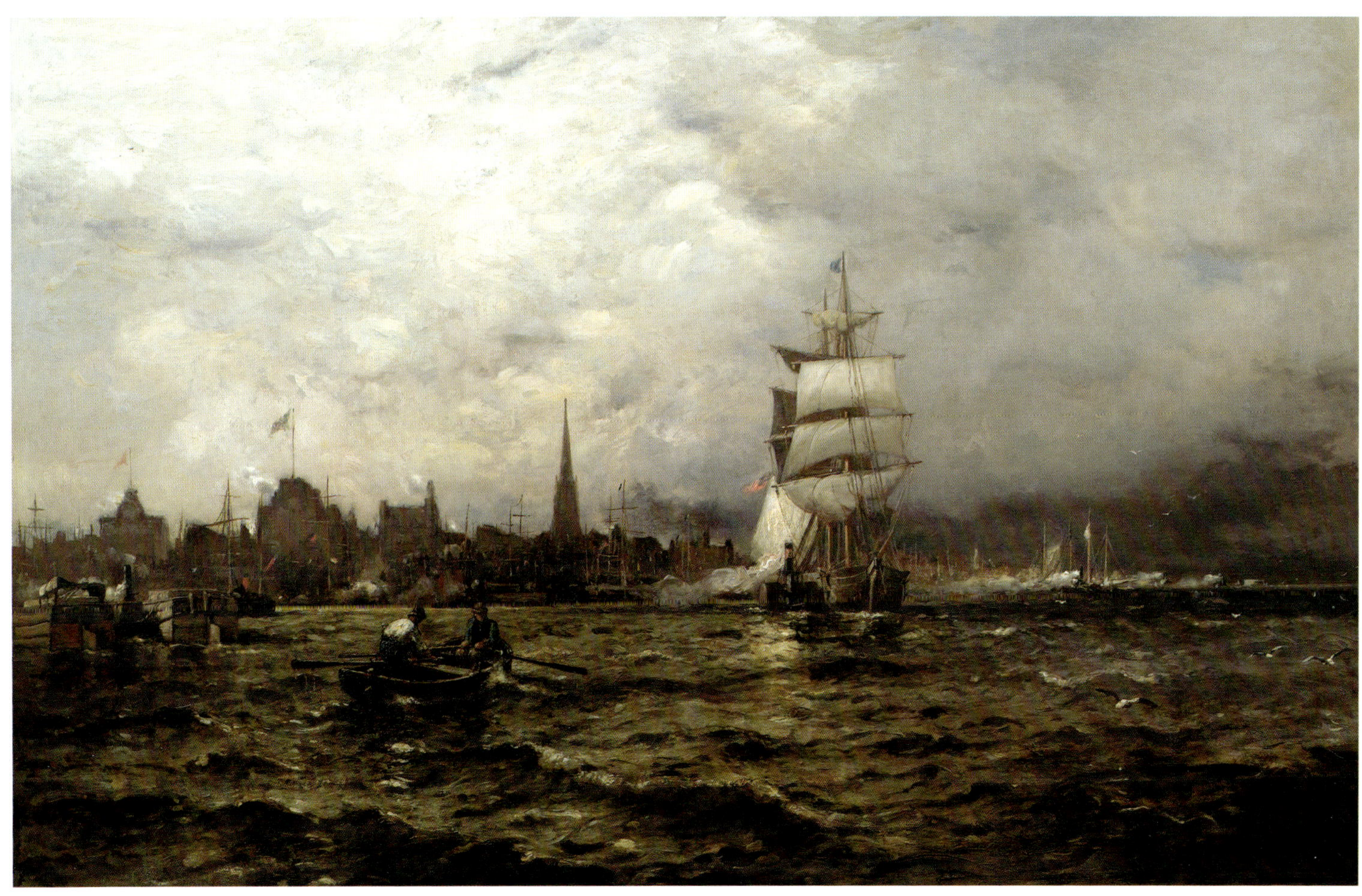

annual exhibition of the National Academy of Design, where it was well described in *American Academy Notes*:

> It is the familiar North River Battery reach, with admirable cloud treatment. From the Bay the lower part of the city is seen in the distance, the mass of buildings rising in dim outline. The spire of old Trinity towers above the rest like a watchful guardian, supported by a band of sturdy companions, represented by the tall buildings for which Manhattan Island is so famous. Away over in Long Island a storm is in progress, and is rapidly approaching the city. The fickle sky, the force and sweep of the wind, and the swollen sea, admirably express the feeling of a characteristic *April Day*.[46]

53. Arthur Quartley (1839–1886)
An April Day, New York, 1881
Oil on canvas, 28⅛ × 44¼ in. (71.4 × 112.4 cm)
Signed lower right: *Arthur Quartley*. Signed and dated verso: *An April Day, / New York / Arthur Quartley / 1881*
X.720

THE GREAT ESTUARY: THE HUDSON RIVER, GATEWAY TO A CONTINENT

> On the 11th [Henry Hudson] passed through the Narrows into the present bay of New York. . . . Toward evening the following day he entered the broad stream, and with a full persuasion, on account of tidal currents, that the river upon which he was borne flowed from ocean to ocean, he rejoiced in the dream of being the leader to the long-sought Cathay. But when the magnificent highlands, fifty miles from the sea, were passed, and the stream narrowed and the water freshened, hope failed him. But the indescribable beauty of the virgin land through which he was voyaging, filled his heart and mind with exquisite pleasure.—Benson Lossing, *The Hudson*, 1866

Henry Hudson's hopes in 1609 would have been partially realized by the completion of the Erie Canal in 1825, which connected the estuary that by then bore his name to the continental interior. When, in October 1825, DeWitt Clinton descended the canal and the Hudson River to pour a barrel of Lake Erie water into the Atlantic, this ceremonial marrying of the waters signaled the ascension of New York to the commercial capital of the United States. A vigorous touring industry would also rise to serve those scenes of "indescribable beauty," much praised in literature and art. The English emigrant artist Robert Havell Jr. portrays the broad estuary from Tarrytown Heights, one of the river's widest points, where sailing craft and steamboats populate the Tappan Zee (fig. 54). While the busy river carried maritime traffic of all kinds, the Hudson's banks provided magnificent views for cottages and villas, marking the rapid development of the upper Hudson as a suburb for New York City. The scenic attractions of the Hudson's entire course, which quickly became famous as a popular picturesque travel route, were celebrated in paintings, prints, and literature.[47]

Tourists boarded luxurious steamboats in New York City, stopping along the river at destinations known for beautiful scenery and historic sites. James Bard, originally in partnership with his twin brother, John, devoted a long and productive career to providing steamboat owners with portraits of the vessels that plied the Hudson. His attention to detail and proportion was such it has been claimed that shipbuilders swore they could use these steamboat portraits to lay down the plans for these so-called floating palaces. Many bore evocative names like the *Cayuga*, after a New York Indian tribe, and offered passengers the combined benefits of luxury travel and high speed (fig. 55). Lossing describes Haverstraw Bay just north of the Tappan Zee: it is "the widest expanse of the Hudson, with all its historic and legendary associations. . . . Here the fresh and salt water usually contend most equally for

54. Robert Havell Jr.
(1793–1878)
View of the Hudson River from Tarrytown Heights, ca. 1842
Oil on canvas, 22 × 30 in.
(55.9 × 76.2 cm)
Gift of Harry Peck Havell, 1946.179

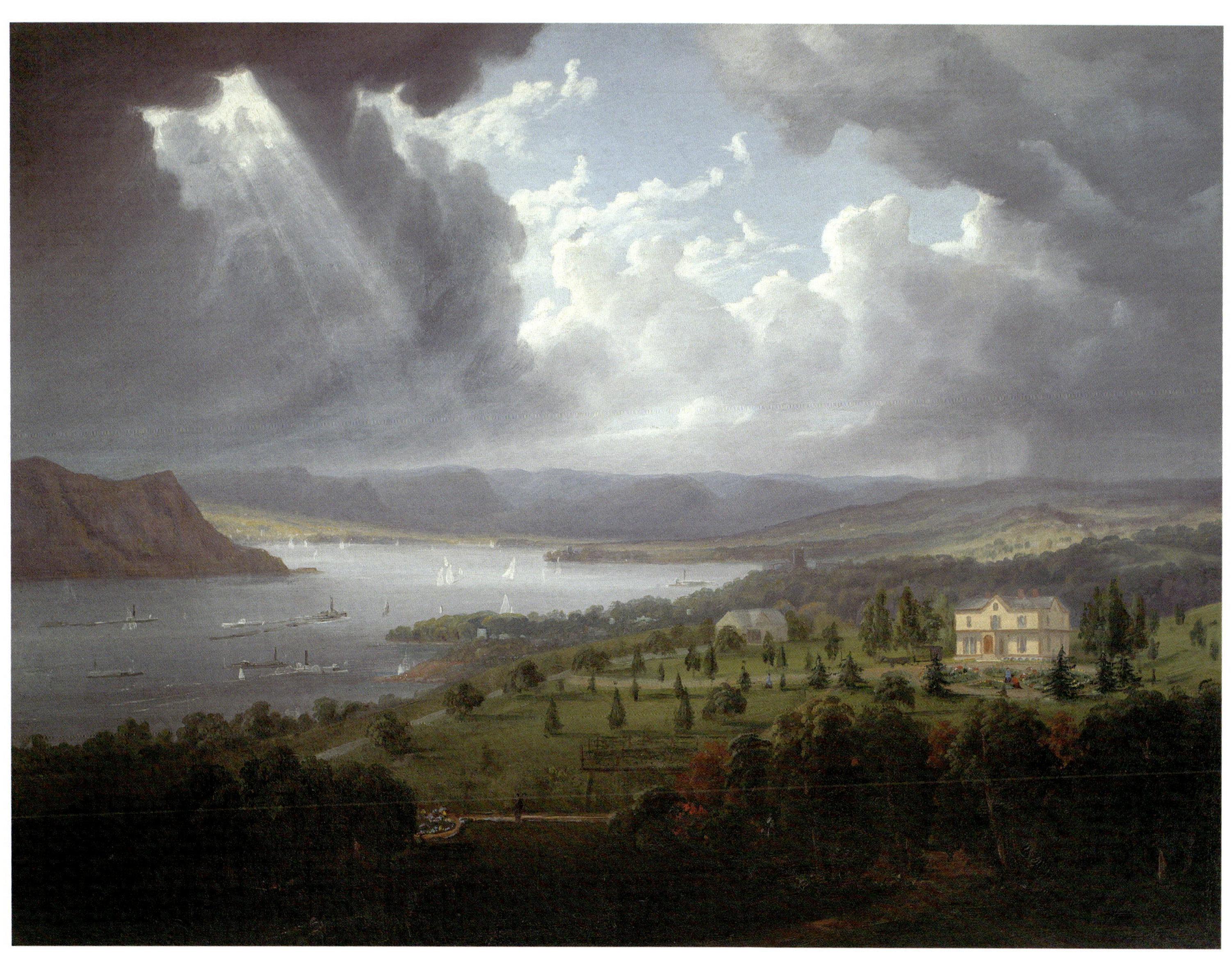

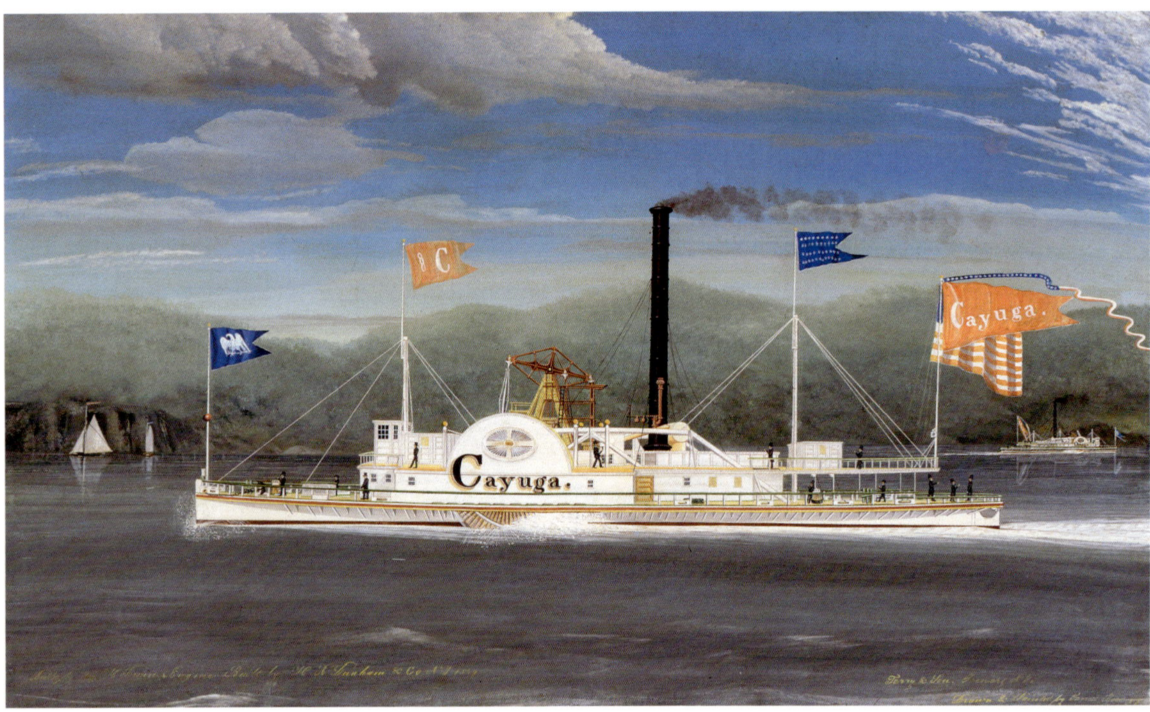

55. James Bard (1815–1897)
Steamboat "Cayuga," 1849
Oil on canvas, 29 × 49⅛ in.
(73.7 × 124.8 cm)
Dated lower left: *1849*; signed lower right: *Painted by James Bard NY*
Purchase, 1924.113

the mastery; and here the porpoise, a sea-water fish, is often seen in large number, sporting in the summer sun. . . . All things considered, this is one of the most interesting points for a summer residence to be found on the Hudson."[48] Bard's lovely *Schooner "Lewis R. Mackey"* shows the boat sailing on Haverstraw Bay in the company of those sporting dolphins (fig. 56). It was likely not a pleasure boat but carried cargo to New York from the brickworks at Haverstraw, reminding us that the Hudson River served many extractive industries in the region and was then, as now, an important commercial as well as a recreational waterway.

Not far north are the Hudson Highlands, the most dramatic passage in the river's course, where forested mountainsides plunge into the narrow channel (technically a fjord), forming spectacular vistas and providing sites for resort hotels into the bargain. The Highlands also evoked historical associations. The United States Military Academy at West Point was nearby, as were the ruins of Fort Putnam, a relic of the Revolutionary War. West Point itself was also (and still is) a popular touring destination rich with history made visible, not only in

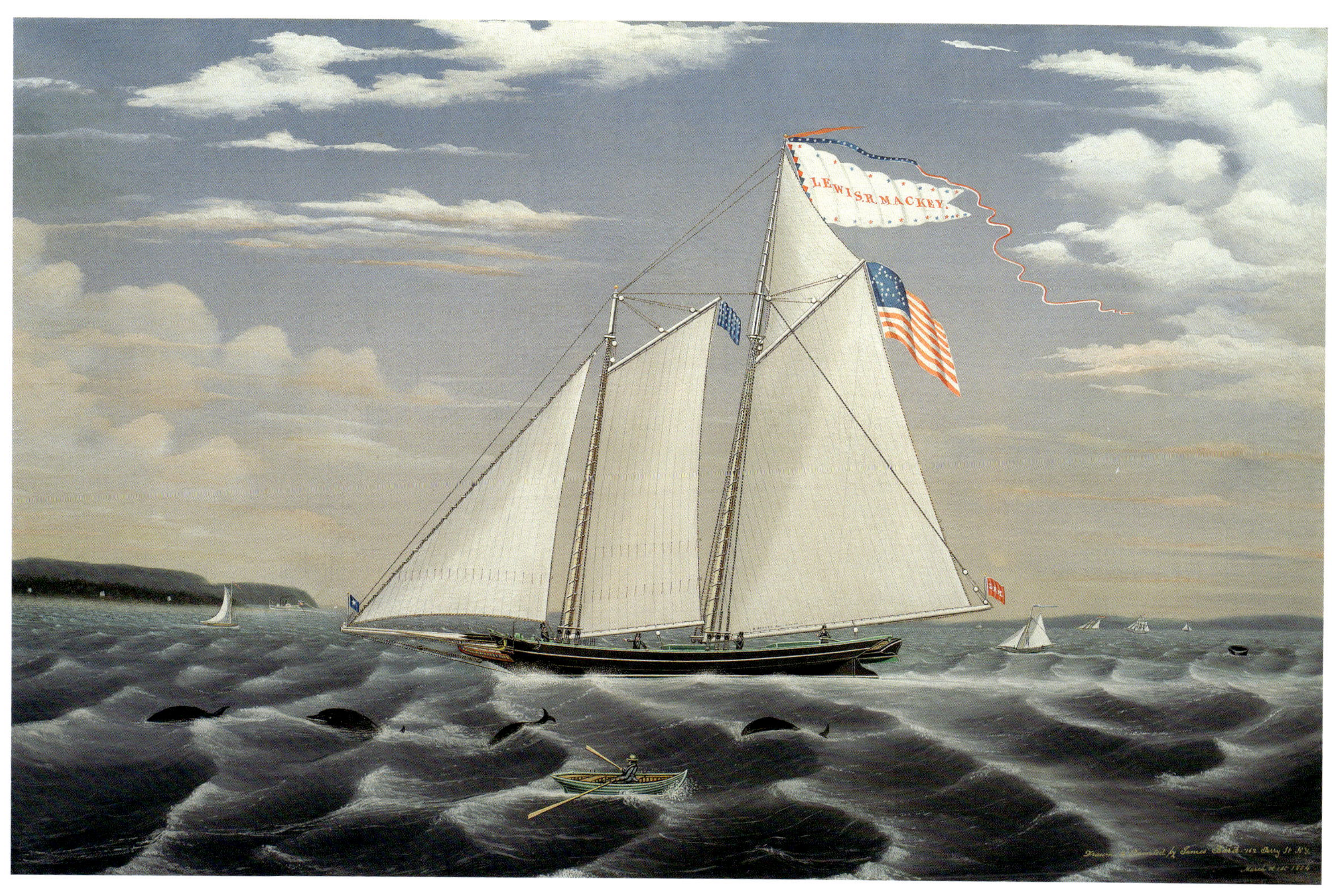

56. James Bard (1815–1897)
Schooner "Lewis R. Mackey," 1854
Oil on canvas, 33¼ × 52⅛ in. (84.5 × 132.4 cm)
Signed and dated lower right: *Drawn and Painted by James Bard 162 Perry St NY. / March The 1st 1854*
Gift of George A. Zabriskie, 1947.66

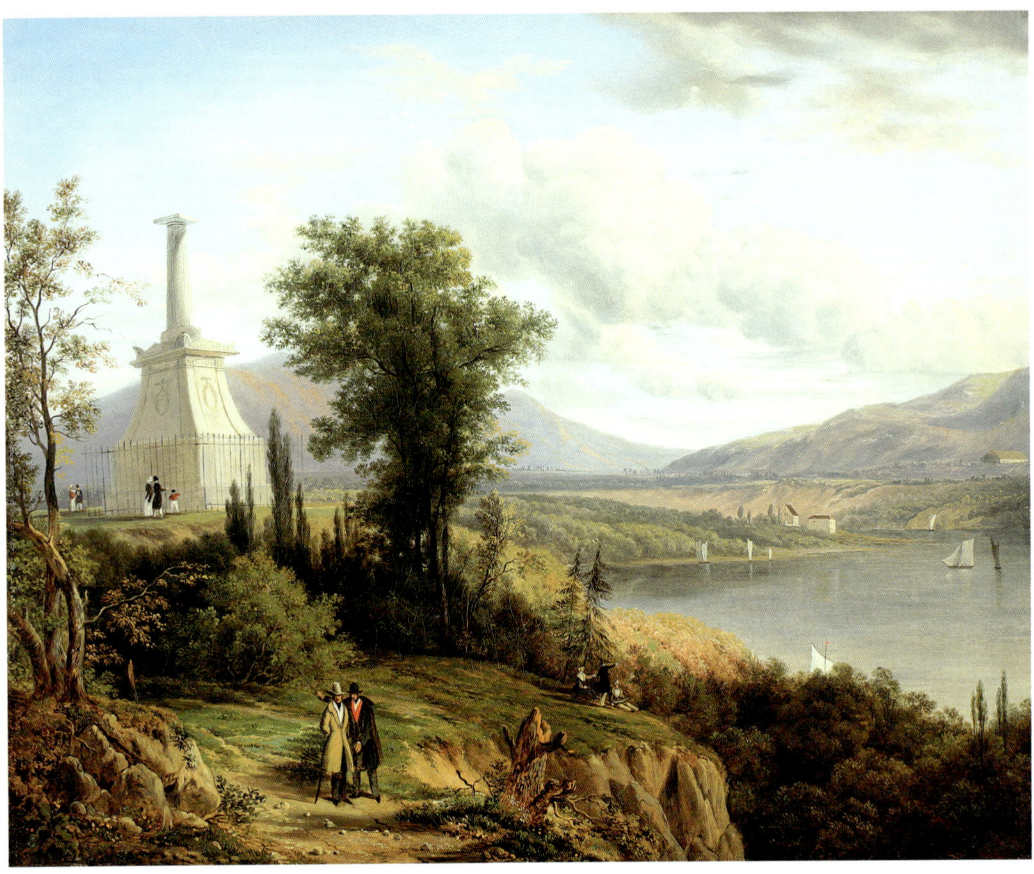

57. Victor de Grailly (1804–1889)
Kosciuszko's Monument, West Point, ca. 1845
Oil on canvas, 23¼ × 28¾ in. (59.1 × 73 cm)
Purchase, 1923.6

the academy's architecture and strategic setting on a promontory above the river but also in the monuments dedicated to military heroes and events on the campus. Victor de Grailly's *Kosciuszko's Monument, West Point* records the stately neoclassical memorial situated high above the river that was dedicated to the Polish patriot Thaddeus Kosciuszko (1746–1817), who served in the Revolutionary army of George Washington (fig. 57). De Grailly was a French artist best known for paintings of American subjects, despite apparently never having visited the United States.[49] This painting and the artist's *View from Hyde Park on the Hudson River*, both from about 1845, are closely based on the engravings published in the book *American Scenery* after William Henry Bartlett's watercolors (fig. 58). Nathan Parker Willis's accompanying text described the site: "A pretty marble shaft stands on the edge of the broad highland esplanade of West Point, over looking the most beautiful scene on the most beautiful river of our country. It commemorates the virtues of Kosckusko [*sic*] who, during his second sojourn in America,

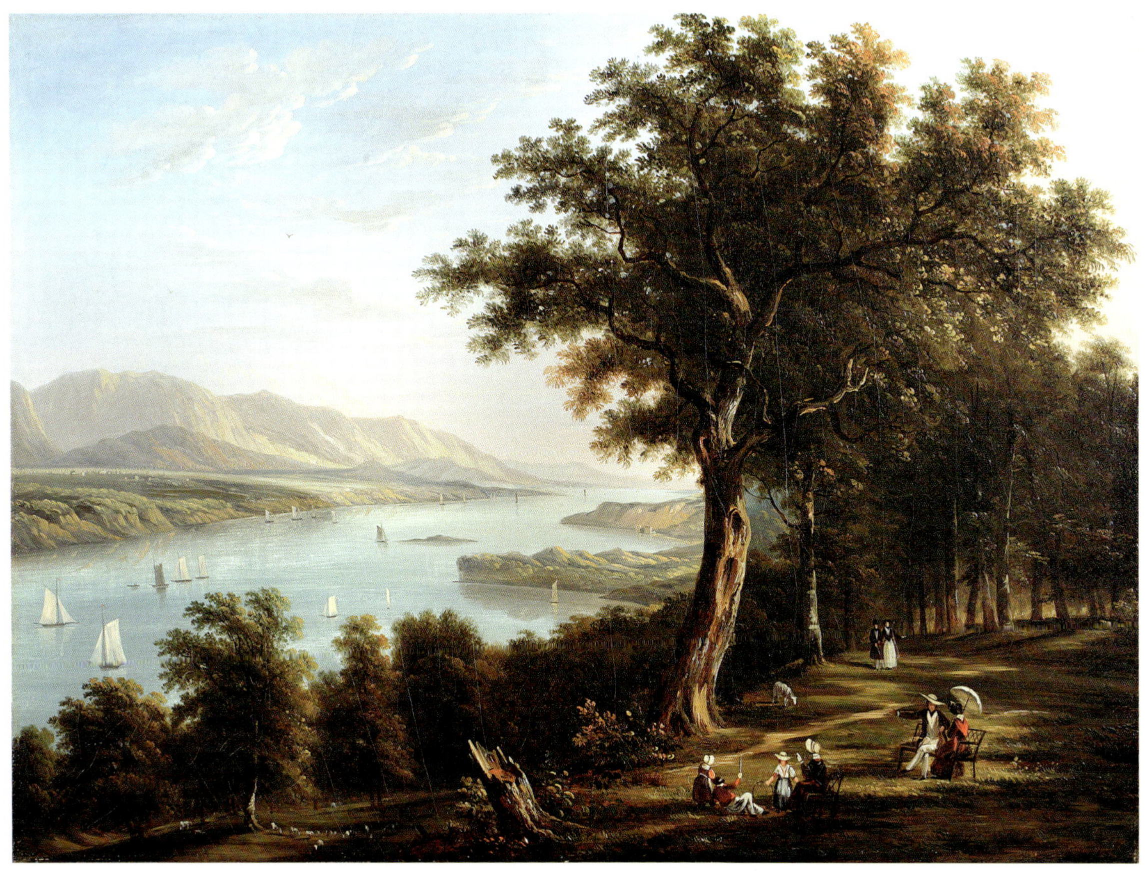

lived at West Point, and cultivated his little garden, near the site of this tribute to his memory." Hyde Park, north of Poughkeepsie, draws its name from one of the riverside estates originally named in honor of Sir Edward Hyde, a royal governor of New York. "The Hudson at Hyde Park," wrote Willis, "is a broad, tranquil, and noble river. . . . [T]he eminences around are crested with the villas of the wealthy inhabitants of the metropolis at the river's mouth. . . ."[50] De Grailly's composition is also based on Bartlett's view: a perspective in service to the high picturesque that emphasizes the breadth of the river and the park-like promenade in the foreground and suppresses any sense of the Hudson as a commercial artery. Hyde Park had long been an elegant preserve for the country houses of New York's oldest elite families; there Dr. David Hosack, a founder of the New-York Historical Society, established an estate renowned for its gardens, where he entertained writers, scientists, and artists, including the founders of the Hudson River School, Thomas Cole and Asher B. Durand.

58. Victor de Grailly
(1804–1889)
View from Hyde Park on the Hudson River, ca. 1845
Oil on canvas, 21¼ × 28¾ in.
(54 × 73 cm)
Purchase, 1923.5

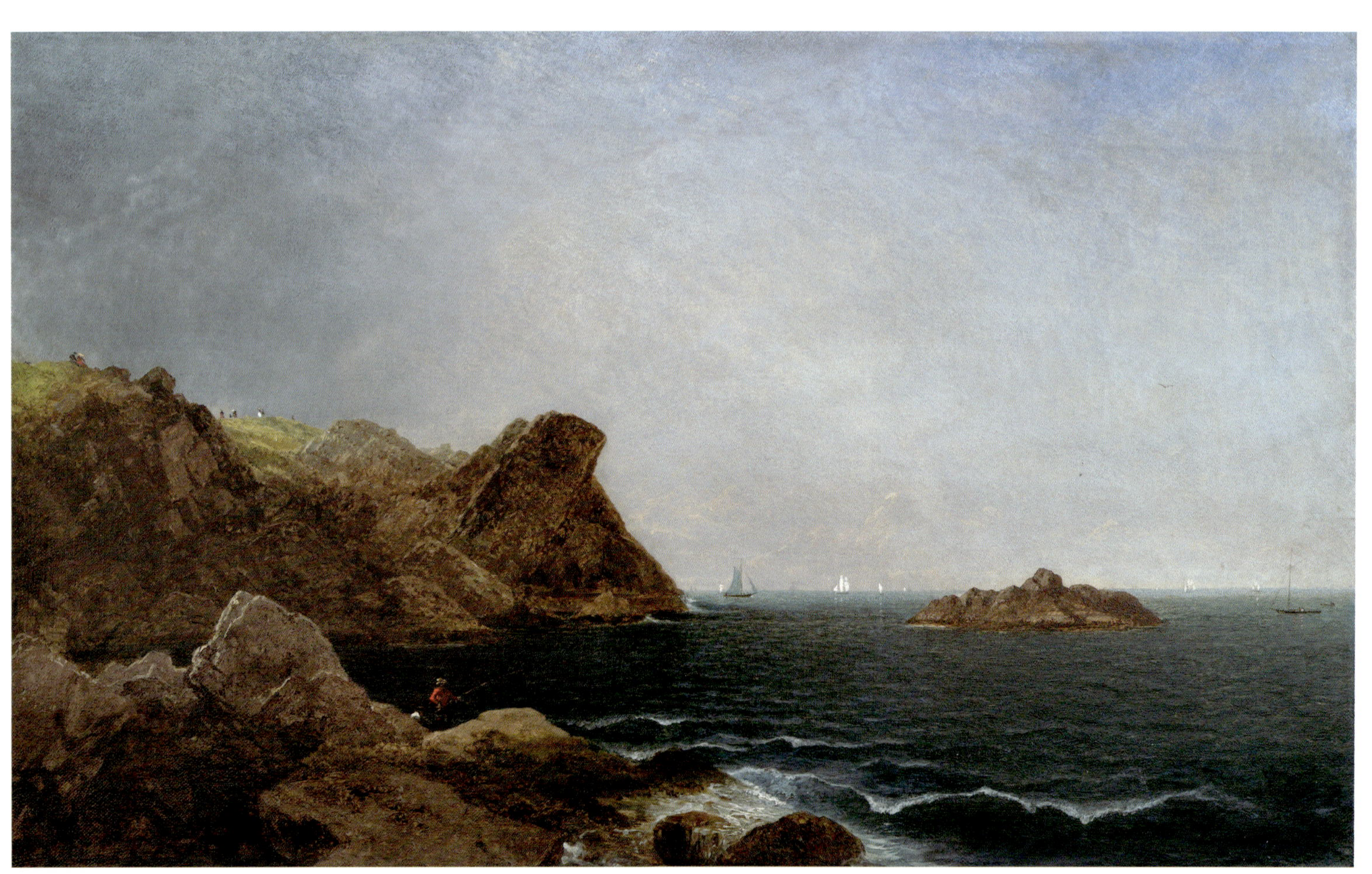

LEISURE AND LIGHT: PAINTINGS OF SEASIDE AND PORT

The second generation of Hudson River School painters would add coastal subjects to their repertoires and summer sketching itineraries, trekking all along the eastern coast from New Jersey to New England. Their routes reflected trends of tourism, as old whaling towns were reinvented as quaint resorts for the urban populations of Boston, Philadelphia, and New York. John Frederick Kensett was one of the first major landscape painters to develop a strong interest in painting coastal terrain, a subject whose popularity grew as seaside tourism developed in the second half of the nineteenth century.[51] Unlike maritime and harbor specialists, he portrayed the New England and New Jersey seaboard with a focus on unpopulated stretches of rocky coast under luminous skies or at fashionable resorts like Newport, Rhode Island, and Nahant, Massachusetts, although his interpretations of those sites were not conventionally picturesque, as we see in *Pulpit Rock, Nahant (Nahant Rock and Seashore)*, 1859 (fig. 59). This summer resort on the coast north of Boston was associated with investigations of natural history by the renowned Harvard geologist Louis Agassiz, who considered the ledges at Nahant to be his outdoor research laboratory replete with signs of ancient volcanic and glacial forces. Kensett portrays a prominent geologic feature known as the Pulpit located on the end of East Point, where it was a local attraction until it was destroyed in 1951 by a nor'easter.[52] This natural landmark is set in the middle distance as a powerful profile against the sky at the end of the point's rocky wedge, where it thrusts into the Atlantic. The composition is Kensett's favored coastal configuration: a compacted mass on one side of the canvas opposing a fluid-filled, empty space on the other, all under the canopy of a huge sky that occupies more than half of the picture. Close viewing reveals that the greensward capping the point is populated with figures whose tiny scale signals the mass of the ledge on which they stand, enjoying a view of the sea. These gaily dressed excursionists are realized with a miniaturist's attention, an attention that Kensett also applied to the fissured and fractured surfaces of the heavily eroded reddish bluffs characteristic of that stretch of coast. The site is further domesticated with sailboats and a fisherman perching on the foreground ledge. Nevertheless, Kensett's vision pushes beyond the standard picturesque format to force the viewer into an awareness of the geologic forces that long ago formed the protruding layer of red-hued volcanic rock. He alludes as well to the relentless actions of the waves and wind that are wearing the Pulpit away, a veiled allusion, perhaps, to the challenges that the science of natural history presented to traditional religious beliefs.

59. John Frederick Kensett (1816–1872)
Pulpit Rock, Nahant (Nahant Rock and Seashore), 1859
Oil on canvas, 18 × 30 in. (45.7 × 76.2 cm)
Signed and dated lower left: *JF.K. / 1859.* [JF conjoined]
The Robert L. Stuart Collection, S-84

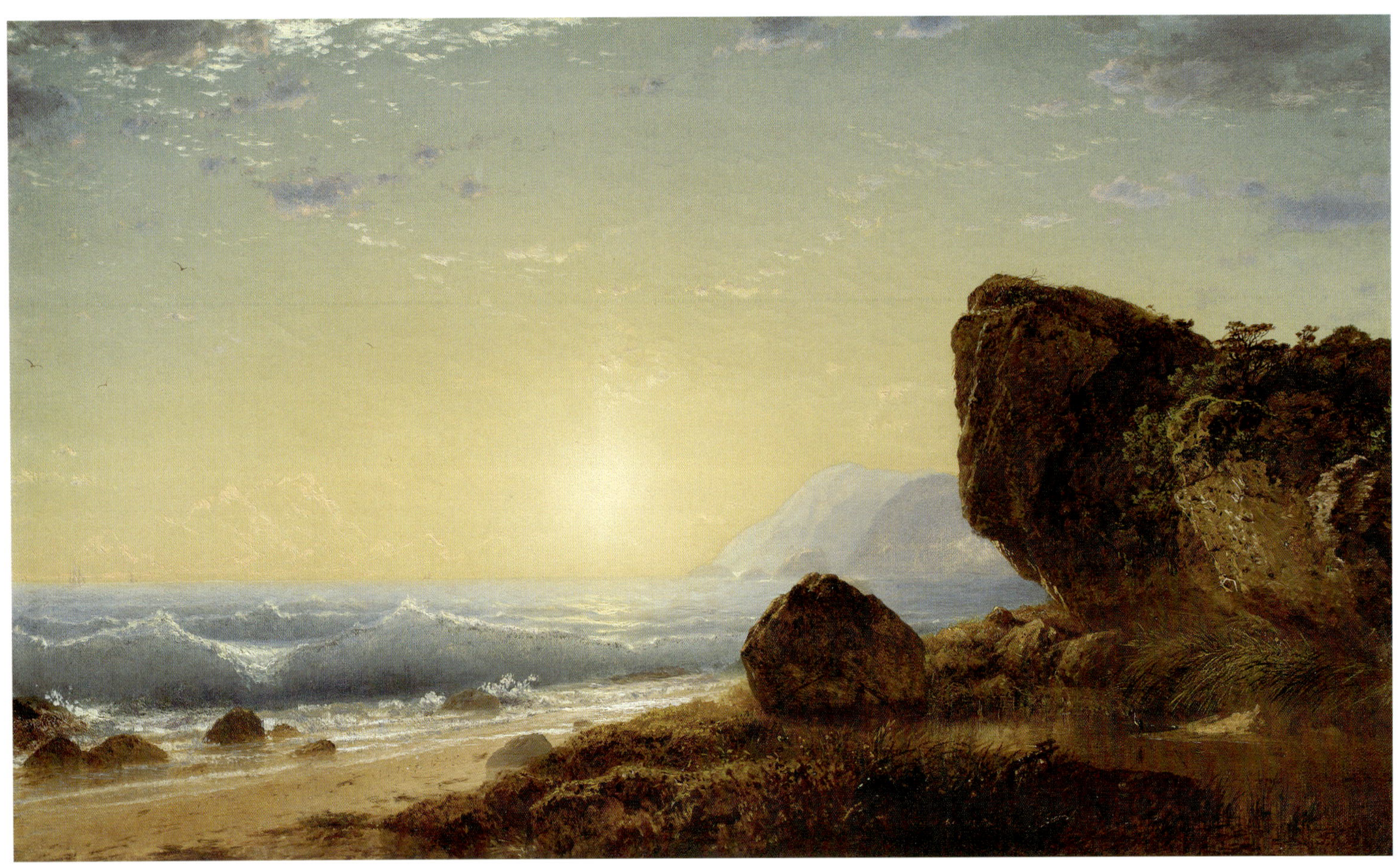

60. John Frederick Kensett (1816–1872)
Sunset on the Coast (Seashore), 1861
Oil on canvas, 18 × 30 in. (45.7 × 76.2 cm)
Signed and dated lower right: *JF.K. '61*. [JF conjoined]
The Robert L. Stuart Collection, S-42

Kensett's *Sunset on the Coast (Seashore)*, 1861, is similar in composition but, as the title suggests, not site-specific: it depicts an isolated coastline unpopulated except for a solitary waterfowl (fig. 60). Distant sails on the horizon do nothing to dispel the sense of solitude on a remote shore bathed in the glow of the setting sun, suggesting a site for romantic meditation on matters both spiritual and geologic, as breaking waves beat on the sands beneath looming rock ledges. The mood here is emphatically poetic, but this work, like *Pulpit Rock, Nahant*, could also evoke a train of thought reflecting Agassiz's observation about the primordial "physical history" of America: "Hers was the first dry land lifted out of the waters," he declared, "hers the first shore washed by the ocean that enveloped all the earth beside."[53]

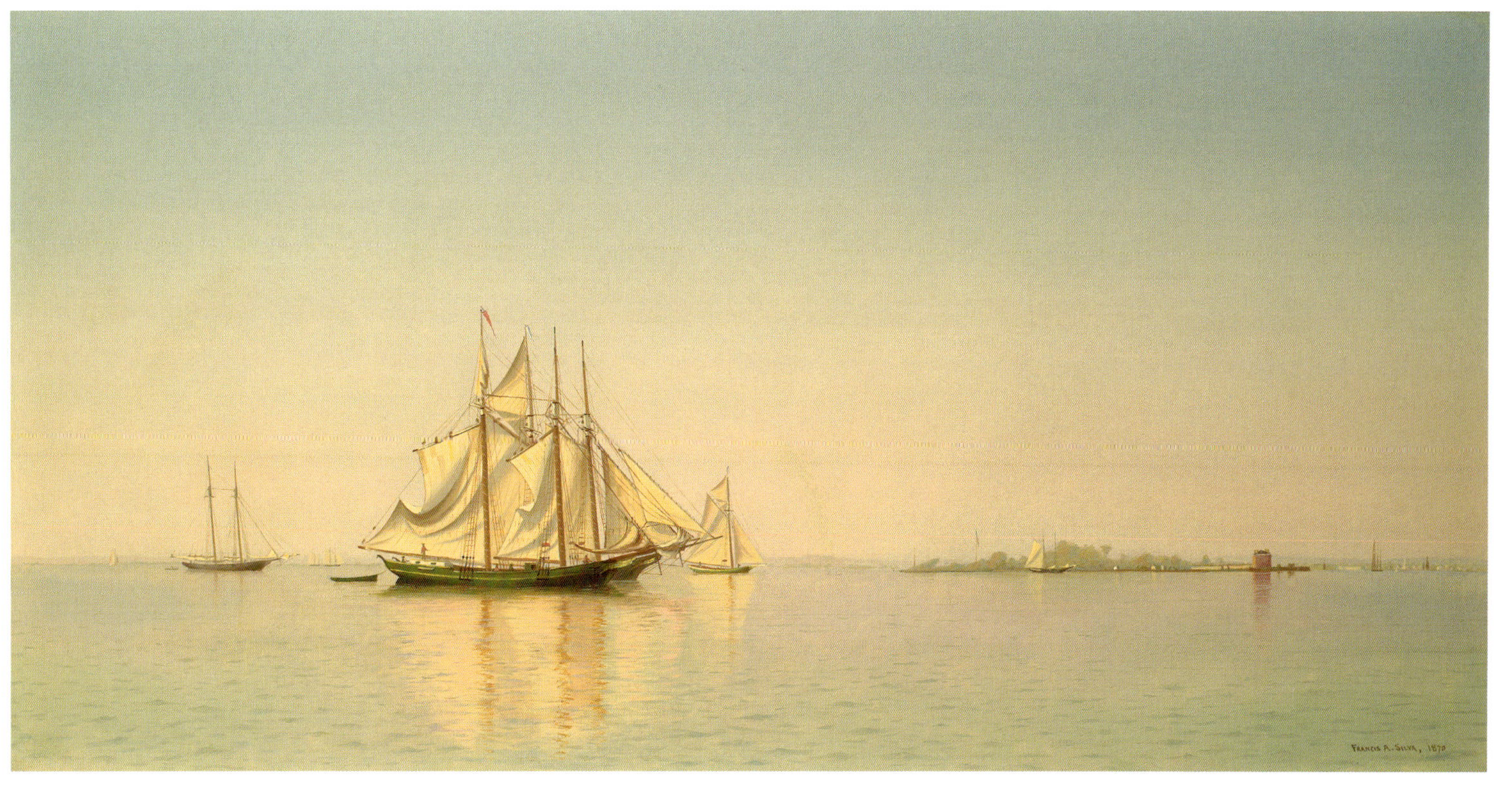

61. Francis Augustus Silva (1835–1886)
Off City Island, New York, 1870
Oil on canvas, 20¼ × 40¼ in. (51.4 × 102.2 cm)
Signed and dated lower right: *FRANCIS A. SILVA, 1870*
Thomas Jefferson Bryan Fund, 1975.22

Francis Augustus Silva was a self-taught but gifted interpreter of marine environments. His repertoire was narrower than Kensett's, but he excelled at capturing certain aerial and atmospheric effects. While his *New York Harbor* of 1880 (see fig. 50) treats the busy waters of the port, typically Silva focused on the more remote stretches of river and coast, where he was able to exploit the great expanse of open sky and the fleeting effects of weather and the time of day to create poetic waterscapes, like *Off City Island, New York* (fig. 61). Even in his harbor view seen above, Silva had suffused the environment in a twilit glow that muted maritime energies, transforming the passage of ships into a stately promenade. In this quiet channel several miles north, the almost still and luminous waters reflect the sails of becalmed schooners and a sloop. City Island is said to be visible in the distance, which places the scene on Eastchester Bay at the western end of Long Island Sound. Located on the busy shipping channel from the sound into New York Harbor, City Island was then a seaport community of oystermen and shipbuilders. However, we are removed from mundane pursuits, out on the water afloat in the realm of maritime leisure, adrift in warmly lit surroundings that evoke a Mediterranean sense of dolce far niente.

GILDED AGE NOSTALGIA: REMEMBERING THE GREAT AGE OF SAIL

Gilded Age nostalgia during the 1880s and 1890s inspired commissions for Julian Oliver Davidson and Carlton Theodore Chapman, two eminent American marine painters who are largely forgotten today, to re-create historic naval battles of the Civil War and the War of 1812 for illustrated histories aimed at a general audience. The Gilded Age is generally characterized as a period of social and economic upheaval in America, when capital was largely consolidated in the hands of a few. These decades also saw elaborate performances of collective nostalgia expressed in a series of national commemorations beginning with the United States Centennial in 1876. These public displays were powerful cultural and political agents for rebuilding a national fabric after the ruptures of the Civil War and Reconstruction.[54] The twenty-fifth anniversary of the beginning of the war was observed in 1886. The quadricentennial commemorations of Columbus's voyage in 1892 and 1893, along with the United States Navy centennial in 1894, turned American eyes back to the Atlantic. All of these events generated widespread interest in history, along with a sentimental longing for simpler times. The latter especially was driven by the nation's increasing industrialization, most powerfully signaled in the maritime realm by the dominance of steam, iron, and steel over wood and sail. All converged to stimulate the writing of popular histories in books and magazines, whose publishers enlisted the talents of the finest American painter-illustrators.

Davidson's meticulously painted reenactments of Civil War naval engagements were reproduced in color by Louis Prang as part of a still-famous suite of eighteen chromolithographs housed in a large easel portfolio titled *Prang's War Pictures* that was announced by the Boston publisher in 1886. Accompanying texts guided the armchair warrior through twelve land battles and six naval actions. Prang's prospectus of 1888 included testimonials of accuracy as well as the "secret process" for reproducing the original works by Davidson and Thure de Thulstrup, who painted the land battles. The publisher also announced that his "Aquarelle Facsimile Prints" could be purchased individually for two dollars each, thereby bringing the prints "within the reach of those who participated in the contests for the preservation of the Union."[55]

When Prang's series was announced, Davidson was at the height of his career as a painter-illustrator. After completing his education at a private school in Connecticut, the young man announced his intention of becoming a marine painter. In preparation, he embarked on a yearlong world cruise, compiling a store of sketches and studies that would serve for years to come. He also benefited from two years of study in New York with the veteran marine painter M. F. H. De Haas. Davidson married in 1877 and settled by the Hudson River at Nyack, where he pursued twin passions for painting and rowing.[56] By the mid-1880s his reputation as a skilled painter and illustrator of modern and historic maritime subjects undoubtedly led Prang to engage him for the six naval encounters planned for *Prang's War Pictures*. If Prang's promotional literature is accurate, Davidson would have traveled up the Mississippi and to Alabama's gulf coast to sketch at both battle sites. Perhaps he spoke with eyewitnesses, and surely he had access to wartime photographs.

Battle of Port Hudson, 1863 documents an episode during the Union campaigns to secure control of the Mississippi River (fig. 62). Steep bluffs beside the small town of Port Hudson located at a hairpin turn in the river some one hundred miles above New Orleans had been well fortified with formidable batteries. Around 11:00 P.M. on the night of March 14, 1863, Admiral David Farragut attempted to run a fleet of seven ships past the Port Hudson batteries in order to block Confederate river traffic. In a spectacular three-hour battle, five of the federal ships were disabled, with one, the *Mississippi*, running aground and being burned by the abandoning crew. The remaining two vessels, Farragut's flagship, *Hartford*, and one gunboat, *Albatross*, were damaged but made it through. Our perspective is from the battery heights with a detailed view of the Confederate position as well as glimpses of the attacking ships through the clouds of smoke and artillery bursts that obscure much of the river below, conveying the confusion and visual drama of a night battle: "Our picture represents the moment in the fight when the 'Hartford' has reached safety above the forts; the 'Monongehela' is turning to drift down, and the 'Mississippi' is bursting into flames as the crew desert her under the fire of the Confederate batteries."[57] *Battle of Mobile Bay* offers a dramatic panoramic view of the gulf coast at dawn on August 5, 1864, with the battle formation of Union warships and ironclads, all under Farragut's command, exchanging fire with the defenders of Fort Morgan, Confederate gunboats, and the ironclad *Tennessee* (fig. 63). Davidson portrays the horrifying moment when the ironclad *Tecumseh* in the middle

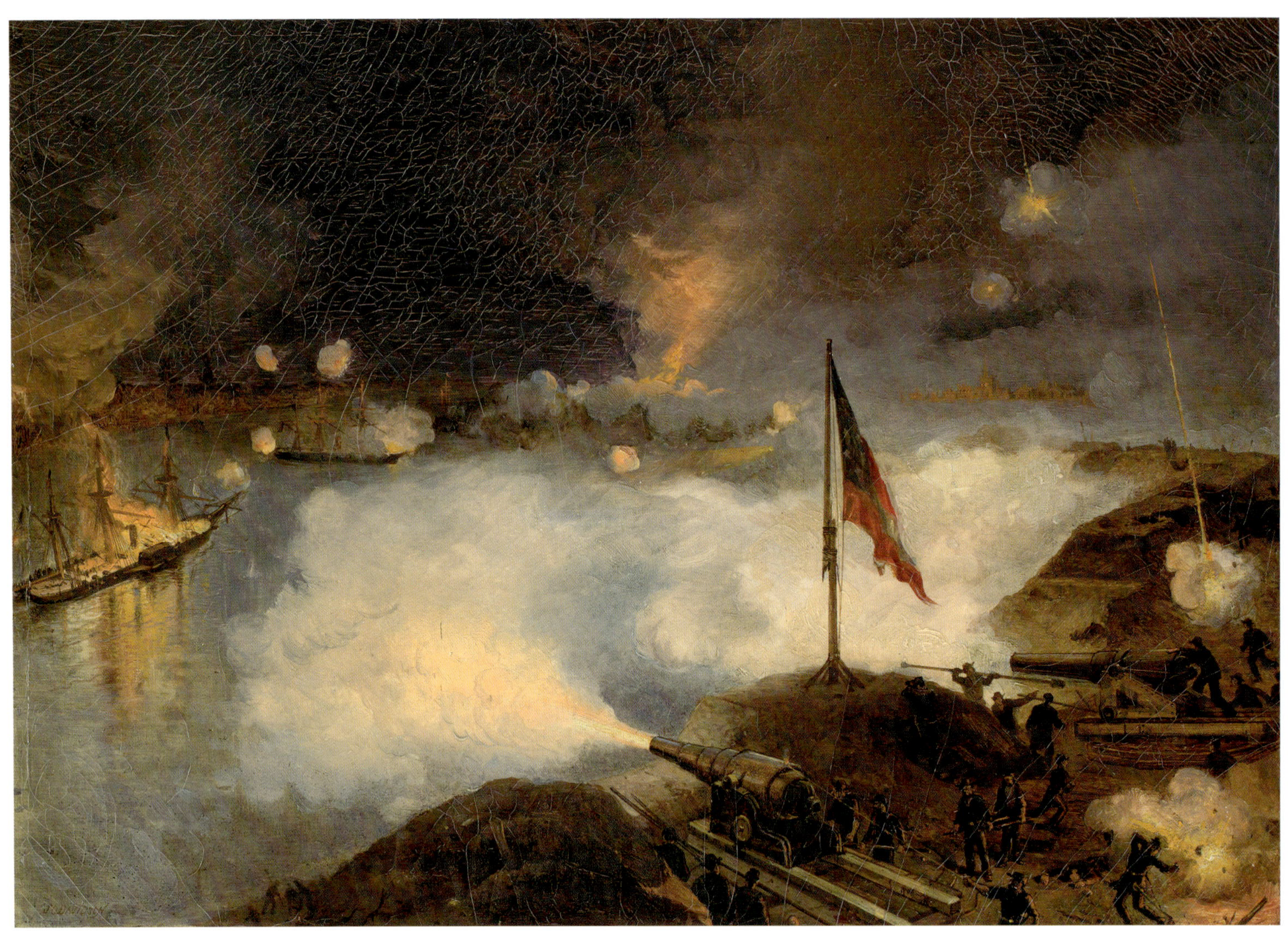

62. Julian Oliver Davidson (1853–1894)
Battle of Port Hudson, *1863*, ca. 1886
Oil on canvas, 15⅝ × 22 in. (39.7 × 55.9 cm)
Signed lower left: *J. O. DAVIDSON*
Gift of the Naval History Society, 1936.801

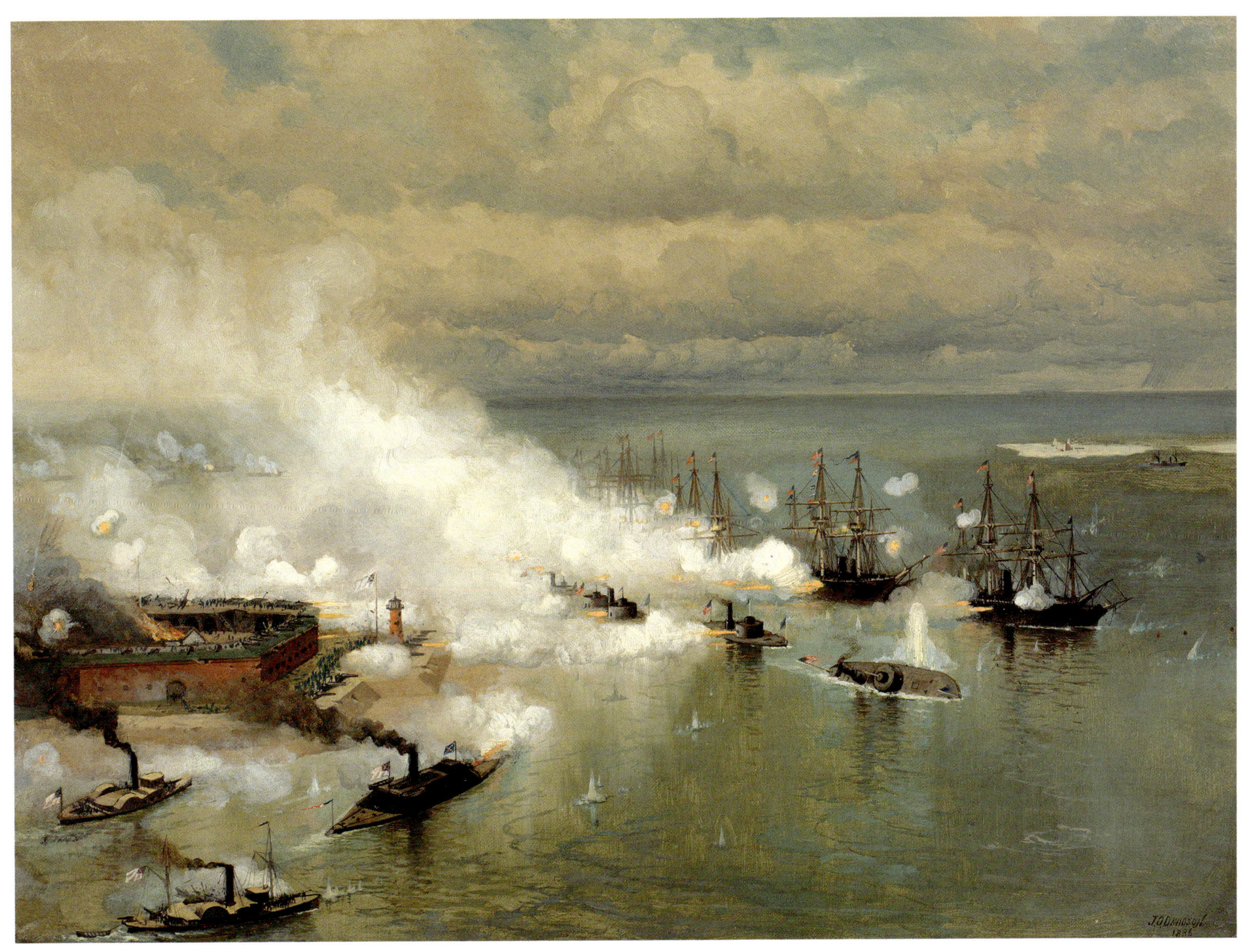

63. Julian Oliver Davidson (1853–1894)
Battle of Mobile Bay, 1886
Oil on linen, 15⅝ × 21½ in. (39.7 × 54.6 cm)
Signed and dated lower right: *J. O. Davidson / 1886*
Gift of the Naval History Society, 1936.802

distance has exploded after striking a torpedo (mine) and is sinking with most of her crew still aboard. Davidson portrays a critical point in the battle, when the attackers are in disarray and the defenders press their advantage; the outcome is uncertain until their valiant commander sails forward to lead the invaders to victory.

> The fleet, under Admiral Farragut, is seen entering the narrow channel, where, between the lines of torpedoes on the left, and close to the guns of Fort Morgan on the right, a passage must be forced to gain an entrance to Mobile Bay. . . . The monitor "Tecumseh" is seen careening from the explosions of a torpedo which she has struck, and, as she plunges beneath the waves with nearly every soul aboard, the leading vessels stop, appalled at the fate seemingly awaiting them.
>
> The enemy, seeing their dilemma, redoubles his efforts, and "the whole of Mobile Point," says one eye-witness, "bursts into a living flame." "What's the trouble?" calls out Farragut to the backing vessels. "Torpedoes ahead!" came the answer. "Damn the torpedoes! Go ahead full speed!" roars the Admiral; and rushing the flag-ship to the head of the line, leads the fleet past the fort, and thus won that great victory, making forever famous the name of Farragut.[58]

The artist's death at forty in 1894 ended a productive career. "Art and publishing circles of New-York have lost a notable figure," lamented the *New York Times*, "as an artist he will be specially missed, because few are capable of painting naval history with his attention to detail."[59]

Davidson's younger contemporary and fellow marine painter, Carlton Theodore Chapman, was one of those few who were also well known by the mid-1890s for portrayals of historical naval engagements. Born in Ohio, Chapman had run away to sea on a Great Lakes schooner in his teens.[60] From a shipbuilding family and himself a collector of ship models, the artist understood ship navigation and construction, a knowledge reflected in his paintings and illustrations. Chapman later studied painting in New York at the National Academy of Design and Art Students League and in 1886 continued his studies in Paris at the Académie Julian. Returning to New York, he set up a studio specializing in marine views, but he also painted landscapes. Chapman first exhibited at the National Academy of Design in 1884, continuing to work well into the twentieth century. Chapman's reputation as "foremost painter of naval warfare and seacraft" had been secured when he was commissioned to provide twenty-one historical marine paintings to illustrate naval historian James Barnes's popular *Naval Actions of the War of 1812* (1896).[61] The Columbian celebrations in 1892 and 1893 along with the United States Navy centennial in 1894 rekindled popular enthusiasm for patriotic narratives of warfare in the age of sail and undoubtedly inspired Barnes's publication and many others. Barnes himself had a special relationship with the New-York Historical Society. As the president of the Naval History Society, he orchestrated the deposit of that organization's large maritime collection at the Society, which included Davidson's paintings of the Civil War as well as Chapman's trio of 1812 battle paintings celebrating victories of the *Constitution*.

The first is *Engagement between the U.S. Frigate "Constitution" and HMS "Guerriere"* (fig. 64), an encounter that took place only a month after the *Constitution*'s daring escape from the British fleet commemorated in Birch's painting of 1838 (see fig. 18). Chapman's painting closely follows Barnes's narrative:

> It was now nearly seven o'clock. The sky had clouded over, the wind was freshening, and the sea was growing heavy. Hull drew off for repairs, rove new rigging, secured his masts, and, wearing ship, again approached, ready to pour in a final broadside. It was not needed. Before the *Constitution* could fire, the flag which had been flying at the stump of the enemy's mizzenmast was struck. The fight was over.
>
> A boat was lowered from the *Constitution*, and Lieutenant Read, the third officer, rowing to the prize, inquired, with "Captain Hull's compliments," if she had struck her flag. He was answered by Captain Dacres—who must have possessed a sense of humor—that, for very obvious reasons she certainly had done so.[62]

We see the victorious *Constitution* in profile on the horizon, approaching and seemingly wholly intact but for damaged sails after the encounter that would earn the American warship her legendary reputation as "Old Ironsides." She towers majestically over the dismasted and devastated British vessel lying in the middle ground on whose deck we are able to see figures of the survivors. The third officer's boat approaches at the left, cautiously avoiding the *Guerriere*'s wreckage afloat in the rolling seas of the foreground.

National commemorations revived public interest in the USS *Constitution*, commissioned in 1797 as one of the six original frigates authorized by the Naval Act of 1794. Her famous exploits during the War of 1812 had stirred a national campaign in the early 1830s to claim the vessel as a national monument. The frigate had been repaired then and continued in service until she was decommissioned in 1881 and had been berthed in the Portsmouth (England)

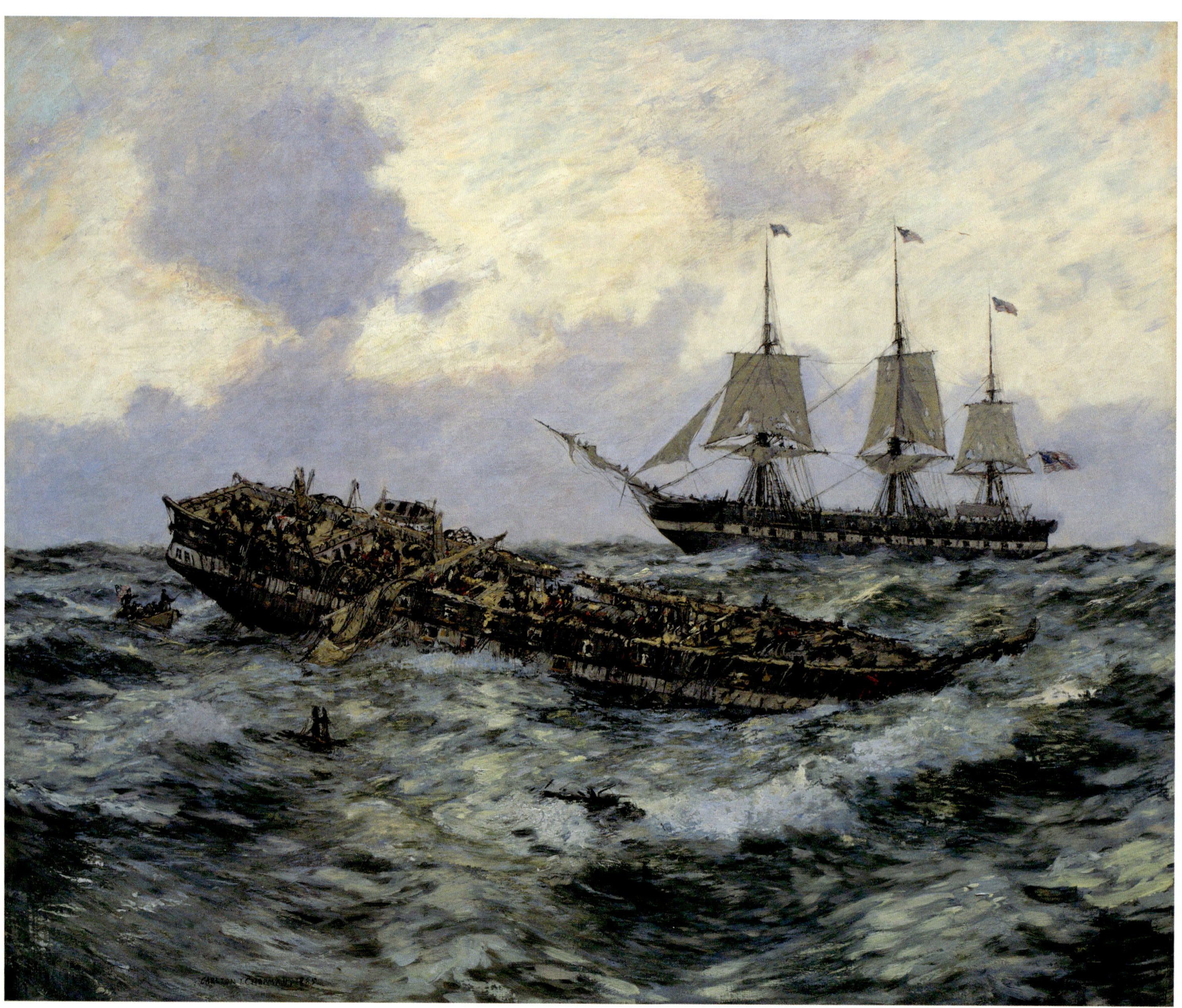

Navy Yard. Renewed efforts to memorialize the vessel brought about the 1897 return of the ship under tow to the Charlestown (Boston) Navy Yard for her centennial. Chapman celebrated the occasion with a pair of paintings that revisited the engagement between the U.S. frigate *Constitution* and the HMS *Java* (figs. 65, 66). Although these works were in the Naval History Society's collection, they postdated the publication of *Naval Actions of the War of 1812*. Nevertheless, they were also conceived much in the spirit of that historical narrative, which included Commodore William Bainbridge's own report of the encounter:

> I have the honor to inform you that on the 29th of December, at 2 P.M., in south latitude 13°6′, west longitude 38°, and about ten leagues distant from the coast of Brazil, I fell in with, and captured, His Britannic Majesty's frigate *Java*, of 49 guns, and upwards of four hundred men, commanded by Captain Lambert, a very distinguished officer. The action lasted one hour and fifty-five minutes, in which time the enemy was completely dismantled, not having a spar of any kind standing. . . . The great distance from our own coast, and the perfect wreck we made of the enemy's frigate, forbade every idea of attempting to take her to the United States. I had, therefore, no alternative but burning her, which I did on the 31st, after receiving all the prisoners and their baggage, which was very hard work, only having two boats left out of eight, and not one left on board the *Java*.[63]

In pendant works, the artist vividly reimagined the engagement of the *Constitution* and *Java* as a pair of stirring cinematic before-and-after marine paintings. The first installment shows the two-hour battle well under way, with the ships exchanging fire and after the *Java* has already lost two masts. One sail hangs useless and the other trails in the water, while shattered spars are afloat in the foreground. Smoke rising from the decks suggests that the *Java* is already aflame (fig. 65). In the second painting, the battle is over. The defeated and destroyed *Java* is burning in the foreground while the rescue operation is being carried out (fig. 66). Two seaboats circumnavigate the ruined vessel transferring prisoners to the *Constitution*. The victorious frigate is poised on the horizon against a dramatic sunset, whose fiery colors are reflected in the waves and echoed in the blazing hulk of the *Java*. We might best summarize Chapman's contributions with the author's own tribute to the artist whose painting transformed his text into vivid images: "Mr. Carlton T. Chapman," Barnes wrote, "has given us back the old days in a way that makes us feel them."[64]

64. Carlton Theodore Chapman (1860–1925)
Engagement between the U.S. Frigate "Constitution" and HMS "Guerriere," 1895
Oil on canvas, 29¼ × 35½ in. (74.3 × 90.2 cm)
Signed and dated lower left: *Carlton T. Chapman. 1895*
The Naval History Society Collection (John Sanford Barnes Foundation), 1925.113
(detail pages 92 and 93)

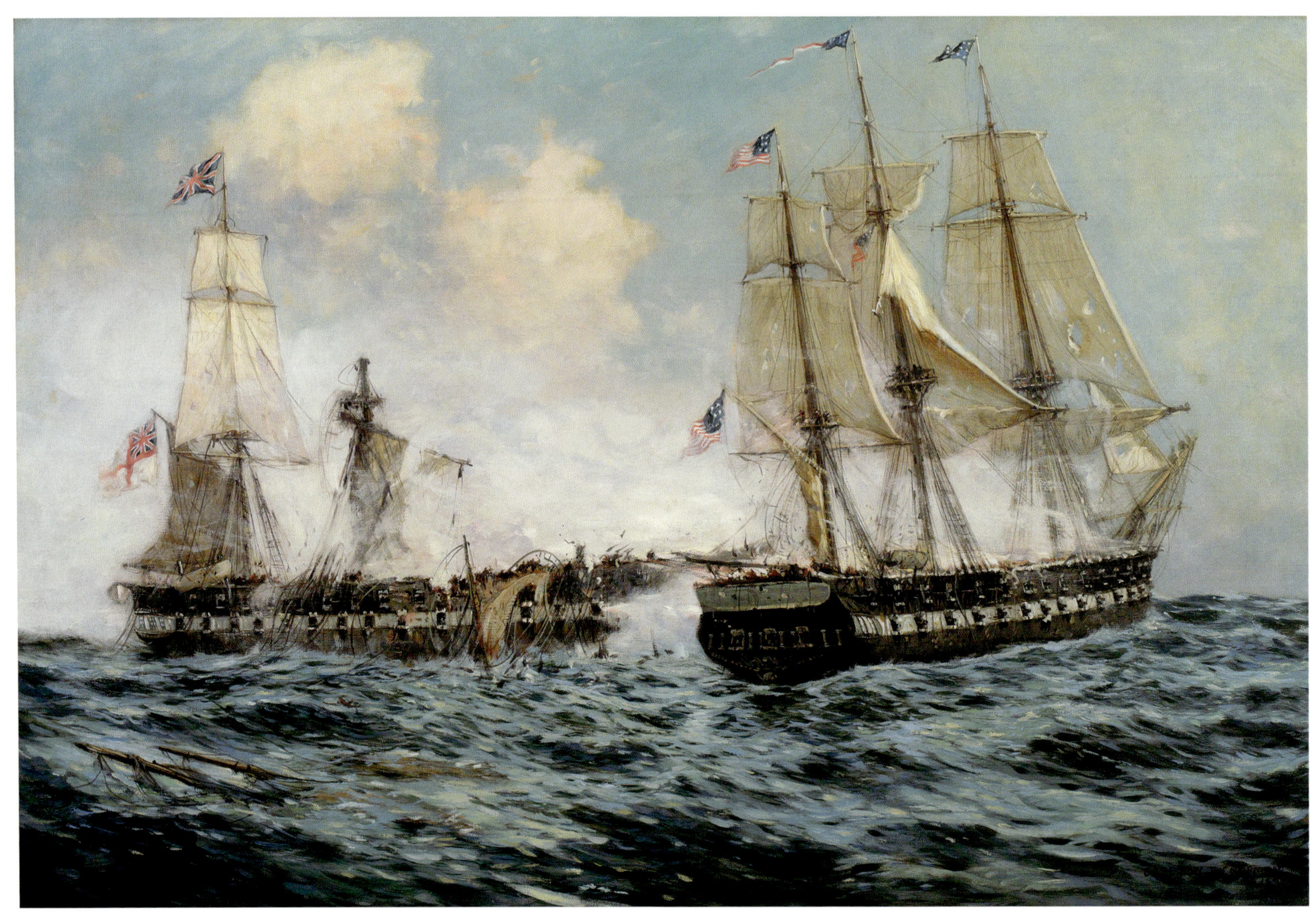

65. Carlton Theodore Chapman (1860–1925)
Engagement between the U.S. Frigate "Constitution" and HMS "Java," 1896
Oil on canvas, 24 × 36¼ in. (61 × 92.1 cm)
Signed and dated lower right: *Carlton T. Chapman. / 1896*
The Naval History Society Collection (John Sanford Barnes Foundation), 1925.114

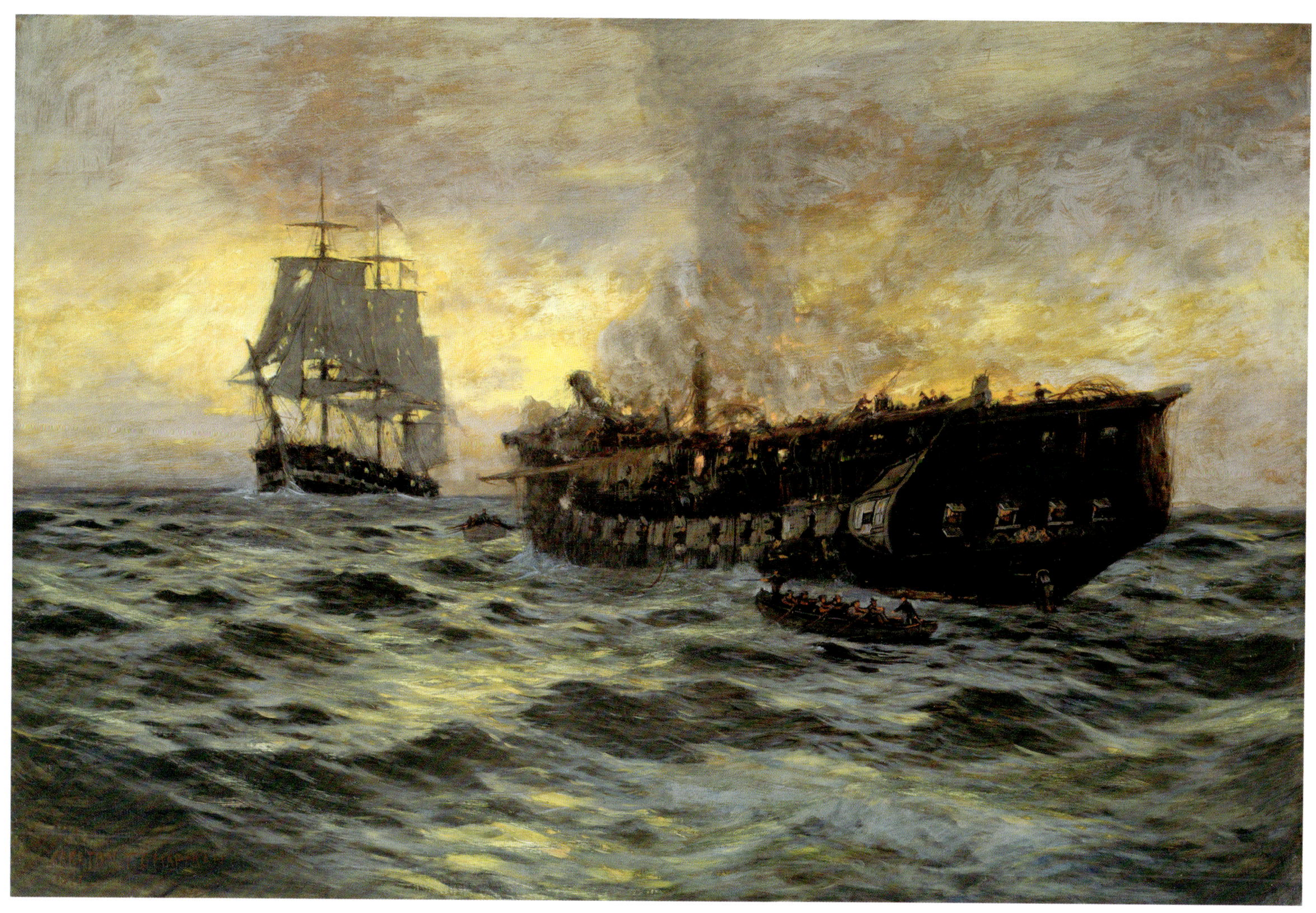

66. Carlton Theodore Chapman (1860–1925)
Engagement between the U.S. Frigate "Constitution" and HMS "Java," 1897
Oil on canvas, 24 × 36 in. (61 × 91.4 cm)
Signed and dated lower left: *Carlton T. Chapman / 1897*
The Naval History Society Collection (John Sanford Barnes Foundation), 1925.115

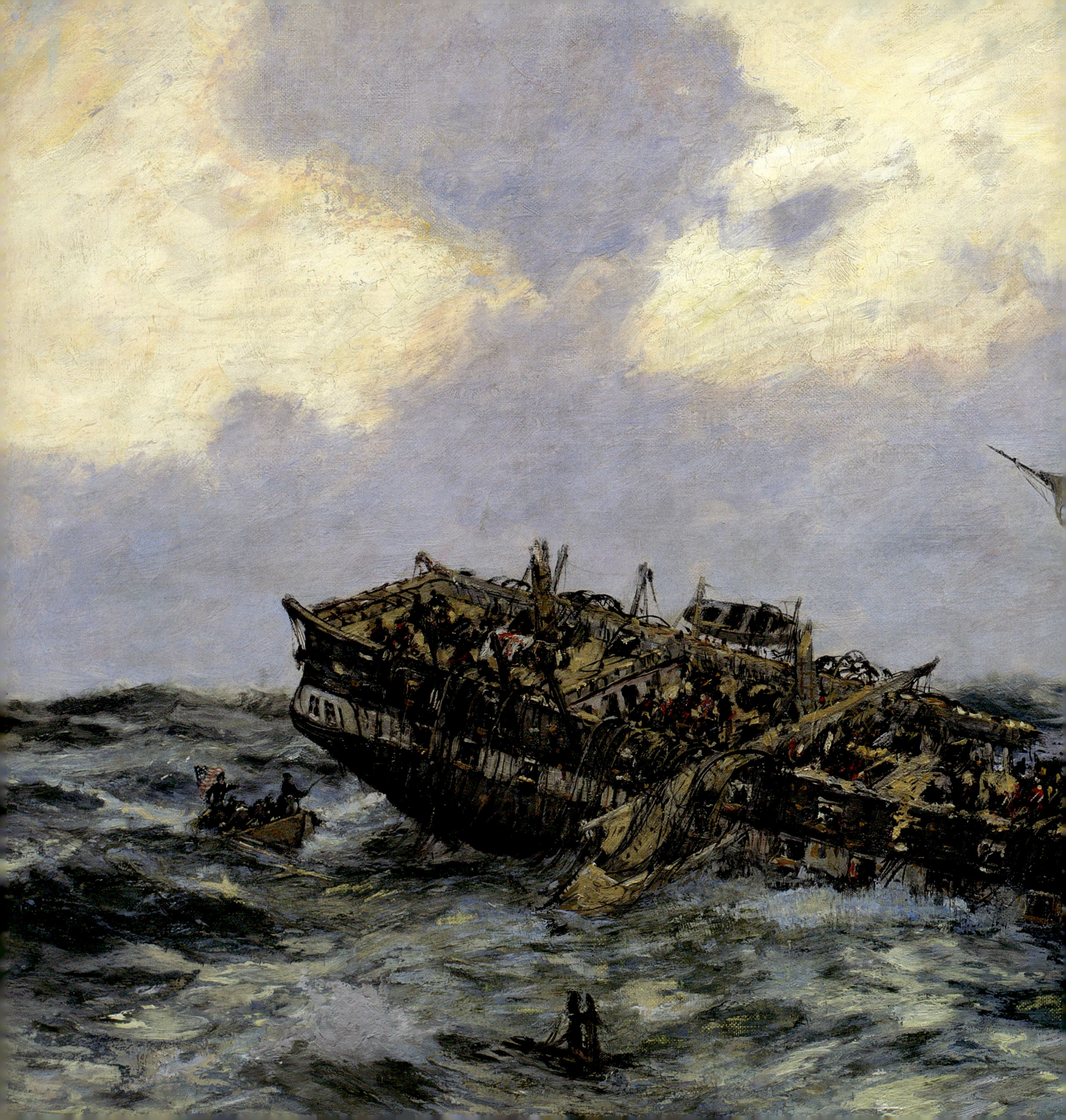

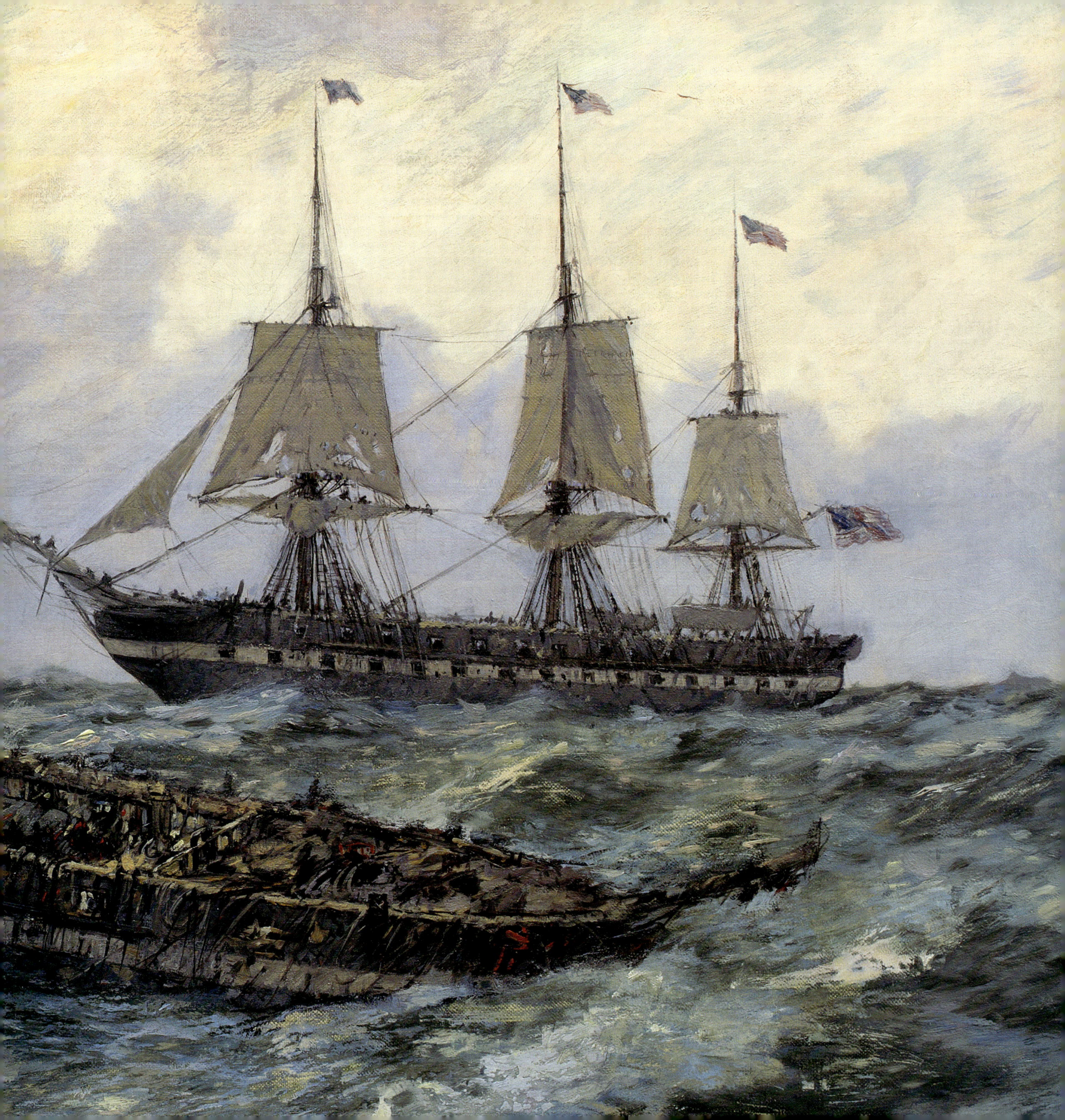

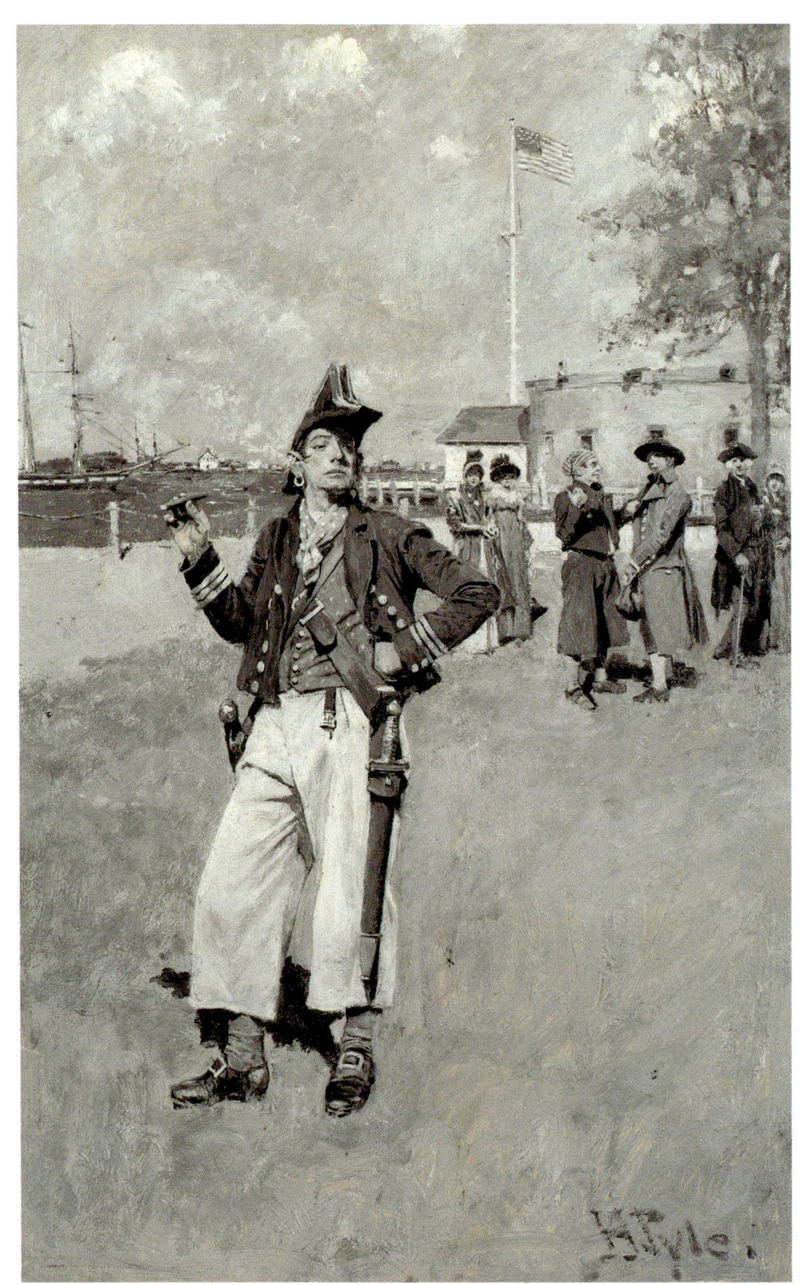

67. Howard Pyle (1853–1911)
A Privateersman Ashore, 1893
Oil on canvas, 18⅞ × 12 in.
(47.9 × 30.5 cm)
Signed lower right: *H. Pyle*
Gift of George A. Zabriski,
1948.28

Interest in the history of New York was also high during these years. Howard Pyle illustrated Thomas A. Janvier's "The Evolution of New York," a two-part chronicle of the port city from its founding under the Dutch to the opening of the Erie Canal that was published in *Harper's New Monthly Magazine* in 1893.[65] After early study in Philadelphia, Pyle came to New York, where his stories and illustrations soon appeared in *Scribner's*, *St. Nicholas*, and the Harper's publications while still a student at the Art Students League. He returned to his native Wilmington in 1879 as an established writer and illustrator. Much research went into the preparation of his pictures, and he passed this practice on to some one hundred students during many years of teaching at Drexel Institute in Philadelphia and at Chadds Ford, Pennsylvania. A gifted and prolific artist, he was well known for his depictions of American historical subjects. Pyle's striking *A Privateersman Ashore*, 1893, is full of historically accurate details with which he re-creates the Battery and Castle Clinton at the time of the War of 1812 as the setting for the audacious privateer who postures in the foreground (fig. 67). Janvier observed, "The one redeeming feature of the situation, in a business way, was the chance that the [War of 1812] offered for privateering." Nevertheless, he recorded that "public sentiment did not unanimously endorse this energetic method of picking up a living on the high seas," and that many New Yorkers saw privateering as nothing so much as "legalized piracy," a shady practice in which "a great amount of property belonging to British subjects was plundered at sea and brought into New York, where for a while the enriched freebooters glittered in their ill-gotten splendor, and exerted a most corrupting influence upon society!"[66] Taking his cue from Janvier's text, Pyle portrays a strutting freebooter in jaunty quasi-naval attire, confronting us boldly while more sober citizens observe their exotic visitor from a safe distance. Their attitudes suggest the ambivalence attached to these raiders who operated on the margins of maritime law at sea and polite society ashore.

EPILOGUE

The Battery as it appeared in 1893 features in a lively vernacular portrayal of New York's harbor as the setting for ceremonial naval pageantry staged as part of the opening ceremonies of the Columbian Exposition. An amateur artist named Andrew Meyer recorded the famous International Naval Review conducted in New York Harbor on April 27, 1893 (fig. 68). President Grover Cleveland, aboard the USS *Dolphin*, reviewed a fleet of thirty-five warships carrying more than ten thousand officers, seamen, and marines from some twenty nations.[67] Crowds lined the shore; excursion boats, shown here in the lower right, carried sightseers out on the water. Perhaps our artist was one of them. We are situated among the crowds on the ramparts of Castle William on Governor's Island seen at the lower left. Meyer's panoramic view charts the vessels as they paraded in double columns before the Statue of Liberty. Frédéric-Auguste Bartholdi's masterpiece was presented by France to the United States and had been dedicated by President Cleveland in 1886. The presence of this colossal

68. Andrew Meyer (active ca. 1893)
Review of the U.S. Fleet in New York Harbor, 1893
Oil on linen, 18¼ × 40¼ in. (46.4 × 102.2 cm)
Signed and dated lower right: *Andy Meyer / 1893*
Thomas Jefferson Bryan Fund, 1986.17

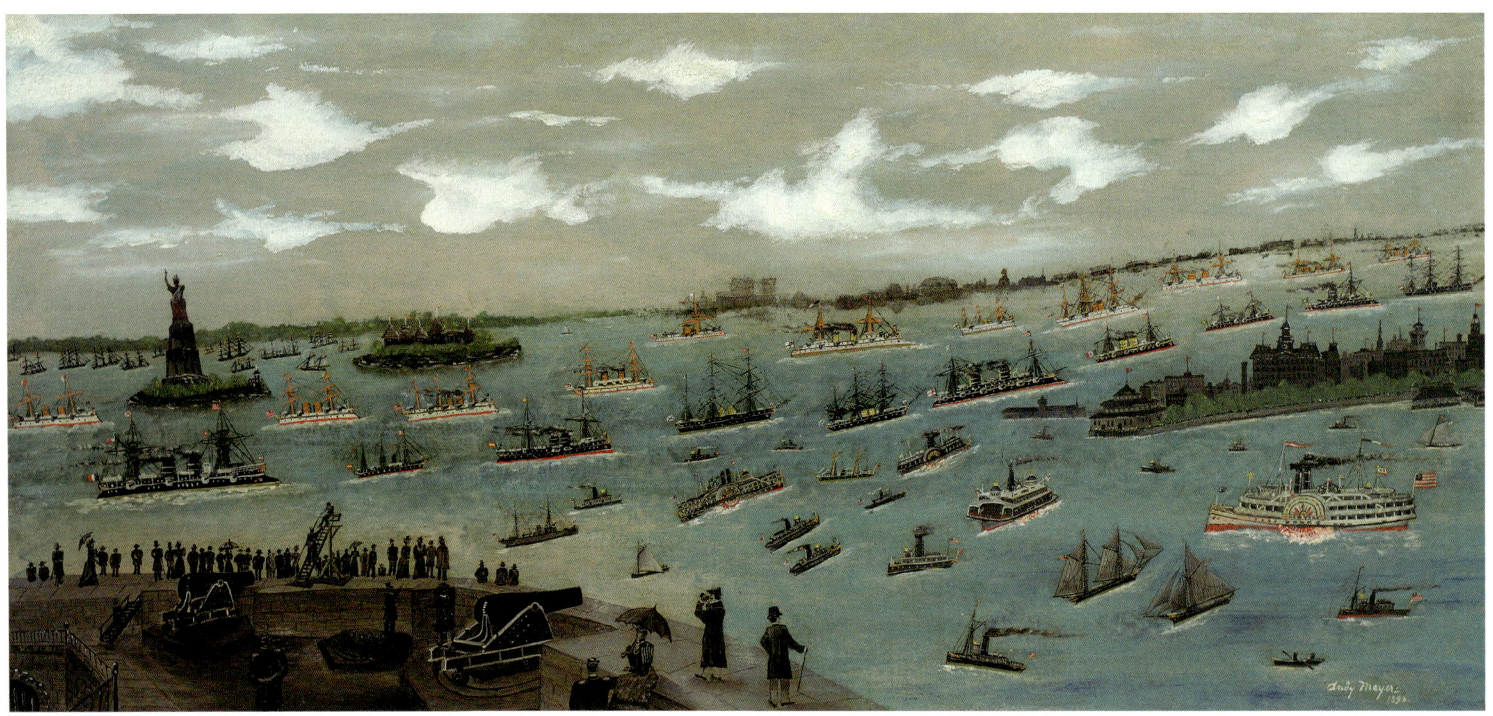

bronze monument has historicized New York's port as a gateway to the New World by co-opting a Roman goddess to perform in the harbor theater as an enduring beacon for voyagers completing or beginning their Atlantic passage. Not far from Bedloe's Island was another new and even larger man-made feature. The Brooklyn Bridge had been completed in 1883, further altering the harbor's configuration by spanning the East River and connecting the cities of New York and Brooklyn. A spectacular feat of modern American engineering, John Augustus Roebling's suspension bridge is supported by a pair of towers whose soaring Gothic arches also nod to the Old World, creating a suitable partnering icon for Bartholdi's colossal goddess of freedom. Chapman's 1904 painting enlists the Great East River Bridge, as it was then called, as an organizing picturesque element to assert a visual experience of New York City (and Brooklyn) as a maritime environment (fig. 69). The Brooklyn Bridge span frames a panoramic vista of the breezy, busy harbor, capturing a view that is still today the classic image of modern twin cities on the edge of the Atlantic.

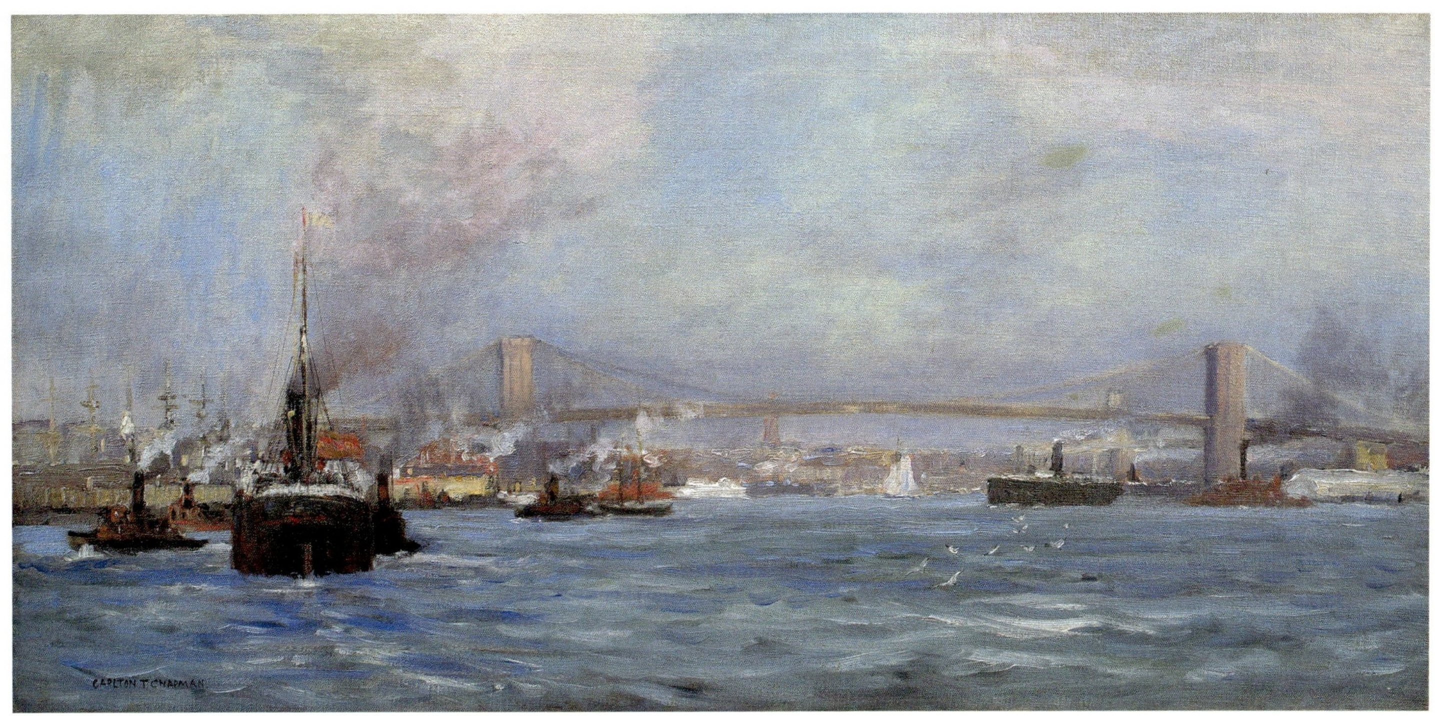

69. Carlton Theodore Chapman (1860–1925)
The East River, 1904
Oil on canvas, 17 × 35 in. (43.2 × 88.9 cm)
Signed lower left: *Carlton T. Chapman*
Gift of Mrs. Carlton T. Chapman, 1938.425

NOTES

Epigraph: James Fenimore Cooper, *The Pilot: Tale of the Sea* (New York: Charles Wiley, 1823), 1:19.

1. For an overview of American maritime history, see Robert A. McCaughey, "By Any Other Name: The Freshening of American Maritime History"; Valery Paley, "An Interview with Nathaniel Philbrick"; and Jenny Gotwals, "A History of Maritime History at the New-York Historical Society," *New-York Journal of American History: The Maritime Issue* 67, no. 1 (2008): 10–23, 58–63, and 109–11.
2. For Hallett, see New-York Historical Society, *Catalogue of American Portraits in the New-York Historical Society* (New Haven: Yale University Press, 1974) (hereafter cited as *Portraits*), 1:321–22.
3. For surveys of American marine and maritime painting, see Roger B. Stein, *Seascape and the American Imagination* (New York: Clarkson Potter in association with the Whitney Museum of American Art, 1975); John Wilmerding, *American Marine Painting*, 2nd ed. (New York: Harry N. Abrams, 1987) as well as the artist's monographs cited below.
4. Nina Athanassoglou-Kallmyer, "New Discoveries: An American Copy of Géricault's Raft of the Medusa," *Nineteenth-Century Art Worldwide: A Journal of Nineteenth-Century Visual Culture* 6, no. 1 (Spring 2007), http://www.19thc-artworldwide.org/index.php/spring07/140-new-discoveries-an-american-copy-of-gericaults-raft-of-the-medusa; and Nina Athanassoglou-Kallmyer, *Théodore Géricault* (London: Phaidon Press, 2010), 218–19. For Uriah Levy, see Melvin I. Urofsky, *The Levy Family and Monticello, 1834–1923: Saving Thomas Jefferson's House* (Chapel Hill: UNC Press Books, 2001); and Ira Day, *Uriah Levy: Reformer of the Antebellum Navy*, New Perspectives on Maritime History and Nautical Archaeology (Gainesville: University Press of Florida, 2006).
5. For *View of a Seaport*, see Richard J. Koke et al., *American Landscape and Genre Paintings in the New-York Historical Society: A Catalogue of the Collection, Including Historical, Narrative, and Marine Art* (New York: New-York Historical Society in association with G. K. Hall, 1982), 3:309, as "Unidentified Artist." A note in the curatorial file suggested an attribution to John Cleveley, the Elder and that the view was of Harwich. We thank Dr. Kevin Fewster, Director of the Royal Museums Greenwich, for directing us to Dr. Nigel Rigby, Head of Curatorial and Research and his colleagues Richard Johns, Curator of Prints and Drawings, and Pieter van der Merwe, National Maritime Museum General Editor, who offered opinions generally supporting an attribution to John Cleveley, the Elder as well as an identification of the seaport as likely to be Harwich.
6. For Birch, see William H. Gerdts, *Thomas Birch (1779–1851): Paintings and Drawings* (Philadelphia: Philadelphia Maritime Museum, 1966); William H. Gerdts, "Thomas Birch: America's First Marine Painter," *Antiques* 89 (April 1966): 528–34; Koke et al., *Landscape and Genre*, 1:57–58; Teresa A. Carbone et al., *American Paintings in the Brooklyn Museum: Artists Born by 1876* (Brooklyn: Brooklyn Museum in association with D Giles Limited, London, 2006), 1:291–94. If Birch's *Marine View* is the work titled *Marine Piece* exhibited by Birch at the National Academy of Design in 1836, Reed could have purchased it from the artist shortly before his death in June 1836; otherwise, the painting would have been acquired by the New-York Gallery of the Fine Arts sometime between 1844 and 1858.
7. For Captain John Waddell, see *Portraits*, 2:845–46, where Wollaston's companion portrait of Mrs. John Waddell (1891.3) is also illustrated and discussed.
8. Koke et al., *Landscape and Genre*, 3:316–17; Marilyn Symmes, *Impressions of New York: Prints from the New-York Historical Society* (New York: Princeton Architectural Press in association with the New-York Historical Society, 2005), 26–27.
9. Alan Russett, *Dominic Serres, R.A.: War Artist to the Navy* (Woodbridge, Suffolk, U.K.: Antique Collectors' Club Ltd., 2001), 106–12; Koke et al., *Landscape and Genre*, 2:236–37; Richard J. Koke, "Forcing the Hudson River Passage, October 9, 1776," *New-York Historical Society Quarterly* 36 (October 1952): 459–66. Another copy after this work by Serres signed by the British artist Thomas Mitchell (1735–1790) is in the National Maritime Museum, Greenwich (BHC0420), and a third, also by Mitchell, was on the market in London.
10. For Abeel, see *Portraits*, 1:1.
11. For Captain David Bush, see ibid., 1:120.
12. For *Mrs. Daniel Truman and Child*, see ibid., 2:807; and Richard Brilliant with Amy Weinstein, *Group Dynamics: Family Portraits & Scenes of Everyday Life at the New-York Historical Society* (New York: New-York Historical Society in association with the New Press, 2006), 116–17.
13. For Jenny, *Foot of Cortlandt Street*, see Koke et al., *Landscape and Genre*, 3:326–27, as "Unidentified Artist," although the entry suggests that Jenny could be the artist. The attribution is supported by comparison of this work with *Wall Street, New York*, 1820, a signed work by Jenny in a private collection (Photograph, Frick Archives, Frick Art Reference Library).
14. For Birch's *New York Harbor*, see ibid., 1:56–57. Henry Tuckerman, *Book of the Artists: American Artist Life* (1867; repr., New York: James F. Carr, 1967), 551.
15. For Evans, see Koke et al., *Landscape and Genre*, 2:14–15; Natalie Spassky et al., *American Paintings in the Metropolitan Museum of Art*, vol. 2, *A Catalogue of Works by Artists Born between 1816 and 1845* (New York: Metropolitan Museum of Art in association with Princeton University Press, 1985), 5–8. Thanks to Tom Parker, Associate Director, and Zachary Ross, Researcher, at Hirschl & Adler Galleries for providing information about Evans.
16. Debra Schmidt Bach, "'Preserved in Perpetuity': Naval History Mementos and Maritime Silver at the New-York Historical Society," *New-York Journal of American History: The Maritime Issue* 67, no. 1 (2008): 94–95.
17. For Buttersworth, see Helen Comstock, "Marine Paintings by Two Buttersworths," *Antiques* 85 (January 1964): 99–104; and Wilmerding, *American Marine Painting*, 86–88. For Buttersworth's *Escape of HMS*

"Belvidera" from the U.S. Frigate "President," see Koke et al., *Landscape and Genre*, 1:123–24.

18. For Buttersworth's *Running Action between the U.S. Frigate "President" and HMS "Endymion,"* see Koke et al., *Landscape and Genre*, 1:124–25.
19. For Birch's *Escape of the U.S. Frigate "Constitution,"* see Koke et al., *Landscape and Genre*, 1:57–59, 118–19; and Sidney Hart, Rachel L. Penman, et al., *1812: A Nation Emerges* (Washington, D.C.: National Portrait Gallery in association with Rowman & Littlefield Publishers, 2012), 118–19.
20. For Unidentified Artist after Thomas Birch, *Capture of HMS "Macedonian" by the U.S. Frigate "United States,"* see Koke et al., *Landscape and Genre*, 1:58–59, there listed as a work by Thomas Birch; and Hart, Penman, et al., *1812: A Nation Emerges*, 126–27, where the painting is identified as by Birch.
21. For Rembrandt Peale, *Stephen Decatur*, see *Portraits*, 1:194. For snuffboxes, see Thomas Hamilton Ormsbee, "Flashback: American Naval Snuff Boxes," *American Collector* (April 1, 2009), http://www.collectorsweekly.com/articles/american-naval-snuff-boxes/.
22. For Cole, see Roberta J. M. Olson, *Drawn by New York: Six Centuries of Watercolors and Drawings at the New-York Historical Society* (New York: New-York Historical Society in association with D Giles Limited, London, 2008), 206–8. For an in-depth, well-documented discussion of the shipwreck subject in art, see Kathleen A. Foster, *Shipwreck: Winslow Homer and "The Life Line"* (Philadelphia: Philadelphia Museum of Art, 2012).
23. Notice of a *Marine View* exhibited at the National Academy of Design in 1833 is cited in Doris Jean Creer, "An American Shipwreck by Thomas Birch," *Brooklyn Museum Bulletin* 20, no. 4 (Fall 1959): 3.
24. For De Haas, see "American Painters. M. F. H. De Haas," *Art Journal*, n.s., 1 (1875): 308–10; "The Methods of a Marine Painter," *Art Journal*, n.s., 4 (1878): 185–87; "Obituary Record: M. F. H. De Haas," *New York Times*, November 24, 1895, 5; biographical sketch in *M. F. H. De Haas Estate Sale* (New York: Ortigies & Co., 1896); and Koke et al., *Landscape and Genre*, 1:265–67.
25. For Staigg, see Koke et al., *Landscape and Genre*, 3:147–49. His audience was undoubtedly familiar with sentimental poems and songs about seafaring life like "The Sailor's Grave" (1850), a short poem describing a burial at sea written by the popular English poet Eliza Cook (1818–1889). Her closing lines evoke the mood of the painting: "A plunge—a splash—and our task was o'er; / The billows rolled as they rolled before; / But many a rude prayer hallowed the wave / That closed above the sailor's grave."
26. The wreck of the *Atlantic* and Homer's illustration are discussed in Foster, *Shipwreck*, 23–26.
27. For *Sinking of the "Ville du Havre,"* see Koke et al., *Landscape and Genre*, 3:251, where the signature is misread as "W. Watt." After cleaning, the signature of Wesley Webber was discovered on the painting. Extensive coverage of the disaster in the pictorial press would have provided the artist with information and images. For example, on December 20, 1873, *Harper's Weekly*, 1133–36, published a detailed report with images of the ships involved and even a plan of the *Ville du Havre*. More important, the issue of January 10, 1874, featured a dramatic double-page spread of the sinking ship that could have guided Webber in his composition (32–34): "a thrilling view of the ill-fated steamer at the moment before she went down beneath the waves. Her masts have just fallen, crushing the boats as they were on the point of being launched, and killing many of the passengers who had crowded about them."
28. For Francis and his invention of the life-car, see Foster, *Shipwreck*, 50. Francis donated his Congressional Gold Medal to the Smithsonian. The example shown here is from the bronze edition that was issued by the U.S. Mint shortly after presentation of the gold medal to Francis in 1890 (fig. 33). The State Department medal (fig. 32) with the design of a shipwrecked sailor clinging to a spar was meant for distribution to Americans who had rescued one or more seamen along the seacoast. For a history of the lifesaving medals issued by the State Department, see R. W. Julian, *Medals of the United States Mint: The First Century, 1792–1892* (El Cajon, Calif.: Token and Medal Society, 1977), 319–31.
29. For Fish, see *Portraits*, 1:267. For scrimshaw, see Stuart M. Frank, *Ingenious Contrivances, Curiously Carved: Scrimshaw in the New Bedford Whaling Museum: A Comprehensive Catalog of the World's Largest Collection* (Boston: David R. Godine in association with the New Bedford Whaling Museum, 2012). We thank Dr. Frank for sharing information resulting from his survey of the Society's scrimshaw collection.
30. For Kane, see *Portraits*, 1:413–14; Letha Clair Robertson, "The Art of Thomas Hicks and Celebrity Culture in Mid-Nineteenth-Century New York" (Ph.D. diss., University of Kansas, 2010), 107–41.
31. For Bradford, see Koke et al., *Landscape and Genre*, 1:79–80; Adam Greenhalgh, "The Not So Truthful Lens: William Bradford's *The Arctic Regions*," in Richard C. Kugler, *William Bradford: Sailing Ships & Arctic Seas* (Seattle: University of Washington Press in association with the New Bedford Whaling Museum, 2003), 73; and Linda S. Ferber, *The Hudson River School: Nature and the American Vision* (New York: New-York Historical Society in association with Skira/Rizzoli, 2009), 159–61, 201.
32. For Benson, see "Portrait of Hevlyn Benson (1805–1858): Captain of Clipper Ships," *New-York Historical Society Quarterly* 17 (April 1933): 21–22; and *Portraits*, 1:72, where the painting is attributed to an unknown Chinese artist.
33. For Chinese portrait painters and "Chinese Chippendale" frames, see Carl Crossman, *The China Trade: Export Paintings, Furniture, Silver and Other Objects* (Princeton: Pyne Press, 1972), 33–35, 80–81, 252. For Lamqua, see Patrick Conner, "Lamqua: Western and Chinese Painter," *Arts of Asia* 29, no. 2 (March–April 1999): 46–64. Thanks to Patrick Conner for suggesting the attribution to Lamqua and to Bryan Oliphant for putting us in touch with Dr. Conner. Comparison of Benson's portrait with those illustrated in the article cited above supports Dr. Conner's opinion expressed in an e-mail to the author, April 7, 2013, that the "portrait

looks entirely typical of the work of Lamqua, the Cantonese follower of the British artist George Chinnery and your dates of 1840–50 seem right. (Could be late 30s since I see that HB was in Canton then.) Many of Lamqua's portraits have a generalized 'China coast' background like this one."

34. For Chinese hong paintings, see Crossman, *The China Trade*, 85, 106–11; David Sanctuary Howard, *New York and the China Trade* (New York: New-York Historical Society in association with Columbia Publishing Company, 1984), 126–27; Patrick Conner, *The Hongs of Canton: Western Merchants in South China, 1700–1900, as Seen in Chinese Export Paintings* (London: Martyn Gregory, 2009). For "flower boats," see Peter A. Van Dyke, "Floating Brothels and the Canton Flower Boats, 1750–1930," *Historiography: Review of Culture* 37, pt. 2 (January 2011): 112–42.
35. For the *Nightingale*, see A. K. Baragwanath, *Currier & Ives Favorites: From the Museum of the City of New York* (New York: Crown Publishers, 1979), 68–69. For clipper ships, see Carl C. Cutler, *Greyhounds of the Sea: The Story of the American Clipper Ship* (Annapolis, Md.: U.S. Naval Institute Press, 1960).
36. For the America's Cup, see John Rousmaniere, *America's Cup Book, 1851–1983* (New York: W. W. Norton, 1983). We thank Thomas Gochberg, Ray Lent, and Bryan Oliphant for providing information.
37. For Bennett, see *Portraits*, 1:69–70; Barbara Dayer Gallati, ed., *Beauty's Legacy: Gilded Age Portraits in America* (New York: New-York Historical Society in association with D Giles Limited, London, 2013), 148–49.
38. For Stearns, see Koke et al., *Landscape and Genre*, 3:150–51; and Millard F. Rogers Jr., "Fishing Subjects by Junius Brutus Stearns," *Antiques* 98, no. 2 (August 1970): 246–50. Rogers must have been unaware of this work, which was already in the Society's collection, since he did not include the painting in his listing of Stearns's fishing subjects.
39. For Cropsey, see William S. Talbot, *Jasper F. Cropsey, 1823–1900* (Washington, D.C.: National Collection of Fine Arts in association with the Smithsonian Institution Press, 1970); Kenneth Maddox, *An Unprejudiced Eye: The Drawings of Jasper F. Cropsey* (Yonkers, N.Y.: Hudson River Museum, 1979); Koke et al., *Landscape and Genre*, 1:229–34; Ella M. Foshay and Barbara Finney, *Jasper F. Cropsey: Artist and Architect* (New York: New-York Historical Society, 1987); and Ferber, *Nature and the American Vision*, 20–22. According to Dr. Kenneth Maddox, Cropsey used the same drawing, dated May 19, 1851 (Collection of the Newington-Cropsey Foundation), for several versions of both the day and night scenes of Castle Garden. The Society's daytime version was presented to Lind by the artist, who recalled his initial inspiration to sketch at the site after hearing Lind's performance and her subsequent visit to him to thank him for the painting ("A Visit from Jenny Lind," typescript, Newington-Cropsey Foundation). Cropsey painted the nocturnal version while living in England, most likely for the London art publisher and dealer Ernest Gambart, who published the painting as one in a series of hand-colored lithographs of American views based on Cropsey's landscapes. The Newington-Cropsey Foundation also holds versions of both scenes. I am grateful to Dr. Maddox for providing this information in advance of the publication of his forthcoming catalogue raisonné.
40. For Melrose, see Koke et al., *Landscape and Genre*, 2:322–23; and Ferber, *Nature and the American Vision*, 22–24.
41. For Colman, see Koke et al., *Landscape and Genre*, 1:212–13; Ferber, *Nature and the American Vision*, 19–20; and Maribeth Flynn, *The Poetic Landscapes of Samuel Colman* (New York: Kennedy Galleries, 1999).
42. For Silva, see Koke et al., *Landscape and Genre*, 3:138–39; Mark Mitchell, *Francis A. Silva (1835–1886): In His Own Light* (New York: Berry-Hill Galleries, 2002), 135; and Ferber, *Nature and the American Vision*, 24.
43. For Moran, see Koke et al., *Landscape and Genre*, 2:385; Paul D. Schweitzer, *Edward Moran (1829–1901): American Marine and Landscape Painter* (Wilmington: Delaware Art Museum, 1979); and Ferber, *Nature and the American Vision*, 24.
44. For Quartley, see Koke et al., *Landscape and Genre*, 3:80 (biography only; this work is not listed); S. G. W. Sheldon, "American Painters —William H. Beard and Arthur Quartley," *Art Journal* (New York), n.s., 4 (1878): 321–24; Carbone et al., *American Paintings in the Brooklyn Museum: Artists Born by 1876*, 2:870–71, where the interview in the *Art Journal* is quoted on 871; and Chloe A. Richfield, "Arthur Quartley (1839–1886), *Afternoon, Rhode Island Coast*, 1877," in *Important American Paintings* 7 (New York: Questroyal Fine Art, Fall 2006), 50.
45. *Baltimore Gazette*, July 1, 1873, review of Moran's work, quoted in Clara Erskine Clement Waters and Laurence Hutton, *Artists of the Nineteenth Century and Their Works* (1894; repr., New York: Arno Press, 1969), 128.
46. Charles M. Kurtz, *American Academy Notes* (New York: Cassell, Peters, Galpin & Co., 1881), 70–71, ill. 70.
47. For Havell, see Koke et al., *Landscape and Genre*, 1:114–16; and Ferber, *Nature and the American Vision*, 40, 59. For picturesque touring on the Hudson River, see John F. Sears, *Sacred Places: American Tourist Attractions in the Nineteenth Century* (New York: Oxford University Press, 1989); Kevin J. Avery, "Selling the Sublime and the Beautiful: New York Landscape Painting and Tourism," in *Art and the Empire City: New York, 1825–1861*, ed. Catherine Voorsanger and John K. Howat (New York: Metropolitan Museum of Art, 2000); Linda S. Ferber, "Landscape Views and Landscape Visions," in *The Hudson River to Niagara Falls: 19th-Century American Landscape Paintings from the New-York Historical Society* (New Paltz, N.Y.: Samuel Dorsky Museum of Art in association with State University at New Paltz, 2009); Nancy Siegel, ed., *The Cultured Canvas: New Perspectives on American Landscape Painting* (Durham: University of New Hampshire Press, 2011); and Bartholomew Bland, Laura L. Vookles, et al., *The Panoramic River: The Hudson and the Thames* (Yonkers, N.Y.: Hudson River Museum, 2013).
48. Benson J. Lossing, *The Hudson: From the Wilderness to the Sea* (1866; repr., Hensonville, N.Y.: Black Dome Press, 2000), 316–17. For the Bard

brothers, see Koke et al., *Landscape and Genre*, 1:16–17, 18–19; and Anthony J. Peluso Jr., in collaboration with the Mariners' Museum, *The Bard Brothers: Painting America under Steam and Sail* (New York: Harry N. Abrams, 1997).

49. For De Grailly, see William Nathaniel Banks, "The French Painter Victor de Grailly and the Production of Nineteenth-Century American Views," *Antiques* 106, no. 1 (July 1974): 84–103; Koke et al., *Landscape and Genre*, 1:263–65; and Ferber, *Nature and the American Vision*, 50, 64.
50. Nathaniel Parker Willis, *American Scenery; or, Land, Lake, and River Illustrations of Transatlantic Nature from Drawings by W. H. Bartlett* (1840; repr., Barre, Mass.: Imprint Society, 1971), both quoted in Ferber, *Nature and the American Vision*, 64.
51. For Kensett, see Koke et al., *Landscape and Genre*, 2:238–42; and John Driscoll and John K. Howat, *John Frederick Kensett: An American Master* (Worcester, Mass.: Worcester Art Museum in association with W. W. Norton, 1985). Both works discussed here were published in Koke with alternative titles; the original titles have been restored here. In his records, Kensett listed the painting of 1859 as *Pulpit Rock, Nahant* and that of 1861 as *Sunset on the Coast* (cited in Melissa Geisler Trafton, "Critics, Collectors, and the Nineteenth-Century Taste for the Paintings of John Frederick Kensett" [Ph.D. diss., University of California, Berkeley, 2003] 455).
52. For Kensett and geology, see Rebecca Bedell, *The Anatomy of Nature: Geology & American Landscape Painting, 1825–1875* (Princeton: Princeton University Press, 2001), 85–108. For Agassiz and Nahant, see ibid., 109–21. We are grateful to Curator Bonnie Ayers D'Orlando at the Nahant Historical Society for confirming the identification of Kensett's subject as Pulpit Rock.
53. Louis Agassiz, "America the Old World," in *Geological Sketches* (Boston: Fields, Osgood, and Co.), 1, quoted in ibid., 6.
54. For the Gilded Age, see Alan Trachtenberg, *The Incorporation of America: Culture and Society in the Gilded Age* (New York: Hill and Wang, 1982); Alan Trachtenberg, "The Incorporation of America Today," *American Literary History* 15, no. 4 (Winter 2003): 759–64; and Sean Dennis Cashman, *America in the Gilded Age: From the Death of Lincoln to the Rise of Theodore Roosevelt* (New York: New York University Press, 1984). For nostalgia in American culture, see Michael Kammen, *Mystic Chords of Memory: The Transformation of Tradition in American Culture* (New York: Alfred A. Knopf, 1991); and Michael Kammen, *Meadows of Memory: Images of Time and Tradition in American Art and Culture* (Austin: University of Texas Press, 1992).
55. A copy of *Prang's War Pictures* is in the New-York Historical Society Library. For a history of this ambitious project, see Harold Holzer, *Prang's Civil War Pictures: The Complete Battle Chromos of Louis Prang* (New York: Fordham University Press, 2001), 1–49; and *Prospectus. Prang's War Pictures. Aquarelle Facsimile Prints* (Boston: L. Prang & Co., 1888).
56. For Davidson, see A. J. Peluso, "Julian O. Davidson: Engineer, Boxer, Sculler, Rower and Marine Artist," *Maine Antique Digest* (February 1980): 24-C–26-C; Koke et al., *Landscape and Genre*, 1:244–46; Lynn S. Beman, *Julian O. Davidson, 1853–1894: American Marine Artist* (New City, N.Y.: Historical Society of Rockland County, 1986); "Julian O. Davidson: American Marine Artist (1853–1894)," *Antiques and the Arts Weekly* (October 10, 1986): 1, 62–64; and Holzer, *Prang's Civil War Pictures*, 32–33.
57. Text to Number Seventeen of *Prang's War Pictures. "Battle of Port Hudson." Passing the River Batteries* (Boston: L. Prang & Co., [1888]), 47; see Holzer, *Prang's Civil War Pictures*, 45–49, for information about the texts that accompanied the chromolithographs.
58. *Prospectus. Prang's War Pictures*, 6–7.
59. "The Obituary Record. Julian Oliver Davidson," *New York Times*, May 2, 1894, 5.
60. For Chapman, see Carbone et al., *American Paintings in the Brooklyn Museum: Artists Born by 1876*, 1:355–56.
61. *Memorial Exhibition of the Works of Carlton T. Chapman, N.A.* (Toledo: Toledo Museum of Art, 1972), 3. James Barnes's father was John Sanford Barnes (1836–1911), a naval officer who was the founder in 1912 of the Naval History Society. In 1936 the Naval History Society was relocated to the New-York Historical Society, where the younger Barnes had already deposited his father's collection in 1915.
62. James Barnes, *Naval Actions of the War of 1812 . . . with 21 Illustrations in Color by Carlton T. Chapman* (New York: Harper & Brothers Publishers, 1896), 41.
63. Ibid., 87–88.
64. Ibid., vii.
65. Thomas A. Janvier, "The Evolution of New York. First Part," *Harper's New Monthly Magazine* 86, no. 516 (May 1893): 813–29; and Thomas A. Janvier, "The Evolution of New York. Second Part," *Harper's New Monthly Magazine* 87, no. 517 (June 1893): 15–29. For Pyle, see Koke et al., *Landscape and Genre*, 3:77–79; Walt Reed, *The Illustrator in America, 1860–2000* (New York: Society of Illustrators, 2001); and Olson, *Drawn by New York*, 359–61.
66. Janvier, "The Evolution of New York. Second Part," 18, 24.
67. D. Jerrold Kelley, "Naval Review Week," *Harper's Weekly*, May 6, 1893, 417–18.

SELECT BIBLIOGRAPHY

Banks, William Nathaniel. "The French Painter Victor de Grailly and the Production of Nineteenth-Century American Views." *Antiques* 106, no. 1 (July 1974): 84–103.

Barnes, James. *Naval Actions of the War of 1812*. 1896. Whitefish, Mont.: Kessinger Publishers, 2008.

Beman, Lynn S. *Julian O. Davidson, 1853–1894: American Marine Artist*. New City, N.Y.: Historical Society of Rockland County, 1986.

Carbone, Teresa A., et al. *American Paintings in the Brooklyn Museum: Artists Born by 1876*. Brooklyn: Brooklyn Museum in association with D Giles Limited, London, 2006.

Comstock, Helen. "Marine Paintings by Two Buttersworths." *Antiques* 85 (January 1964): 99–104.

Crossman, Carl. *The China Trade: Export Paintings, Furniture, Silver and Other Objects*. Princeton: Pyne Press, 1972.

Cutler, Carl C. *Greyhounds of the Sea: The Story of the American Clipper Ship*. Annapolis, Md.: U.S. Naval Institute Press, 1960.

Driscoll, John, and John K. Howat. *John Frederick Kensett: An American Master*. Worcester, Mass.: Worcester Art Museum in association with W. W. Norton, 1985.

Ferber, Linda S. *The Hudson River School: Nature and the American Vision*. New York: New-York Historical Society in association with Skira/Rizzoli, 2009.

Flynn, Maribeth. *The Poetic Landscapes of Samuel Colman*. New York: Kennedy Galleries, 1999.

Foshay, Ella M., and Barbara Finney. *Jasper F. Cropsey: Artist and Architect*. New York: New-York Historical Society, 1987.

Foster, Kathleen A. *Shipwreck: Winslow Homer and "The Life Line."* Philadelphia: Philadelphia Museum of Art, 2012.

Frank, Stuart M. *Ingenious Contrivances, Curiously Carved: Scrimshaw in the New Bedford Whaling Museum: A Comprehensive Catalog of the World's Largest Collection*. Boston: David R. Godine in association with the New Bedford Whaling Museum, 2012.

Gerdts, William H. *Thomas Birch (1779–1851): Paintings and Drawings*. Philadelphia: Philadelphia Maritime Museum, 1966.

Hart, Sidney, Rachel L. Penman, et al. *1812: A Nation Emerges*. Washington, D.C.: National Portrait Gallery in association with Rowman & Littlefield Publishers, 2012.

Holzer, Harold. *Prang's Civil War Pictures: The Complete Battle Chromos of Louis Prang*. New York: Fordham University Press, 2001.

Julian, R. W. *Medals of the United States Mint: The First Century, 1792–1892*. El Cajon, Calif.: Token and Medal Society, 1977.

Koke, Richard J., et al. *American Landscape and Genre Paintings in the New-York Historical Society: A Catalogue of the Collection, Including Historical, Narrative, and Marine Art*. New York: New-York Historical Society in association with G. K. Hall, 1982.

Kugler, Richard C. *William Bradford: Sailing Ships & Arctic Seas*. Seattle: University of Washington Press in association with the New Bedford Whaling Museum, 2003.

Memorial Exhibition of the Works of Carlton T. Chapman, N.A. Toledo: Toledo Museum of Art, 1927.

Mitchell, Mark D. *Francis A. Silva (1835–1886): In His Own Light*. New York: Berry-Hill Galleries, 2002.

New-York Historical Society. *Catalogue of American Portraits in the New-York Historical Society*. New Haven: Yale University Press, 1974.

Olson, Roberta J. M. *Drawn by New York: Six Centuries of Watercolors and Drawings at the New-York Historical Society*. New York: New-York Historical Society in association with D Giles Limited, 2008.

Peluso, Anthony J., Jr., in collaboration with the Mariners' Museum. *The Bard Brothers: Painting America under Steam and Sail*. New York: Harry N. Abrams, 1997.

Richfield, Chloe A. "Arthur Quartley (1839–1886), *Afternoon, Rhode Island Coast*, 1877." In *Important American Paintings* 7 (New York: Questroyal Fine Art, Fall 2006), 50.

Rogers, Millard F., Jr. "Fishing Subjects by Junius Brutus Stearns." *Antiques* 98, no. 2 (August 1970): 246–50.

Schweitzer, Paul D. *Edward Moran (1829–1901): American Marine and Landscape Painter*. Wilmington: Delaware Art Museum, 1979.

Stein, Roger B. *Seascape and the American Imagination*. New York: Clarkson Potter in association with the Whitney Museum of American Art, 1975.

Wilmerding, John. *American Marine Painting*. 2nd ed. New York: Harry N. Abrams, 1987.

INDEX

Page numbers in **bold** indicate illustrations.

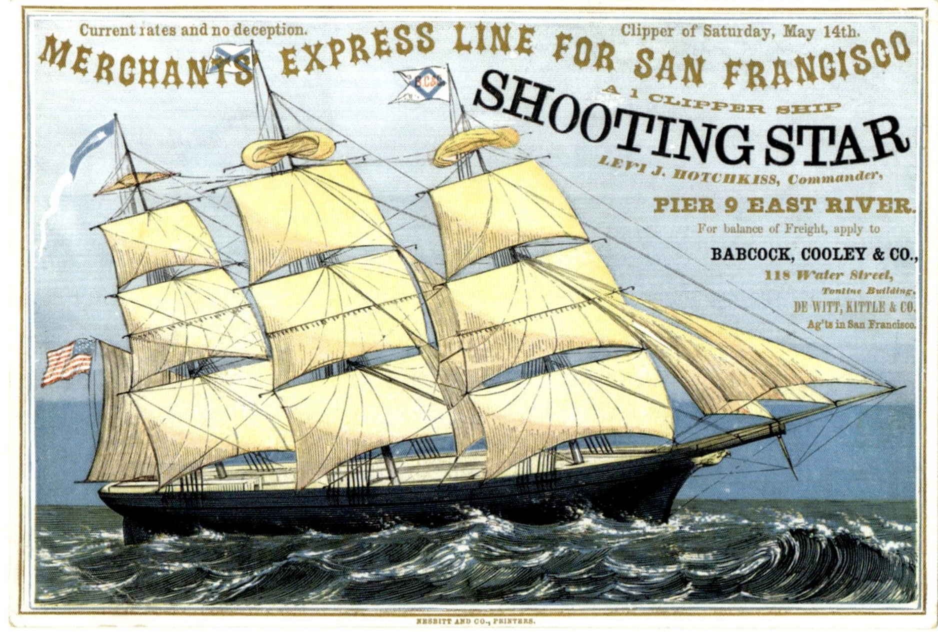

George F. Nesbitt & Co., Printers
Clipper Ship "Shooting Star," 1859
Clipper ship card, 5¾ × 8 13/16 in. (14.7 × 22.3 cm)
New-York Historical Society, Department of Prints, Photographs, and Architectural Collections